Sept 2002

To: Judy Davies,

A token of gratitude

for your support.

Tom Fat

Praise for *Pentecost in Asia*

"*Pentecost in Asia* is a must reading for those who fear the Holy Spirit might have fled the Church!"
Francisco F. Claver, S.J.
Vicar Apostolic of Bontoc-Lagawe, Philippines

"*Pentecost in Asia*, written by a true friend of Asia, is a most delightful and hopeful book. Tom Fox succeeds in presenting the vision and the praxis of the People of God in this part of the world to show readers in the West how 'Asian Catholics provide enormous opportunity to the universal Church.'"
Filo Hirota
Mercedarian Missionaries of Berriz

"Tom Fox's journalistic skill and passion for Asian heritages have resulted in a book that traces the development of the Asian vision in our church: a pastoral vision that seeks dialogues with other cultures, other religions, and the poor; a vision that continues to rediscover the Asian face of Christ."
Ricky Manalo, C.S.P.
Liturgical composer and editor, Singing from the Heart

"*Pentecost in Asia* is an insightful book written by a Westerner who understands and appreciates the Asian way of being church. . . . I would recommend the book even to Asian Catholics to experience the joy of rediscovering our contribution to the universal church."
Archbishop Stephen Fumio Hamao
President, the Pontifical Council for the Pastoral Care of Migrants and Itinerant Peoples

"*Pentecost in Asia* . . . describes how to tap Asian mysticism, discipline for dialogue, and solidarity with the poor — and how we must, if we are to be faithful to our destiny as a living Church. This is a vital study that will fascinate, instruct, and energize both pastoral workers and engaged Catholics. Everyone will learn from it."
Rev. Paul Philibert, O.P.
Professor of Church and Society, Aquinas Institute of Theology

"It is rare to find an outsider who is capable of feeling the pulse of Asia let alone guide others through the labyrinth of minority communities that is the Catholic Church in Asia. Tom's is an outsider's inside story of the ongoing renewal undertaken by Asia's pastors and theologians through the aegis of the Federation of Asian Bishops' Conferences (FABC). This is in-depth journalism at its best."
John Prior, S.V.D.
Secretary, Candraditya Research Centre for the Study of Religion and Culture, Indonesia

Pentecost
in
Asia

Pentecost in Asia

A New Way of Being Church

Thomas C. Fox

ORBIS BOOKS

Maryknoll, New York 10545

Founded in 1970, Orbis Books endeavors to publish works that enlighten the mind, nourish the spirit, and challenge the conscience. The publishing arm of the Maryknoll Fathers & Brothers, Orbis seeks to explore the global dimensions of the Christian faith and mission, to invite dialogue with diverse cultures and religious traditions, and to serve the cause of reconciliation and peace. The books published reflect the opinions of their authors and are not meant to represent the official position of the Maryknoll Society. To obtain more information about Maryknoll and Orbis Books, please visit our website at www.maryknoll.org.

Library of Congress Cataloging-in-Publication Data

Fox, Thomas C. (Thomas Charles), 1944-
  Pentecost in Asia : a new way of being church / Thomas C. Fox.
      p. cm.
Includes bibliographical references and index.
  ISBN 1-57075-442-X
1. Catholic Church—Asia. I. Title.
  BX1615 .F69 2002
  282'.5'09045--dc21
                                        2002003391

I dedicate this book to two scholars and journalists,
both wisdom figures:
Nguyễn Đĩnh Đâù
and
Gary MacEoin.
I am grateful to both.

CONTENTS

ACKNOWLEDGMENTS

This book grows out of the visions of Asian Catholics I have met and known through the years. I hope that by bringing their thoughts and stories to a wider audience I do them proper justice. I ask their indulgences for any shortcomings for which I take complete responsibility.

I am grateful to my colleagues at the *National Catholic Reporter* who have offered their support, including Jean Blake, Sister Rita Larivee, Pat Marrin, Tom Roberts, Arthur Jones, and John Allen.

A special thank you goes to publisher Michael Leach and all the professionals at Orbis Books for their enthusiasm and care, particularly Catherine Costello for her attention to every detail in getting the manuscript ready for production, and to Doris Goodnough and Bernadette Price.

I am especially indebted to Father Peter C. Phan, professor of theology at the Catholic University of America, who has also offered helpful encouragement and suggestions.

Most of all, I am indebted to my wife, Hoa, my best friend and life companion. Through her grace and love, she keeps me dreaming and, when necessary, returns my feet to the ground.

Apostles among Us

The wise person travels with maps. It makes sense to chart the course ahead. This book is about people who are traveling with maps. Moreover, these same people have drawn the maps they are using. The journey of which I write is the journey of the Catholic Church into the twenty-first century. The people who have drawn the maps are Asian Catholics. The course they have set is a faith-driven, wondrous, and imaginative one, and it responds to the needs of the times. In fact, they have been drawing their maps for more than three decades now, yet the wider church knows relatively little about their work—their journeys of faith. I hope this book will help change this. It is the story of the compelling vision of the Asian Catholic leadership since the end of the Second Vatican Council in 1965.

For several reasons the West has not adequately heard the story of the church in Asia, not least of which is that the Asians go about their work quietly. The wider church got a brief look at some of the Asian ideas regarding church during the synod in April 1998, but these were offered without context—and then seemed to disappear from public view when the synod closed. There are other reasons we have not heard a lot out of Asia. Only slowly in recent decades has the West awakened to Asia. Only slowly in recent years have Western Catholics awakened to Asian Catholics, who, after all, represent a tiny fraction of the Catholic Church. It would be wrong, however, to let those small numbers conceal the creative and dynamic faith visions coming out of Asia.

I am of the opinion that Asian Catholics today have something very important to share with the wider church. If we open our minds, if we challenge the way we think about church, we could begin to see Catholicism from a whole new perspective, a non-Western perspective—an Asian perspective. This non-Western, Asian perspective is already a blend of West and East, because nearly all Asian Catholics have inherited Catholicism from the West. In this sense, the Asian vision of church is an

East/West vision. One might even call it global, the product of both East and West, though Asians are not necessarily trying to export their vision. They would be happy if the West (meaning Rome) simply allowed them to develop their Asian vision for their own Asian churches.

My hope is that the Asians are allowed to inculturate the faith as they desire. My further hope is that the West pays attention to the insights that are coming out of the churches of Asia. It makes sense that the West listens to the East. The East has listened to the West for centuries. For one thing, we live in a new global age. East and West face common challenges. Meanwhile, increasingly fast transportation, instant electronic communication, shared scientific insights, and the planet's eco-systems all play roles in both bringing us together and making us more interdependent. For another, Catholicism has also entered a new global era as church. The church is widespread and some of the most creative theologies are coming out of places like Asia.

Consider for a few moments some aspects of the Asian Catholic vision. Free from the weight of Western tradition, it looks into the future with fresh eyes. The Asian vision is grounded in Asian reality—and that reality is the reality of widespread poverty and hunger. This is especially painful given Catholicism's belief in an incarnation God who took on a human body. From this bedrock place of faith, Asian Catholics feel secure to reach out freely to find the Christ of history in Asian cultures and religions. They seek rich spirituality, carved from a belief that the Holy Spirit graces Asia, acting through good people and religions everywhere. Asian Catholics believe there is much to be discovered from Asia's ancient heritage. The Asian vision places high value on harmony. It is the state of life as God intended. The Asian vision has difficulties with Western dualistic thinking because it tends to separate rather than to join together. Traditional Catholic scholastic theology distinguishes and distinguishes again until all is divided neatly into "truth" and "error." Asians generally do not feel at home with this approach to thought. They prefer "both/and" ideas to "either/or" ones. Asian Catholics resist neat categories—and resist being defined in such categories. This Asian "fuzziness" confuses some Westerners who like neat boxes and sharp lines. This is not the Asian approach to life.

The Asian vision attempts to integrate. It seeks to draw all existence together, including mind, body, and spirit. It is holistic. It is more humble, allowing a lot more room for mystery, for the unanswerable Tao. The emerging Asian Catholic vision operates through a belief in dialogue, the idea that there is always more to be revealed. In this sense, dialogue takes place not just to "explain," but even more fundamentally to "discover." It is an approach characterized by respect and humility.

Asian evangelization, similarly, is not out to confront and convert, to distinguish and discard, as much as it is to discover and embrace. Why? Because the Holy Spirit is active everywhere—calling all to reconciliation and harmony. Asian Catholic evangelization witnesses to the Gospels by attempting to live them, by building the reign Jesus came to announce— peace, justice, and solidarity with peoples. Since the Asian Catholic vision sees the Holy Spirit in other religions, it wants to learn from them. The Asian bishops are very much attuned to the fact that cultures, including religions, are changing, are very much in motion. The Asian bishops want to understand these changing cultures and cooperate with their leaders. In the final analysis, the Asian Catholic seeks to bring about the reign of God that Jesus announced to the world within the contexts and cultures that fit the Asian soul.

SOME WE HAVE KNOWN

It is said that there are always apostles among us. Each age has them. If we pay attention we will know who they are and hear what they are telling us. They speak to the times. They speak truth. Archbishop Oscar Romero of San Salvador, El Salvador, was one such apostle. He spoke out on behalf of the oppressed of his nation. "If they kill me, I will rise up in the Salvadoran people," he said shortly before his martyrdom. Bishop Dom Helder Camara of Recife, Brazil, similarly spoke truth. He loved all people, especially the poor. Said Dom Helder: "When I give food to the poor, they call me a saint. When I ask why the poor have no food, they call me a communist." "From Hope to Hope," has been the motto of Paulo Evaristo Cardinal Arns of Sao Paolo, Brazil, whose love for the poor moved him to take up the lonely cause against military dictators on behalf of the imprisoned and tortured. They have called him "the people's cardinal." He too has lived as a modern apostle. Another Brazilian, Bishop Pedro Casaldáliga, has endured numerous death threats as he has spoken truth to injustice. Bishop Samuel Ruiz of Chiapas, Mexico, has been another voice for the voiceless and an ardent defender of the indigenous peoples. Said Ruiz: "The Holy Spirit is already present in the indigenous people of the world. It is our job to listen to that Spirit in them and in our own selves . . . then to go forward from this point."

North America has experienced its own apostles. With the Cold War and nuclear arms race at an intensely dangerous phase, the world heard the lonely voice of one U.S. prelate, Archbishop Raymond Hunthausen of Seattle, who called the Bangor Naval Base in his archdiocese "the Auschwitz of Puget Sound" and the Trident submarines housed there "the global crucifixion of Christ." Facing the rise of U.S. arms sales, the death penalty, inner-city poverty, and abortions at an all-time high, Chicago

Cardinal Joseph Bernardin spoke as a modern apostle when he preached on behalf of a "seamless garment" of life. Other U.S. bishops have stood against the tide of U.S. militarism, preaching nonviolence. The most notable has been Detroit Bishop Thomas Gumbleton, co-founder of Pax Christi USA and past president of Bread for the World. He has faced numerous arrests and jail cells as he has provided light and hope to countless peacemakers for decades. All these bishops have walked in the sandals of the early apostles. Each has reminded the world of the Christian challenges contained in the Gospels.

One intention of this book is to introduce the West to a few of the Asian apostles, some who are with us now and others who have died in recent years after initially helping to set the course for contemporary Asian Catholicism.

WHY LOOK EAST?

Were one to shrink the earth's population of just over six billion people into a village of 100 people, then 58 would be Asians, 33 would be Christians, and 17 would be Catholic. At the beginning of the twentieth century, 80 percent of all Catholics lived in the northern and western hemispheres—in Europe, North and South America; the other 20 percent lived elsewhere. By the 2020, 80 percent of all Catholics will live in the Eastern and Southern Hemispheres, with Europe and North America containing the 20 percent minority. In a period of only 120 years, the demographics of the Catholic Church are being turned upside down. The locus of Catholicism has already shifted dramatically in our lifetimes to such nations as India, Indonesia, the Philippines, Sri Lanka, Pakistan, Vietnam, and South Korea. Already some 70 percent of the world's Catholics live outside Europe and North America.[1] In the year 2000, the number of Jesuits in India exceeded for the first time the number of Jesuits in the United States. These changes provide enormous new opportunities for the church to walk with and speak out on behalf of the marginalized. Church leaders will increasingly be called to voice the deepest aspirations of their peoples, as apostles do. How the church encounters the ever-increasing numbers of poor, how it lives out its mission, how its leaders provide vision and hope are the most pressing of questions it must answer at the start of a new century and millennium.

Meanwhile, some 3.7 billion of the planet's 6.1 billion people live in Asia. According to the World Bank, 840 million are not eating enough today to sustain even modest health, and 2 billion are living malnourished lives. Some 1.3 billion are living in what is called "absolute poverty," existing on less than one dollar a day. Seventy percent of these hungry people live in Asia. Most Asian Catholics live in material poverty. Like most Asians, most Asian Catholics feel they live in spiritual abundance.

The Catholics of Asia make up only a small fraction of the total Asian population, approximately 2.7 percent of its people, or 106 million in all, two-thirds of these in the Philippines. Curiously, it is the small numbers that makes the Asian story all the more compelling. Asian Catholics live at the edge—and it has always been by going to the "edge" that the church rediscovers itself. By most measures, Asian Catholics hardly count in the total Catholic population of over 1 billion worldwide. However, living as distinct minorities their communities have reflected those of the early Christians. And like the early Christians, the Asian Catholics have struggled with issues of self-identity, defensiveness, and mission. Just as the early Christian disciples did centuries ago, today's Asian Catholic apostles have transformed their mission and, indeed, their very identity. In the process, they have moved out of defensive postures, once set up by Western mentors, and are now looking for ways to encounter their own "Asianness," their own cultures and religions. They are compelled to do this by spirit and faith.

TRANSFORMATION

Many Catholics, asked what has most changed Catholicism in our lifetimes, might answer that it was the Second Vatican Council. Perhaps true, but increasingly simple demographic changes are having revolutionary effects as well. Once a church comprised of the white and the well-positioned of the world, it is increasingly a church of color and of the marginalized. We can run from this change—or willingly embrace it as a gift of God. Either way, it is happening. Shortly after the Vatican Council, Jesuit theologian Karl Rahner, acknowledged by many as one of the greatest theologians of the twentieth century, had an insight. He realized that he had caught an early glimpse of the dawn of a new and truly universal, global Catholicism. Reflecting on the council, he called it "the first major official event in which the church began in fact to actualize itself precisely as a world church." He defined that church as one that "begins to act through the reciprocal influence exercised by all its components."[2] His was a prescient observation. Curiously, Rahner's image and definition mirror the image and definitions of church that the Asian Catholic leadership has brought to light and life in the years since Rahner spoke. The church the Asian bishops have in mind is not the one they inherited from the West. Generated by the desire to embrace the poor and walk with the countless millions of poor on their continent, the Asian bishops envision a life-sustaining, networked church, one that integrates and celebrates local cultural and religious gifts and shares these gifts with the wider church. This church is the voice of those without voices. This church is a voice of hope. This church acts courageously because it is inspired and bolstered by the collective strength and wisdom of all the local churches. This church speaks out of faith as followers of Christ, in concert with other religious leaders and people of good will who are also guided by the Spirit. This church works for what the Asian bishops call "integral liberation."

ONE FAMILY

Entering a new century, the human family has critical choices to make and little time left in which to make them. The world's religious leaders are among those who will shape this young century for better or for worse. The tragic events of September 11, 2001, and the months that followed offered ever more ample evidence that choices matter and that human beings write history one day at a time. How this century eventually unfolds—whether the human family can meet the formidable challenges ahead—will depend in no small measure on whether good people, inspired by the ageless religiously motivated ideals of generosity, justice, and mercy can build a better world.

How the Catholic leadership first envisions and then lives out the church's mission will make an enormous difference. If the Catholic church can help bridge the intellectual, spiritual, and material gaps between East and West and rich and poor, this century can be the most fruitful and glorious in history. This opportunity exists as never before, and the Catholic Church is one of the very few global institutions with the structual ability and moral authority to serve in this global capacity.

For this to happen, today's apostles and their inspired messages must be heard. In this regard, I believe the Asian Catholic leadership, riveted by the suffering and hopes of the poor, by an abiding respect for the richness and diversity of cultures, and by an East/West global vision, needs to be heard. This is about vision. This is about leadership. This is about having the wisdom to know when and how to listen.

Asian Odyssey

The chapel off the inner courtyard at the Jesuit theologate in Chennai, India, was chilly and damp at six in the morning. One by one the young Jesuits entered, sitting on small pillows, crossing their legs lotus-style around a small altar that stood only two feet off the floor. The celebrant wrapped his shoulders in an amber-colored cloth and sat in silence for several minutes before speaking.

"We welcome today special guests, two friends, Kim Hoa and Tom Fox. They have come from America. We receive them into our community this morning with much affection. Welcome, Kim Hoa, sister from Vietnam; welcome, Tom, son-in-law of Asia." We bowed slightly, acknowledging our welcome, and I remember that special feeling of acceptance. This would not have been possible were it not for my wife's Asian heritage, our Catholic bonds, and the hopes we shared for the future of Asia.

Even now I remember thinking of Rudyard Kipling's often cited words: "Oh! East is East and West is West; never the twain shall meet." Not this time. Not at this moment. These twains were meeting. In my many travels in Asia I have found most Asians open and accommodating, willing—even eager—to accept strangers, provided they show modest respect for Asian customs and culture.

I have been richly blessed, having experienced both the East and the West. Five years in Asia and a thirty-one-year marriage to a Vietnamese from the Mekong Delta have assured this. Our time together has been a grace—and a cultural eye-opener. I have had the chance to travel through much of Asia and have studied Southeast Asia in graduate school at Yale University. I willingly confess my admiration for Asia, my enchantment with its peoples. I think Asia, with its rich histories, sense of the sacred, diverse cultures, patience, and endurance, has much to teach us. If only we slow down enough to listen and learn.

My own ties to Asia go back almost forty years. It was in June 1963 that I, as an idealistic nineteen-year-old, first stepped onto Asian soil. At the

1

time I had just completed my first year at Stanford University. The dean of freshmen invited two dozen freshmen to join him to work as volunteers for the summer in Asia. We flew on a Pan Am 707 one long night and landed in Tokyo. I still remember that first hot, muggy night at Haneda airport.

Japan seemed so exotic. We toured temples in Tokyo, Nara, and Kyoto, the ancient capital. We took a train to Hiroshima, where we walked beneath the air space where the first atomic bomb exploded August 6, 1945, changing history forever. I expected Japanese resentment but found none. That summer I ended up teaching English to young Chinese refugees, the sons and daughters of parents who had fled China, crossing into the British-controlled New Territories during years leading up to the brutal Mao-inspired Cultural Revolution.

When I graduated from Stanford University in 1966, the Vietnam War was raging. I was deeply troubled by the U.S. involvement and felt the best way to come to terms with Vietnam was to volunteer as a civilian to work with war refugees. So I joined a Mennonite-, Brethren-, and Quaker-inspired non-profit organization, contracted to the Agency of International Development, called International Voluntary Services. After a month of intensive language training, I was assigned to assist refugees outside a small coastal town, a provincial capital in central Vietnam, Tuy Hoa. I lived there and worked for two years, witnessing the war close up. I saw the iron fist under the velvet glove of U.S. foreign policy. Some said we refugee volunteers were window dressing on the genocide that was taking place in Vietnam. They had a point. I felt like that at times, but I also knew I could make at least a small difference in the lives of needy people. The Vietnamese have a saying: "When the elephants fight, the ants get crushed." I lived with and tended to the wounds of the ants.

Since my first trip to Asia I have returned there more than a dozen times. In all I lived in Vietnam for nearly five years. My Vietnam War experience led me into journalism and on to Asian studies. Eventually, having returned again to Vietnam, I met a Vietnamese social worker, a Catholic convert who had grown up in the Mekong Delta town of Can Tho. Her name was To Kim Hoa. One year later we married, following all the Vietnamese customs, including prayers and offerings before her family's ancestral shrine. Two years later, in 1973, Kim Hoa was pregnant and we returned to the United States to begin our family in a less chaotic environment. By then I was pursuing journalism as a career, but never lost my interest in Asia.

The seeds of this book can be traced to a *National Catholic Reporter* project on which I worked with veteran journalist Gary MacEoin. In early 1998, we jointly wrote several articles in preparation for a spring synod on Asia. I attended that month-long gathering and during it reencountered up close the depth of the emerging Asian Catholic vision of church. It was then that I first began to grasp the wider possibilities of that vision and its importance for the wider universal church.

The synod ended up as a tug-of-war, prelates on two ends of a long rope seeming to pull in opposite directions as they took on the issues of church mission and in particular the role of evangelization within that mission. On the one end were the Asian bishops; on the other were the curial prelates. While participants were always friendly and polite, the synod revealed deep disagreements among the Catholic hierarchy and potentially differing and critical choices for the future of the local churches of Asia. As a result of the synod's bureaucratic process, it produced fifty-two propositions that were only echoes of echoes of the most exciting ideas the Asian bishops had brought with them to Rome. These were then forwarded to the pope for his consideration.

A year and a half later in New Delhi, in November 1999, Pope John Paul II offered his responses to the synod. A few months later, in January 2000, the Asian bishops met for the seventh plenary gathering of the Federation of Asian Bishops' Conferences. I had the distinction of being the only Western journalist to sit through the entire gathering, even at one time being called to work as a workshop recorder. I was drafted because I was one of the few at the meeting to come equipped with a laptop computer! During that week and a half I had the rare opportunity of seeing close up how the bishops and religious and lay leaders of Asia worked together to craft a new pastoral document.

Shortly after I returned from Thailand, Michael Leach, working for Orbis Books, suggested I write this book. This is a reader-friendly story. In the process I have tried to turn theology into journalism. It is not an easy task. I can imagine some Asian theologians grinding their teeth as they read this book. My goal has been to bring a very important pastoral-theological story to a wider audience, to popularize it. If in this book I have captured a small fraction of the energy of the dreams and hopes of the Asians I encountered along the way I will be satisfied. For anything good to happen, it first must be imagined. Asian Catholics have moved beyond imagination. Their vision is coming to life, slowly and unevenly, but it is happening. It's time to take notice. We will be enriched by the effort.

Some final notes: This book is meant to serve as an introduction to a large topic. As an introduction, it is bound to generalize. For example, virtually any use of the word "Asian" as an adjective is an overstatement. There is almost no single "Asian" anything. Rather there are an infinite number of *Asian* experiences, attitudes, cultures, and beliefs. Yet the use of "Asian" as an adjective continues in common parlance. It helps make sense of reality. This stated, most Asians—products of millennia of Asian philosophies and religions—do, in fact, approach life differently from many in the West. Asians tend to be more patient—or fatalistic. They pay considerable attention to family, which they view as a wider unit than do most Westerners today. Western spirituality has sought holiness and salvation. Eastern spirituality has sought enlightenment and transcendence. There are differences between East and West.

It is not an easy task to take theology and translate it into popular journalism. Nuances necessarily get lost. My hope is that the essentials remain intact. Nevertheless, I offer my apologies to those who might feel the need to cringe at times as they read the narrative.

Finally, while I refer throughout this book to Asia, I focus on East Asia, not those Asian lands we call the "Middle East." This book deals with eastern, southeastern, and southern Asia, those lands we once referred to as the "Far East." These lands comprise those where the Catholic leadership joined together in 1970 to begin to forge a new vision of church, an Asian vision of church. Just as the early apostles after Pentecost began their journeys to spread a hopeful vision of faith in their time, the Asian bishops, moved by the same Spirit, are on a wonderful journey today.[1]

PART 1

CHAPTER 1

New Way
of Being Church

Blessed are the peacemakers, for they
shall be called children of God.
                    —*Matthew 5:9*

Oh God, You are Peace.
From You comes Peace,
To You Returns Peace.
Revive us with a salutation of Peace,
And lead us to your abode of Peace.
            —*A saying of the Prophet used*
            in daily prayer by Muslims

Imagine a Buddha-like man, stocky, bald, round-faced, intelligent, and wise. His disposition is cheerful; his manner mild. He has a history of working for peace with a record of speaking out against militarism. His focus is caring for others, especially the weak and marginalized.

Meet Archbishop Fumio Hamao, two decades bishop of Yokohama, Japan, and currently the president of the Vatican's Pontifical Council for the Pastoral Care of Migrants and Itinerant Peoples. Hamao is the first Japanese to head a Vatican office. I first interviewed this Japanese prelate at the synod of bishops for Asia in Rome in April 1998. We spoke again at the seventh plenary gathering of the Federation of Asian Bishops' Conferences, or FABC, in Sam Phran, Thailand, in January 2000.

Dressed in sandals, tan trousers, and a short-sleeved shirt, Hamao was in good spirits and seemingly quite relaxed at the Thailand gathering as he talked to longtime friends, a glass of Singha beer in hand. Late afternoon prayer, a mixture of Gospel readings and Taizé chants, had ended. So too had a cafeteria dinner of white rice, vegetables, and a fish soup.

A bright moon lit up a clear sky under which some seventy-five bishops and archbishops were milling about on a large patio near a still pond graced with water lilies and swans. The setting was as peaceful as the dispositions of those who filled it out. This January night was typical for Thailand, mild and not too humid, good socializing weather. That's precisely what the Asian bishops were intent on doing. They had come from all over the continent to combine work and play. The mix produces pastoral-oriented reflection and enhances their fascinating vision of church.

For Hamao, this particular evening was special. After months in Rome he had just returned to Asian soil. A smile on his face, he noted that he always feels more comfortable in Asia. The Asian bishops tend to be less formal in their episcopal dealings than their Western counterparts. It is rare for these men to wear their Roman clothes at home—and on this night I saw no Roman collars or red-buttoned cassocks.

In many ways Hamao is typical of the Asian bishops, pastoral to the core. Before being assigned to his curial post, he headed the Yokohama diocese from 1980 to 1998. For decades he had been a major voice for peace and justice issues among the Japanese Catholics. He has spoken out strongly against Japan's growing military ties with the United States. He has protested at the U.S. Navy's Yokosuka naval base. Addressing the synod on Asia in 1998, Hamao said the work of peacemaking is central to the Catholic mission. He noted that the virtues of spiritual and social harmony run deep in Asia and likewise through the veins of the Asian bishops. The whole concept of harmony, he said, has become foundational to the nature and expressions of the local churches of Asia. Hamao's synod intervention was one of the more passionate to be delivered before the bishops. His words rang out as an expression of humility and a call for Christian forgiveness and reconciliation, affording listeners a window on an Asian soul.[1]

When the atomic bombs were dropped on Hiroshima and Nagasaki in August 1945, hundreds of thousands of lives were snuffed out in an instant. We Japanese are victims of the war, but at the same time we were also the aggressors who trampled on the lives of people in many areas of Asia and the Pacific. We must admit that the church of Japan failed to realize and courageously proclaim how inhuman and out of harmony with the Gospel values were the elements of that war. The church failed in her prophetic role of witnessing to the will of God in protecting human life. Today we live in a "global village," an interrelated network of nations, cultures, ethnic groups, traditions and religious families. This is true especially of Asia. Peace cannot be attained unless it cuts across these multi-cultural, multi-religious nations. Peace is a gift, the fruit of a healthy human community. Peace is the final gift, the result of a harmonious and mature integration of fairness, justice, love, truth, liberty and respect for all. It must include mercy (compassion) towards the weak and powerless, tolerance and a patient waiting for growth. Peace never occurs in isolation. It is the fruition of a good life for all. For that reason, working for peace is considered to be a highly esteemed spiritual value. Peace is the greatest blessing of God to a people. Working for peace should be a central concern of the church.

Ecological concerns are also very important elements in the evangelization conducted by the church. Environmental concerns are not just for the benefit of future generations, but all creatures and nature itself are "our brothers and sisters" as St. Francis called them, and they are our companions on this earth with which we must strive to live in harmony. . . . It is our earnest desire, and that of the bishops of Japan, that this synod puts peace at the center of our evangelization and mission in Asia today. Our Lord said: "Blessed are the peacemakers; they shall be recognized as children of God."

At the time of Hamao's Rome appointment, some of his friends suggested that he was being kicked upstairs so that his voice could be muffled. He laughs mischievously at the thought. Once in Rome, Hamao turned down an offer to live in a Vatican villa. Instead he chose quarters at the Santa Marta, a hotel-like residential building for visiting clergy inside the Vatican walls. Unlike other curial prelates, Hamao has no chauffeur, drives a car, and sometimes uses local public transportation. It's his way, he told me, of staying closer to the people of Rome.

Hamao is one of the Asian apostles who have been shaping the local churches of Asia since the Second Vatican Council (1962–1965), the brainchild of Pope John XXIII. Within three months of his election, Pope John announced a general council, summoning 2,500 bishops from around the world to "throw open the windows" of the church and let fresh air in. Stressing the need for episcopal collegiality, the council fathers drew up documents filled with fresh expressions of faith and a belief that the church had to be a transformative force within the wider world community. The council ignited the imaginations of millions of Catholics worldwide. Asian Catholics were no exception. After all, the council not only offered the pledge of church renewal, but tore down the walls it had erected over centuries to protect itself from the world.

As much as anything else, the Vatican Council signaled to Asia's Catholics that the church had become sensitive to issues of culture and ethnic identity. The council also marked something else for the churches of Asia. It signaled a new era of equality and ecclesial fraternity. Out of this came the expectation that church machinery would now be turned over to local leaders. The days were ending when European bishops were appointed to run Asian dioceses. Local leaders were abundant and ready to take charge of their own lives and those of their faithful.

These new Asian bishops faced serious challenges. Their overwhelming problem was pretty basic: Christianity, inspired by the Asian Jesus, his disciples and the evangelists, had taken on a European template before returning to Asia. The challenge for the Asian leaders was now to find those paths that would allow them to nurture the essence of their faith while separating it from the trappings of the colonial experience. This task was further complicated by the fact that many older Asian Catholics had grown accustomed to their European saints, statues, and holy cards. Many had little interest in changing the personal pieties they had grown up with through their lifetimes.

Fundamentally, the Vatican Council was about renewal; however, implementing that renewal required both energy and vision, whether in Europe, North America, or Asia. Nearly all Asian bishops and theologians who attended the council supported church renewal. Despite varied national and ethnic differences, they returned home to face similar questions: What steps should they take to implement the council documents? Which elements of church renewal would most enrich the faith lives of their people? What actions would they need to take to ensure that Catholicism would flourish in the years ahead?

With a few notable exceptions, the Asian bishops had been mostly passive participants at the council. The expertise of the Asian theologians was generally not sought out at the council.[2] For the Asian church leaders the council was largely a learning and incubation period, opening their minds to new possibilities later on. It was during this same period that a fresh postwar generation of young Asian theologians was leaving graduate schools and seminaries and was beginning to make an early imprint on the developing theological and pastoral conversations. The list of young Asian theologians was already quite extensive—and impressive. The most prominent of the new thinkers were D. S. Amalorpavadass, Aloysius Pieris, George Soares-Prabhu, Felix Wilfred, Samuel Rayan, Michael Amaladoss, Tissa Balasuriya, and C. G. Arévalo. Each wrote out of a specific discipline, but all shared the conviction that the Word of God had to be viewed anew through *Asian* eyes and within the context of *Asian* history—with its gaping wounds caused by widespread poverty, hunger, violence, and oppressive structures. These theologians were calling for radical change. They were calling for liberation—total spiritual and physical liberation! And they sought freedom not only from centuries-old injustices, but also from a newer disease, a creeping Western-inspired materialism that was starting to tear deep at the fabric of Asian society. These theologians were borrowing freely from Latin American liberation theology, particularly seizing upon its fundamental insight that theology grows out of the local experience of the believers, that all theology is local. All theology is contextual. However, these Asian theologians were adding to the liberation theology they had inherited because their context was different. To the social analysis found in Latin American liberation theology, the Asian theologians were adding a uniquely Asian context. They were adding Asia's rich sense of contemplation and spiritual and religious heritage. This was theology within the context of Asian poverty, culture, and religion.

Following the Vatican Council, the Asian leaders faced many very practical as well as theological questions. They were spread out across the continent of Asia. They had to find the means to meet on a regular basis. They lacked the publishing tools and journals in which to share their ideas. They had to build pastoral centers and theological reviews. And in the new era of collegiality, with Rome no longer necessarily at the center, the bishops needed to form and run national episcopal conferences. These would have to become the instruments for coordinating church renewal. But even these conferences were isolated from other Asian bishops' conferences. Ideas had to be exchanged and shared across Asia. All these mechanisms were yet to be learned, let alone successfully used on behalf of renewal.

No challenge seemed too large at the time. There was much will and energy. In virtually every Asian nation discussions among the Asian leadership led to decisions to set up academic and planning centers. Throughout Asia, biblical, liturgical, pastoral, and catechetical institutes began to pop up: in the Philippines, the East Asian Pastoral Institute and the Paul VI Institute of Liturgy; in Japan, Nanzan University's Institute for Religion and Culture; in India, Ishvani Kendra in Pune, and the National Biblical Catechetical and Liturgical Center in Bangalore; in Sri Lanka, the Tulana Research Center. These centers soon became platforms for dialogue and further calls for renewal. Many started publications that allowed the theologians and other visionaries to share their ideas. It was at the first general meeting of the Indian bishops in 1966 that the leadership, fresh from the council, decided to form a national center solely aimed at fostering church renewal. The bishops chose Bangalore, in central southern India, for its mild climate and its proximity to the relatively large population of Catholics in the region. So it was that the widely acclaimed National Biblical, Catechetical and Liturgical Center came to life. A thirty-three-year-old Indian visionary, Father D. S. Amalorpavadass, would soon head the center. His ideas would spearhead pastoral thinking in India and elsewhere for decades to come.

This was a very heady time for the local churches of Asia. The years

were full of expectation and hope. The excitement was further aug-
mented by Rome's own growing interest in Asia, most graphically symbolized by Pope Paul VI's 1964 trip to Bombay for a Eucharistic Congress.
International papal travel was a rarity at the time. A trip to Asia was
unprecedented. Paul VI, traveling in India, became so moved by the
poverty he encountered that he gave his white Lincoln limousine to
Mother Teresa, who in turn staged a raffle and spent the proceeds—
$100,000—to aid the poor. Today, a large bronze bell stands in front of the
Bombay (now called Mumbai) cathedral, commemorating the pope's
1964 visit. The influence of that visit on Pope Paul VI was significant. In
1967, he mentioned the trip in his encyclical on development, *Populorum
Progressio*:

> There can be no progress towards the complete development of man
> without the simultaneous development of all humanity in the spirit
> of solidarity. As We said at Bombay: "Man must meet man, nation
> meet nation, as brothers and sisters, as children of God. In this
> mutual understanding and friendship, in this sacred communion,
> we must also begin to work together to build the common future
> of the human race." (§43)

The 1964 Asian trip turned out to be a mere warm-up, however, for
what came six years later. Paul's penchant to travel soon earned him the
nickname of the "missionary pope." It was in November 1970 that he
returned to Asia. That trip was Pope Paul's seventh outside of Italy, the
longest and most grueling of the then seventy-three-year-old pontiff's
seven-year pontificate. It was a 28,400-mile adventure that took him to
East Pakistan, Iran, the Philippines, Samoa, Australia, Indonesia, Hong
Kong, and Ceylon. The clear high point of the journey was a three-day
stopover in Manila, where 180 Asian bishops had gathered from fifteen
nations to receive him.

Vatican II had inspired Catholics, but not always in the same way. In
the early 1970s Asia was only one generation removed from colonialism.
Its national leaders, including Catholics, were feeling strong nationalist
sentiments, and they were proud to take the reins of their governments
and their very lives. In the eyes of many Asians, the Catholic Church was
a privileged institution, one that had benefited enormously from centuries of foreign presence. Even though Christianity had Asian roots, it
was viewed throughout most of Asia as a foreign implant, an outgrowth
of European colonialism. In reality, the history of the church in Asia during colonial times was more complex than outward appearances would
have it.

Nevertheless, during the 1940s, 1950s, and 1960s, decades of eruption of nationalistic fervor, the challenge Roman Catholics faced was enormous. In many instances it was virtually impossible for Catholics to convince their fellow compatriots that they too were patriots, or that Catholicism in Asia could support Asian ethnicity and Asian nationalist pride. Little did it matter that Jesus had been an Asian, or that the first Christians had been Asians. With few exceptions, Catholicism had arrived with or soon after Western conquerors. This was—and continues to be in many places in Asia—a bitter pill for Asian Catholics to swallow. Western Catholics who fail to understand this fundamental Asian reality cannot begin to understand the dynamics of Asian Catholic thought as they continue to be played out in Asia today. Failure to understand this reality makes it impossible to comprehend the need for and value given by Asian Catholics to the inculturation of faith.

That said, the West needs to understand another fundamental aspect of Asian thought before it can began to approach the Asian Catholic psyche. Recorded Asian history dates back several millennia. Asians are very proud of their long histories. The stories they pass from generation to generation shape Asian art, culture, language, and religion. These stories and histories are deeply ingrained into the Asian mind and heart and are a large part of the fabric that brings Asians to a common worldview. Any outside force, be it political, economic, or religious, viewed as causing harm to Asian heritage—or not taking it seriously—will be viewed with little respect and even quiet hostility.

All these factors have shaped the story of the growth of Asian Catholicism in recent decades. The essential notion here is the importance Asian Catholics give to planting their Catholicism in Asia, that is, giving it Asian characteristics. On the other side of the coin, they take pride in their Asian heritage and want to bring it to the wider faith community. From the Asian Catholic point of view, Catholicism in Asia will become authentic only when it ceases to be "Western." In other words, the primary Asian emphasis is on building the local Asian faith community.

The *American Heritage Dictionary* defines "theology" as "the study of the nature of God and religious truth." In the years that followed the Vatican Council, local religious experience and local reflections on the nature of God were becoming essential ingredients of the work of the churches in Asia. In other words, Asians were beginning to do theology. They were "contextualizing" their experiences of the divine, set in the circumstances of Asia, specifically of their local church. Like Latin American theologians, Asian theologians seized on an insight that would revolutionize theology within the Catholic Church and beyond—that their collective experiences, their search for God in the Asian context, were the basis of their theology. Meanwhile, when the Asian church leaders began to speak of their initiatives as "a new way of being church," they were actually affirming the insight that theology is local—coming out of local history, local culture, and local social and economic experiences. What also seemed to energize the Asian leadership in the years that followed the council was the notion that while their experiences of church were fundamentally "local," they were not to be alone. What was growing at the time was a pan-Asian call for cooperation and further exchange of ideas. In all these things, one finds the early seeds of what would grow into the wider Asian vision of Catholicism as a network of local churches working in harmony, sharing spiritual insights and, when necessary, material resources, as they attend to the deepest longings of the human family. This was, of course, a radically new vision of Roman Catholicism, especially in Asia, where for centuries Catholics had lived under a European ecclesial umbrella.

The ideas and theologies that were beginning to be generated in Asia at the time in some ways were not unlike other notions of church sprouting up elsewhere in the world. At the same time, however, the Asian theologies had their own unique views. One could honestly call them "post-Western." More accurately, the Asian leadership saw itself as more interested in engaging the future than rejecting the past. It just happened to be that the vision of a globally networked church, should it come to fruition, should it stress the richness of local culture and theology, could have the effect of reducing the burden of Western colonialism in Asia. Further, such a vision of church would be timely and would reflect the maturing process of thought in the late twentieth century, a period in which new insights into the importance of culture and ethnicity reshaped the human imagination. While not saying it, and probably not yet imagining it at the time, the Asian Catholic leadership was in the early stages of setting down a possible course for the universal church to follow in the twenty-first century, a post-Western pathway for a church increasingly ready to celebrate human dignity and equality throughout the world. It is not as if the council fathers who toiled in Rome for years did not recognize such a possible vision of church. Some did. It may be, however, that what the Asian bishops were being called by history to do in the wake of the council, given its fresh ideas and faith images, was to take the implicit and make it explicit. They were to take theory and flesh it out in living faith communities.

Jesuit Karl Rahner, the prominent German-born theologian, was one of the first to grasp the revolutionary importance of the shift that was occurring in Catholicism as a result of the Vatican Council. He wrote that the church, in the wake of the council, could transform itself. Vatican II, he stated, finally made a Catholic global church possible. In Rahner's view the one element that made the transformation possible was the change in language, the move to the use of local languages in local liturgies. He believed this change, called for by the council, would open the door to the inculturation of faith as never before imagined. This, in turn, he believed, would lead to the emergence of a truly global Catholicism. In fact, he wrote that the Vatican Council was "the first major official event in which the church began in fact to actualize itself precisely as a world church." Pondering the meaning of a global church, he continued that it would "act through the reciprocal influence exercised by all its components . . . even if only in an initial and tentative way: this is what we observe in Vatican II."[3]

POPE PAUL VI IN MANILA

Some truly historic moments are recognized immediately. The Second Vatican Council was one. Others become recognized after the fact, as their impact is felt in the years that follow. This was the case of Pope Paul VI's second trip to Asia, in 1970. As the pope went about the preparations for that journey, it was only a peripheral concern to most Western Catholics. At that time the West in general and the United States in particular had their hands full thinking about the fate of only one Asian nation, Vietnam.

Meanwhile, in November 1970, on the eve of the papal trip, the U.S. bishops were dealing with more mundane matters. At their annual meeting in Washington they were debating "communion in the hand." By a margin of 115 to 107, they rejected the option. It would be another seven years before they could muster the required votes. In November 1970, Jesuit Robert Drinan, former dean of Boston College Law School, made history by becoming the first Catholic priest to win a seat—from Massachusetts—in the U.S. House of Representatives. Not all Jesuits succeeded in their political quests. In the same election, Jesuit John J. McLaughlin (now of the *McLaughlin Group*), lost his bid to unseat Democratic Senator John O. Pastore of Rhode Island. By far the largest church issue most Western Catholics were facing in 1970 was the fallout from Pope Paul's July 1968 encyclical, *Humanae Vitae* ("On Human Life"), in which he reaffirmed the church's ban on artificial contraception. While it rocked many Western Catholics, it had a far smaller impact in Asia. At least two reasons can be cited for this. First, birth control measures were less available in Asia. The pill was not an option. Second, the press in largely non-Catholic Asia gave the encyclical relatively little attention. Generally speaking, the Asian bishops and their peoples follow the birth control policies of their respective governments.

It was another of Pope Paul's encyclicals, *Populorum Progressio* ("The Development of Peoples") that stirred the wider Asian Catholic imagination. In that encyclical the pope called upon the world's nations and organizations to take up the cause of justice worldwide. As far as Asian

Catholics were concerned, Pope Paul was directing attention to their impoverished continent. *Populorum Progressio* was written in a decade of unparalleled idealism. "International development" had virtually become household words. They were on the lips of economists and government leaders everywhere. If only nations could work together, if only they would pledge aid, if only the peacemakers would have their way, then hunger and warfare could be eliminated. Or so it was believed.

Pope Paul reflected this spirit in *Populorum Progressio*. Peace, the pontiff wrote, "cannot be limited to a mere absence of war, the result of an ever precarious balance of forces. No, peace is something that is built up day after day in the pursuit of an order intended by God, which implies a more perfect form of justice among people" (§76). Years later, Pope Paul's idealism lingers but seems to have been reduced to a bumper-sticker slogan: "If you want peace, work for justice."

It was still uncommon for the Asian bishops to gather together in 1970. Most lived in very isolated locations, and satellite communication was still in its infancy. It was more common for an Asian bishop to know a cleric in Rome than to know a bishop from another Asian country. That isolation, of course, began to break down at the Vatican Council. It was during those sessions that some Asians shared their common concerns. They developed a stronger sense of common resolve as they were infected by the council's fresh spirit of collegiality. Yet five years after the council, even as a new spirit of church renewal was breaking through, the outer shell of the older ecclesial realities seemed to hold sway. On the eve of Pope Paul's journey correspondents of the *New York Times*, asked to assess Catholicism in Asia, found little to praise. One writer summed up Catholicism in Asia in stark and uninviting terms, writing, ". . . in Asia, Catholic churches suffer from limitations on proselytism, unimaginative leadership and failures to develop enough indigenous priests and bishops."[4] That was soon to change.

The pope's Alitalia DC8/62 jetliner set down in Manila on the morning of November 27. Some Catholics might recall that day in Manila although without associating it with a gathering that would outline a vision for decades to come.[5] What they might remember is the vicious attack on the pope as he moved through the Manila airport. A dagger-wielding thirty-five-year-old Bolivian named Benjamin Mendoza y Amor Flores lunged at the pontiff in an unsuccessful attempt to take his life. The pontiff emerged shaken but unhurt. Later Flores explained that he had tried to kill the pope because he represented religion, which, he said, was superstitious. Despite the assassination attempt, Paul went ahead and read a prepared arrival speech, thanking President Ferdinand Marcos for a warm reception. He would later call upon Marcos to share more of the nation's wealth with the poor.

The pope explained the purpose of his mission in a broadcast over Radio Veritas, the Catholic network, in Manila. Addressing "all the peoples" of Asia, as opposed to just Catholics, he made it known that his intentions were primarily pastoral and went beyond the boundaries of the church. "To the countless millions of men and women, our brothers and sisters who live in Asia, this cross-roads of cultures, ancient and modern, and in a special manner to those among you who are women and children in Christ—the blessing of God, abiding peace and fraternity." The "countless millions" were not just a figure of speech. Asia at the time made up 60 percent of the world's population.[6] Yet Catholics in Asia were a distinct minority, 1 to 2 percent in most countries. The Philippines was the exception, with thirty-two million Catholics, representing nearly two-thirds of Asia's Catholics.

For their part, the Asian bishops had chosen as the theme for their gathering the pope's encyclical *Populorum Progressio*. It was a remarkable moment, providing a rich new opportunity for a blending of visions. Never before had the Asian bishops gathered on Asian soil to exchange their experiences and deliberate on common matters facing them.[7] Many seemed to sense the unique importance of the occasion, including the pope himself, who called it a "historical moment full of mystery."[8] The Manila gathering marked a new maturity in thinking among Asian Catholic leaders. Felix Wilfred, a systematic theologian from St. Paul's Seminary in Tiruchirapalli, India, would later write that the meeting "marked the beginning of a new consciousness of the many traditional links that united the various peoples" of Asia. He explained that in spite of many differences, the peoples of Asia are bound together "by a spiritual affinity and sharing of common moral and religious values." He attributed this to the cultural, religious, and ethical influences of India and China, while adding that in addition to these links, "the peoples of Asia experience today the same patterns of sociopolitical conditions, face common challenges and share similar concerns."[9] The Manila gathering was momentous. It seemed as if the stars of heaven had lined up, and for a moment in time the Catholic leadership of Asia gathered together to pledge solidarity with the poor and cast their lot with millions of marginalized Asians.

The three-day gathering fostered a strong sense of solidarity among the bishops themselves as they met to discuss a variety of development issues.[10] Oblate Miguel Marcelo Quatra years later wrote, "It was as if they had finally awakened to the reality of the many cultural, historical and contemporary bonds that united the local churches of the continent, despite their indisputable diversity."[11] Of course, all this was made possible by the pope's presence. He had written the original text for their deliberations in his encyclical and in those passages had pleaded for humanity to respond to world hunger, oppression, and injustice. Given that strong papal lead, the Asian bishops felt empowered to do the same. As a result, few of the topics they took up during the meeting dealt with institutional church matters. Their starting point was, in the words of the pontiff himself, "the needs and aspirations of our peoples."

As the bishops approached the end of their meetings, they were feeling liberated and resolute. Following their discussions they agreed to send a "message of the conference" to their peoples. In it they confidently listed a set of concrete tasks to which they solemnly committed themselves in the presence of the pope. It is noteworthy that at the top of their list—their number one resolution—was their common commitment to become a "church of the poor."

> It is our resolve, first of all, to be more truly "the church of the poor." If we are to place ourselves at the side of the multitudes in our continent, we must in our way of life share something of their poverty. The church cannot set up islands of affluence in a sea of want and misery; our own personal lives must give witness to evangelical simplicity, and no man, no matter how lowly, or poor, should find it hard to come to us and find in us their brothers.[12]

Coming just two years after the Latin American bishops announced their own "preferential option for the poor" in Medellin, Colombia, the Asian bishops were now following suit. Facing a similar gulf between rich and poor, between the "haves" and the "have-nots," the Asian bishops made the same choice the Latin American bishops had made. They aligned themselves with their peoples—and most of these peoples were poor and hungry and oppressed. They decided to enter into Asian poverty. For a group of bishops, many of whom had known little other than privilege, it was a giant step forward—but not without risk.

However, that was only part of the historic decision making that emerged from the Manila gathering. The bishops also placed on their task list commitment to youth, to dialogue, and to the process of inculturation. They decided that to spread the Word of God in Asia, to share the faith more widely, they had no choice but to enter deeper into Asian culture. In a move still remarkable at the time, they urged their local churches to maintain "a deep respect for the culture and traditions of our peoples."[13] That statement marked the end of centuries of Asian Catholic defensiveness. The call was nothing short of revolutionary—even, some critics argued, bordering on the heretical.

The bishops' final Manila message stressed the importance of cooperation with all people of good will in search for human development, freedom, justice, and peace, so that the church may "help bind together the new world of Asia as a true family of nations in this part of the earth, linked not only by lines of geography, but by mutual understanding and respect, by the nobler bonds of brotherhood and love."

What happened in Manila was nothing short of inspirational. Some observers later wrote that being part of it, they could see the hand of the Holy Spirit at work. But how would the energy that emerged during the Manila gathering be harnessed? How could it be assured that the work of Manila would continue? What means of collaboration would allow the vision to go forward? What would happen after the excitement of the papal visit subsided? How would the bishops stay in touch? How would they continue to share their common concerns and learn from each other's experiences? Wise leaders had asked these questions quietly early on; some even anticipated these questions before the bishops came together in Manila.

Cardinal Stephen Kim, archbishop emeritus of Seoul, was one such modern apostle. Years later he recalled that, looking forward to Manila the bishops of Korea were very anxious.

> We feared that the important event would be restricted to a wonderful celebration without any follow up. To prevent that sad possibility, we decided to propose the creation of a permanent body as an instrument of communion and dialogue among all bishops of Asia. . . . I thought then that for the future and evangelization of Asia in a rapidly developing world, its bishops' conferences needed cooperation among themselves. . . . Such mutual help would not only contribute greatly to the development of the Catholic Church in Asia, but it would have the potential of making a major contribution to human development, advancing justice and creating a human being-centered society, all of which were badly needed in many countries.[14]

And so it was that while in Manila, as the wider body of bishops met daily to develop a common document, a vision of church that would take them forward, during the evenings a smaller group of bishops, interested in establishing a permanent Asian bishops' organization, gathered at the Jesuit Xavier House to discuss the possibilities. "One day during the assembly, Archbishop Sergio Pignedoli, then secretary of the Congregation for the Evangelization of Peoples, approached me to say he knew of our plan," Kim recalled. He asked that we formally present it, as he favored it. If the bishops agreed on the proposal, he said, he would give it positive support. "For me, those words were like a million reinforcements."

So, gathering courage, I made the proposal at a meeting attended by Pope Paul. In the ensuing discussion, Bishop Francis Hsu of Hong Kong, who had attended the meetings at Xavier House and spoke fluent English, explained the proposal. After sharing opinions, a resolution was passed at the general assembly to establish a permanent [Asian bishops'] organization. The nature and title of the organization were not yet decided, but Bishop Hsu was asked to convene a meeting of national conference presidents before the end of March 1971 to being drafting a plan.

Jesuit C. G. Arévalo, professor of theology at Loyola School of Theology in the Philippines, was in Manila at the time as a young theologian. In subsequent years he would become a central deposit of information for the Asian bishops. He recalls that the bishops involved in the early discussions at Xavier House included three extraordinary Asian visionaries, Cardinals Kim, Valerian Gracias of Bombay, India, and Justinus Darmojuwono of Semarang, Indonesia. Also present were Bishops Francis Hsu of Hong Kong and Mariano Gaviola of the Philippines, as well as Father Horacio de la Costa, the Jesuit Provincial to the Philippines.[15]

The outlines of the new organization were slowly emerging. They called for a loose network of Asian bishops who would come together under a central secretariat. But during early discussions questions of authority arose. During one debate, Darmojuwono, chairman of the Indonesian Bishops' Conference from 1965 to 1979, assured the bishops that the central secretariat would not have authority over the episcopal conferences, but rather would act more modestly, attempting to serve the conferences. With these assurances offered, the bishops chimed in and offered their full support. All that was needed was papal approval, seemingly a mere formality. On November 28, in the presence of the pope, the resolution was approved. Pope Paul was very supportive. It was further decided that Bishop Hsu be given the responsibility of organizing the first meeting of the new organization's central committee.[16]

Before ending their meeting, the bishops released a set of episcopal resolutions. Showing the importance they gave to their new organization, they placed at the top of their list a call for the establishment of "a permanent structure for the effective implementation of the decisions of this meeting." The organization that was soon to be called the Federation of Asian Bishops' Conferences, or FABC, was coming to life.

Looking back, it is unlikely that the FABC would ever have come to life without Pope Paul's support. Not only did he protect the idea of the organization early on, but steps he took during his pontificate helped set the stage for the FABC. Its development fits very well with the establishment under Paul VI of the International Theological Commission as well as the clear and substantial structure that he gave to episcopal synods. *Ecclesiam Suam* from 1964 has a sophisticated explanation of the meaning of dialogue, which was reiterated in 1968 by the Secretariat for Non-Believers in the document *Humanae Personae Dignitatem.*

During Manila the directions that gathering was taking did not please some Vatican prelates. Cardinal Gracias later told the story of a curial official who offered objections to parts of the texts as they were developed in Manila. Hearing this, Gracias privately asked the pope if he shared those reservations. Pope Paul, he said, reassured him that he had taken the time to read personally the documents and made it clear to all that there would be no changes whatsoever in the original texts.[17]

Besides deciding to create a permanent Asian bishops' organization, the Manila resolutions offered episcopal pledges to defend human rights, to throw in their lot with the workers and peasants, to begin to converse with the other religions of Asia, and to develop indigenous Asian theologies. Spawned by a quest for answers to problems of human development and social justice, the resolutions became the first truly collegial act of the Asian churches. Each of these resolutions was taking the Asian leadership into uncharted waters. Having come together, the bishops were emboldened by one another, becoming collectively stronger than any one imagined alone. They were setting out on a profoundly new pastoral course—a more religiously, culturally, socially, and politically attuned course, responding to the needs of the times. They would soon be calling it a "new way of being church."

CHAPTER 2

Triple Dialogue

What does the Lord require of you,
but to do justice, love mercy and
walk humbly with God?
　　　　　—Micah 6:8

In whatever way and path humans
worship Me, in that same path do I
(meet) and fulfill their aspirations
and grace them. It is always My Path
that humans follow in all their
different paths and journeys, on all
sides.
　　　　　—Bhagavad-Gita IV:11

Nearing eighty and living in retirement, South Korean Cardinal Stephen Kim Sou-Hwan is bamboo thin, but like the plant is agile and well grounded. It was on a bitter cold morning in January 2001 that my wife and I met him on the campus of Seoul's Catholic University. With winds rattling the windows we sat down and were quickly offered hot green tea. Kim wore a black scarf around his neck as he sat on a sofa covered with white linen. Korea at the time was experiencing its coldest weather in a dozen years. A Siberian cold front was moving through. In Korea, unlike in other East Asian nations to the south, weather can be a major hardship, but the locals have adjusted. They've learned to live with the cold.

That morning the cardinal was characteristically cordial. He told me he was familiar with the *National Catholic Reporter*, the news weekly for which I have written for these past two decades. He asked my wife about our family. In Asia, family talk precedes business. The practice not only breaks the ice but also speaks to the high value Asians place on family. Identity comes out of family. After ten minutes of friendly conversation we settled in well, so I decided to ask the cardinal if he would share with me his memories of the military dictatorships in the 1970s and 1980s. Through those brutal years, Kim was perhaps the nation's most vocal advocate of democracy and human rights.

"Those were tough years," he said in English.

"And lonely years?" I asked.

"Yes, sometimes our bishops did not always agree on the statements we needed to make."

There were divisions within the ranks of the Korean bishops at that time. Not so much on the nature of the regimes, as on how to respond to their widespread violations of rights. Some bishops wanted to stay relatively quiet and work from the inside. Kim thought otherwise. He felt compelled to speak out, to be a voice for the people, he said. As archbishop of Seoul, he was at times in a lonely place as he stood—sometimes all alone—against the generals. During that time he opened the Seoul cathedral, offering it as a place for political sanctuary. In the process he extended his episcopal cloak of protection to tens of thousands of students, workers, and political dissidents. The Myongdong cathedral, an old French gothic structure in the heart of Seoul, became a beacon of light and hope through years of darkness, not only in Korea but also symbolically throughout Asia. The generals responded by jailing hundreds of lay activists and dozens of priests. Once they sentenced a Korean bishop to fifteen years in prison.

In 1975, in one memorable cathedral confrontation, police arrested opposition leader (and later Korean president and Nobel Peace Prize laureate) Kim Dae Jung and two dozen other protesters as Bishop Kim Sou-Hwan led two thousand supporters in a prayer service. A decade later, one of South Korea's largest newspapers, *Dong-a Ilbo*, expressing gratitude for the nation, named Kim "Man of the Year." Said the paper: "His vision of democracy—his vision that people be respected, his going out to seek the marginalized and the oppressed, to be with them, to comfort and pray with them—is the reason we have chosen Kim Sou-Hwan man of the year." Kim continues to be respected throughout South Korea, where Catholics make up about 8 percent of the nation's forty-eight million people. Today the Catholic Church in Korea is experiencing the highest annual adult baptism rate in the world, a trend also true among Koreans living in America. Catholicism in Korea has had a remarkable history. It began through the initiative of Korean Confucian scholars in 1784 who had visited China and became Christians after reading Christian texts found in Beijing. Korean laity not only kept the faith alive, but also shared it with others until the first missionaries arrived in 1836.[1]

It was Pope Paul VI who appointed Kim archbishop of Seoul in 1968. The following year the pontiff made him, at the age of forty-seven, the youngest member of the Sacred College of Cardinals. Kim has watched the South Korean Catholic population more than double to four million. Many say it was his courageous commitment to justice and human dignity that drew converts to the church. Curiously, despite Kim's public profile, few Korean Catholics seem to be aware of the important role he played in determining the course of the Catholic Church in Asian history. Few know, for example, that it was Kim who first imagined, and then lobbied to bring to life, an organization that would unite and galvanize all the Asian bishops' conferences. Looking back over three decades, he chuckles and says that it was nothing short of a miracle that the Asian bishops' organization he dreamed up ever got off the ground. Distrust in Rome almost did it in, he told me.

"Would you like some more tea?" he asked.

"Of course," I responded, wrapping my fingers around the small porcelain cup for warmth.

Kim then recalled an important gathering of the presidents of eleven Asian bishops' conferences some four months after Pope Paul VI's visit to Manila. The bishops were in Hong Kong to nourish the idea of forming an umbrella organization to unite all the bishops of Asia. Specifically they wanted to draw up statutes so they could present them in Rome. Once in Hong Kong, however, Cardinal Edward Cassidy, the Vatican diplomat of Taipei, Taiwan, at the time, gave the Asian bishops some unexpected and shocking news. He told them that key members of the Roman Curia were so opposed to the idea of the proposed organization that they wanted all work on it to stop immediately.

"Cassidy told us that there was nothing that could be done. The only thing left [for us] to do was to go shopping—or leave Hong Kong right away. We were shocked," Kim continued, adding that he was equally determined to stay the course. "I asked Cassidy to imagine the reaction of the mass media when word got out that Rome had canceled the meeting of the Asian bishops," Kim said. "They knew we were in Hong Kong to discuss the organization," he went on. "If we stopped it would be very negative. It would be very bad publicity for the Roman church."

Cassidy listened and pondered Kim's remarks—and eventually agreed with him. He had been won over and, in fact, went on to say that he would personally take responsibility for the *continuing* of the bishops' meeting. With Cassidy's new reassurance, the bishops began their work. First they formed an organizational working committee that would draft statutes. The group named Kim committee president. It went on to name as committee members Jesuit Cardinal Justinus Darmojuwono of Indonesia, Archbishop Teopisto Alberto of the Philippines, Bishops Francis Hsu of Hong Kong and Patrick D'Souza of India. Hsu, who was fluent in English, was chosen to be committee secretary.

By the end of April 1971 the committee had completed a first draft of the statutes. Later, after receiving feedback and suggestions from the Asian episcopal conferences, the group sketched out several revisions. By November 1971, it had written a proposed constitution and had again distributed papers to the various national conferences. The statutes, reflecting the wider Asian conferences' sentiments, were well received. The only reservation at the time was that some bishops wanted assurances that membership in the new organization would be strictly voluntary.

By the end of August 1972, less than two years after Manila, the presidents of twelve bishops' conferences had given their approval, and it was decided that the four Asian cardinals—Valerian Gracias of Bombay, Thomas Cooray of Colombo, Darmojuwono, and Kim—would go to Rome to present the approved constitution to Pope Paul.

"The pope was supportive," Kim recalled. However, not everyone in the Vatican was so pleased. "By then CELAM (the Latin American Bishops' Conference) had been established [in 1955] and some in Rome did not accept it," said Kim. "They did not want another CELAM. It was a matter of control. Rome didn't want to lose control."

There was another sticking point. The Vatican, Kim said, did not want the proposed bishops' organization to have, in church parlance, "binding authority." Rome did not want the bishops involved in strict moral or doctrinal matters.

"We assured the pope," Kim said, "what we envisioned was an organization that was pastoral in nature, an advisory body aimed at facilitating communication." Kim also told the pope that the new body would work for social justice and human development, that it would promote and defend the greater good of Asia.[2] Implicit in Kim's description to the pope was an idea close to the pontiff's heart—an organization committed to practicing collegiality, putting the ideals of the council to work. The new group would help forge a Vatican II vision of church.[3]

Ironically, the fact that the nascent organization did not, in the final analysis, end up with the official authority Rome had feared turned out to be a real plus. Some in Rome clearly feared a countervailing Asian authority, another power center. The truth is that the Asian bishops were not really seeking "power" as much as they were seeking better communication. They were looking down a pastoral path. From Rome's viewpoint, however, the Asian churches were still mission territory, young churches—and not to be trusted. (The Asian churches, as mission territory, continue to fall under the aegis of the Vatican's Congregation for the Evangelization of Peoples, which supports them with money and ecclesial direction. Many argue—with good reason—that this financial dependence limits somewhat the independence of the local churches of

Asia.) There was a twist to this story. As it turned out, by *not* having "binding authority," the Asian bishops, not burdened with the weight of such authority, were able to act much more freely—and agree more quickly—to the many statements they were to issue in the years that followed. For the Asian bishops the important issues, it turned out, would be pastoral in nature, not doctrinal. They would deal with mission, spirituality, dialogue with other religions, and peace and justice issues. They would have to do with charting the direction of the church in Asia. These were essentially pastoral matters. Curiously, these issues would turn out to be far more "subversive," at least from Rome's point of view, than the "binding" matters of morality and doctrine that Rome feared. Another point needs to be mentioned here. When it came time to write their documents, the approach the bishops used was consensus building. After much socializing, many hours of talks and votes, the bishops were always able to agree on basics. The beauty of not having "binding authority" is that you are freer to speak your mind, your beliefs, and your passions. You can share these thoughts, put them in writing, and, when working with other bishops, even publish them as pastoral documents. As a result, the Asian episcopal vision, after decades of work, is not found in any single document. Rather it has evolved out of many.

In the years that passed the Asian episcopal vision took form. Explained Kim: "Because there was no binding authority there was more freedom and more willingness to act in a cooperative spirit." It was in this spirit of cooperation and freedom—beneath Vatican radar—that the Asian vision of church took hold.

In November 1972 Pope Paul gave his final approval to the proposed statutes—for a two-year experimental period. At the end of two years, however, the question of whether to continue or not was moot. But questions had to be answered. What was to be the precise mission of the new organization? The bishops had answers. Section A of Article I of the FABC statutes read:

> The Federation of Asian Bishops' Conferences (FABC) is a voluntary association of episcopal conferences in South, Southeast, East and Central Asia, established with the approval of the Holy See. Its purpose is to foster among its members solidarity and co-responsibility for the welfare of Church and society in Asia, and to promote and defend whatever is for the greater good.

Section B read:

> The decisions of the Federation are without juridical binding force: their acceptance is an expression of collegial responsibility.

From the outset, the statutes made it clear that the bishops wanted to solidify interchurch bonds and place their local churches at the service of the wider society.

The Federation of Asian Bishops' Conferences, or FABC, as it began to be called, was now taking shape to include bishops' conferences in South, Southeast, and East Asia, including the bishops of Bangladesh, Taiwan, India-Nepal, Indonesia, Japan, Korea, Laos-Cambodia, Malaysia-Singapore-Brunei, Myanmar, Pakistan, the Philippines, Sri Lanka, Thailand, and Vietnam. With the Vatican approval in hand, the Asian bishops quickened their pace. On February 13, 1973, presidents of ten Asian bishops' conferences met again in Hong Kong. This time they worked out FABC's formal structures. They established a central committee of all episcopal conference presidents. A smaller five-bishop standing committee would govern the organization. To avoid old regional rivalries it was decided that the committee would have no president. Instead, it would appoint a secretary general and would convene plenary assemblies. These assemblies would be made up of all the episcopal conference presidents as well as additional elected bishop delegates based on the size of each national conference. Only a plenary assembly, the supreme governing body of the FABC, could modify the statutes. (There have been seven plenary gatherings in all of FABC history, the last held in Samphran, Thailand, in January 2000.) While in Hong Kong, members of the newly formed central committee chose Bishop Hsu as its first secretary general. However, he died a year later and was replaced by Taiwanese Bishop Stanislaus Lokuang.

TAIWAN PLENARY

One of the first tasks the new organization faced was to choose a theme for its first plenary session. The bishops soon decided on "Evangelization in Modern Asia" for their inaugural gathering, to be held in Taiwan in April 1974. At that first meeting the bishops were to elect their first FABC secretary general, Bishop Mariano Gaviola of the Philippines. Some say the bishops, in choosing evangelization, wanted to send a signal to the wider church regarding the importance they gave the subject. There was a more practical reason, however. Rome had scheduled a synod on evangelization for later in the year. The plenary gathering would allow the bishops to gather their best ideas and to jump-start their responses.

The bishops arrived in Taiwan with both excitement and trepidation. There was no precedent for the meeting; it would be wide open; they would work out of instinct. It would be an extraordinary period for the bishops at the end of which they would issue a statement intended to give direction to their local churches. The gathering would also set precedent. They had to get it right. Much was riding on the outcome. What they would write could help define the new Catholic organization. It would test them to see if they were really ready to take Catholicism into the future in Asia. They knew they had questions yet to be resolved. Would they be able agree on a direction? Would old national rivalries derail their efforts? Could they set common priorities? Could they form a coherent strategy?

The bishops had several factors working with them. First, they were generally tolerant men. Asians are known for their tolerance and patience. Vietnamese, for example, liken themselves to bamboo, saying they stand firm but bend in the wind to assure their survival. Furthermore, the continent's rich diversity of religion and culture, coupled with its density of population, has forced Asians to value tolerance. Otherwise, there would simply be too much conflict. It is also true that Asian history has had its share of intolerance and violence resulting from intolerance. One only need recall the bloodbaths in Cambodia in the 1970s or the outbursts of religious intolerance that have plagued such nations as Pakistan, India, and the Philippines, or the political intolerance of China. Nevertheless, the bishops, in forming the FABC, had sent out signals that they wanted to cooperate across ethnic and national lines. Now they had a chance to prove it.

Without question, ethnic rivalries have continued throughout the FABC's history. These have always played roles. The organizational structure has managed to hold most of these in check. Where there has been strife, there has also been a larger desire to work for the common good. This has meant setting aside some of the older national rivalries, if for no other reason than to prove to the wider world that Catholic bishops and theologians from different Asian ethnic backgrounds can work together for the greater mission of the church. Those bishops who established the FABC were aware of the potential for national rivalries. That is why they avoided establishing a powerful executive director. From the beginning, the FABC headquarters has been in Hong Kong, a somewhat neutral and accessible location. It has been there that FABC Assistant Secretary General Father Edward Malone, a Maryknoll priest, has carried out much of the organization's administrative work. Having a "non-Asian" in such an important position has raised other issues, especially in more recent years. At the same time, Malone's presence has meant that the Asian bishops have not had to choose an Asian national to carry out the FABC work. This seems to have been a larger issue in the earlier days of the FABC. Today, with a three-decade record of solid cooperation, worries within the FABC of maintaining strict "neutrality" appear to have faded. Many

Asian Catholic leaders seem more than ready to take over the final administrative functions of the organization.

To understand the challenges—and through them the accomplishments of the FABC—it helps to get a feel for the enormous cultural diversity that exists within the organization. Such diversity is bound to mean that bishops would bring widely different experiences and needs to the group. How different? Vietnam, for example, sits only five hundred miles across the South China Sea from the Philippines, but the two nations are worlds apart in history and culture. The same is true of many of the Asian nations that make up the FABC. Sometimes Asians, referring in jest to eating styles, divide themselves into three culinary regions: the "chopstick" nations of East Asia, the "spoon" nations of Southeast Asia, and the "finger" nations of South Asia. Each region has its own heritage. It takes strong common purpose, a shared mission, to make effective cooperation a reality. And all the Asian Catholic leaders share at least one fundamental reality: their churches are located in nations facing widespread poverty and injustice.

But there is more. Virtually all Asians share rich religious heritages and cultures that highlight religion and religious impulse. It is said that spirituality is the rhythm of Asia. This has been true for millennia. Personal pieties and family rituals shape the flow of life throughout Asia. This is true for Asian Catholics as well, for whom devotion plays a central role in their life of faith. Asian Catholics pass on devotions from generation to generation in the same way that they pass on stories and proverbs intended to teach values and enhance family ties.

With a few notable exceptions, the Catholic story in Asia is relatively young—at least by Asian standards. One exception is the story of Catholics in southern India, where some Indians believe that Christianity dates back to Thomas the Apostle. Tradition has it that Thomas founded Christian communities in the area and that his remains are buried in a crypt below an altar in a small church in the seaside city of Chennai, India. The modest church draws Catholics from throughout India to pray at and touch the crypt. For the most part, Christianity first came to Asia in the sixteenth and seventeenth centuries and spread as European colonialism took hold. By contrast, Asia's other religions date back three to six millennia and now have deep roots in "timeless" Asia. Pondering such a lengthy history and ways that cultures and religions become deeply intertwined, one can more easily understand that "conversion" experiences from one major religion to another are not common. Often conversions to Christianity, where they have occurred in Asia, have been among tribal peoples or other minorities who have been excluded from mainstream culture. The Asian bishops who gathered in Taiwan were educated men, and they brought with them considerable historical and cultural awareness. In this sense, they were realists as well as idealists. They well knew the vulnerability Christianity faced in their nations. They also knew—and had personally experienced—the power of its hopeful message, if only ways could be found to allow the message to enter the Asian psyche.

The Taiwan meeting was something entirely new. It was the very first FABC plenary gathering. At the same time, it represented a continuation of conversations that had begun in Manila four years earlier. In Manila, each of the bishops had come as a representative of his local church. From the start, the sum of the FABC experience was the total of the local church experiences. This is an important point. Each local language, local ethnicity, local culture, and local religious context became the starting point for an episcopal contribution to the whole. The FABC from the start was a "bottom-up" organization. It would not be surprising, then, to find that the FABC facilitated a "bottom-up" approach to theology and problem solving. This made sense to the bishops, who believed that such an approach was precisely what the documents of the Second Vatican Council had called for. Furthermore, by the time of the Taiwan meeting the Latin American and Asian theologians were influencing each other.

There were other models of church, of course. The contrary model, the "top-down" model, had been the more traditional one. This was a model of church some Asians and others have referred to as the "cookie-cutter" model, a one-size-fits-all model exported from the center to the periphery. When the early missionaries came to Asia, with few exceptions their concern was to establish mini European churches in Asia, using the same language and same rites as Europeans had used for centuries. The conditions and needs of local culture simply played no role; they were not to be factored in at all. This top-down model remained the predominant model of the churches in Asia until the time of the council. The First Vatican Council (1869–1870) and the promulgation of the doctrine of papal infallibility had enhanced this centralized model. When a pope can declare one truth for all time there is less room for negotiations involving the subtleties that grow out of culture, ethnic attitudes, and local histories. The local model of church fostered by the Asian bishops placed greater value on a decentralized authority structure, one that recognizes that Easterners do not always think like Westerners—and the thoughts of Easterners are products of local conditioning.

The men who came to Taiwan were certainly among the privileged few of Asia, having lived most of their lives within religious structures that set them apart from most other Asians. At the same time, nearly every one of these men carried with him pain caused by personal experiences of discrimination. On the one hand, many Western Catholics still looked at Asian Catholics as their "offspring," as youngsters who were still in need of direction. The very administrative structure of the church, with Asian churches listed as still being in "mission" territory, enhanced this notion. On the other hand, the Asian bishops, as Catholics in non-Catholic Asia, as offshoots of a colonial era, were often viewed by their fellow Asians as suspect, as somehow less than patriotic. These are painful realities that most Catholics in Asia are simply forced to live with. In many instances in the histories of the Asian Catholic churches prejudices led to mass violence and attacks directed against Catholics. They even led to mass martyrdom.

For example, consider the sheer terror Vietnamese Catholics felt in 1954 at the end of the French Indochina War as defeated French troops left Vietnam and the nation was cut in two. Most Catholics had sided with the French, their longtime patrons, against the insurgent nationalist Vietminh. So frightened were the Vietnamese Catholics living in northern Vietnam that nine hundred thousand fled south, fleeing Communism, to seek the protection of the newly created, American-supported Saigon government being formed by a former New York Catholic seminarian and Vietnamese mandarin aristocrat, Ngo Dinh Diem. The mass flight was in large measure the result of an intense American psychological campaign that involved dropping leaflets over North Vietnam telling Catholics that "Christ has gone to the south" and "the Virgin Mary has departed from the north."[4] Nevertheless, the exodus speaks to the way some Asian Catholics, many of simple faith, cast their lot with Westerners. With eventual independence, these Catholics were forced to adjust to new and sometimes quite harsh realities. Some had fought against the colonial powers, but most had not. Being tiny minorities in most Asian nations—only 2 percent or so—Catholics have felt isolated and vulnerable. They have been easy targets for exploitive politicians seeking quick scapegoats. The bishops who came to Taiwan brought with them their peoples' sense of vulnerability as well.

To a greater or lesser degree, each of the bishops who came for the first FABC plenary, sometimes called FABC I, brought with him a complex bundle of historical, cultural, and social factors that had shaped his local church differently from others. Until Manila and Taiwan, each Asian bishop had lived in isolation, carrying these prejudices, vulnerabilities, and fears, cut off from others who might somehow understand. Yet each had been empowered by a faith that offered hope and a belief that they would prevail. For the first time, Manila and Taiwan were breaking down that sense of isolation. While individual circumstances might vary, each Asian bishop was finding others sharing the same feelings, the same insecurities, the same hopes and aspirations. In other words, the FABC was like a fruit on the vine, ripe and ready to be picked. It was set to come to the table. It is as if the forces of history demanded it. The Asian bishops needed each other more than they had ever imagined. Sharing so much, they were ready to get down to work.

What followed in Taiwan were acknowledgments of those forces that had shaped their local churches—for better or worse. To understand those forces, to celebrate them when possible, to challenge them when necessary, the bishops knew they had to confront them head-on. The way they decided to do this was, in the final analysis, very Asian. They decided they would enter into dialogue with them. It made perfect sense to them to develop a pastoral approach that would engage them deeply in their respective societies. Preaching from a distance simply would not work, and they knew it. They had to walk in the rice paddies, understand the needs of their peoples, live fully as other Asians—and, most of all, denounce the privileges they had inherited from their European mentors. While in Taiwan, the bishops indeed made hard decisions and began to lay out their own vision of church mission. People who recall the gathering say that the work accomplished in Taiwan was nothing less than inspired, for it would set the course for the decades that followed. Arguably, the Asian bishops during their time together in Taiwan were drawing up the first blueprints for a Catholicism that had spilled beyond Europe and could no longer fit into a European temple. In this sense, these Asians, without fanfare, were starting to imagine a "post-European" model of church.

One of today's most notable Asian theologians was a young Jesuit Filipino priest in 1974. His name is Catalino Arévalo, currently professor of theology at Loyola School of Theology in Manila. He recalled the uncertainty of that first FABC plenary meeting and its tentative nature. He also recalled how somehow, after more than a week of deliberations, a final document emerged that captured the feelings of the bishops and served to launch the FABC. It was, he said, "one of the most memorable happenings in my life."[5] Arévalo recalled:

> It was the first time the Asian bishops had gathered like this, trying to put together their thoughts and resolutions with regard to evangelization in modern day Asia. The discussions, tentative at first, became livelier, more spontaneous, as the days went on. At the end, all the reports of group-sessions, proposed resolutions, aspirations were written up hurriedly and without much order. Some fifty pages of closely written material. All of it had to be put within a clear, synthetic framework faithful to what had been said at the assemblies . . . all something of the spirit. [Jesuit] Bishop Joe Rodericks of Jamshedpur [India], head of the drafting committee, then left all the material to be brought together, summarized, and col-

lated within a structure. It was seven in the evening. The finished statement had to be taken up for discussion and approval by eight the next day.

Five, six hours of struggle, until the vision found shape: the local church at the center; dialogue as the way; three dialogues as the spelling out of the talks; the final theological synthesis presented within a prayer to the Crucified and Risen Christ, Lord of our Asian peoples, head of the Church, shaper of history. By three in the morning it was done; by eight-thirty, in mimeographed form, it was read and discussed on the floor, and passed almost without alteration. To this day I truly believe the Holy Spirit was at work on the text.[6]

What emerged initially was the importance of local context. Theological reflection grows out of experience and place, the bishops affirmed. Theology is contextual. Seizing upon this idea, the Asian bishops were, in fact, using Vatican II and the Latin American liberation theologians as primary guides. From FABC I onward, virtually every paper that the Asian bishops would pen would start with an examination of context. Thus, the bedrock—the starting point—of theological reflection is not the church itself, but the people and the circumstances in which they live and seek life and God. In fact, one can say that "context" became the FABC hallmark. Assessing "context" in most of Asia means, before all else, recognizing its enormous poverty and hardships. These shape virtually every aspect of life. In this sense, the Asians were choosing to run on a parallel path with their Latin American episcopal counterparts who only a few years earlier had adopted their "preferential option for the poor." In the years that followed, the Catholic theologians of Latin America and Asia would support and encourage one another—although the Latin American theologians would play a more public role in the church in the 1970s and early 1980s. There is little question that the influence of Latin American liberation theology upon the Asians was significant from the late 1960s onward.

However, poverty was not the only factor affecting the lives of Asians in the 1970s, and the bishops in Taiwan noted this. They also saw taking place around them a "swift and far-reaching transformation" caused by unprecedented economic forces seemingly well beyond their control. These forces were breaking up traditional societies, ravaging traditional values, especially among the young. This transformation, according to the bishops, was resulting from the industrialization of Asian society. They wrote that it was causing "irreparable alienation and the disintegration of patterns of life and social relationships built up over the centuries." Here they saw two threats of enormous proportion: poverty and the breakup of the traditional sociocultural fabric of society. How, the bishops asked out loud, in the face of these twin menaces, do we enhance meaning and human dignity? How do we build our churches?

In one of the most formative statements ever written by the Asian bishops, they answered emphatically: We enhance life and build community—we become church—by entering into dialogue with local cultures, local religions, and local peoples.

Here are the words they used:

> [Our] primary focus . . . is the building up of a truly local church . . . incarnate in a people, a church indigenous and inculturated. And this means concretely a church in continuous, humble and loving dialogue with the living traditions, the cultures and religions. . . . In Asia especially this involves a dialogue with the great religious traditions of our peoples. In this dialogue we accept them as significant and positive elements in the economy of God's design of salvation. In them we recognize and respect profound spiritual and ethical meanings and values. Over many centuries they have been the treasuries of the religious experience of our ancestors from which our contemporaries do not cease to draw light and strength. They have been (and continue to be) the authentic expression of the noblest longings of their hearts, and the home of their contemplation and prayer. They have helped to give shape to the histories and cultures of our nations. . . . How then can we not give them reverence and honor? And how can we not acknowledge that God has drawn our peoples to Himself through them? . . .
>
> This dialogue will allow us to touch the expression and the reality of our peoples' deepest selves, and enable us to find authentic ways of living and expressing our own Christian faith. Finally, this dialogue will teach us what our faith in Christ leads us to receive from these religious traditions, and what must be purified in them, healed and made whole, in the light of God's Word. . . .
>
> A local church in dialogue with its people, in so many countries in Asia, means dialogue with the poor. For most of Asia is made up of multitudes of the poor. . . . Deprived, because they live under oppression, that is, under social, economic and political structures, which have injustice built in them. . . . This dialogue . . . demands working, not for them merely (in a paternalistic sense), but *with* them, to learn from them (for we have much to learn from them!) their real needs and aspirations, as they are enabled to identify and articulate these, and to strive for their fulfillment, by transforming those structures and situations which keep them in that deprivation and powerlessness.

This dialogue leads to a genuine commitment and effort to being about social justice in our societies. . . . The Synod of Bishops of 1971, in the document *Justice in the World,* has affirmed that "action in behalf of justice and participation in the transformation of the world fully appear to us as a constitutive dimension of the preaching of the Gospel, that is, of the mission of the Church for the redemption of the human race and in liberation from every oppressive situation." We affirm this teaching again, for we believe that this, in our time, is part and parcel of "preaching the Good News to the poor" (Mt 11:5; Lk 4:18).

Once again in relation to the tasks we have emphasized, the construction of a genuinely Asian theological reflection must be given a special priority. For the discernment of theological imperatives and the formulation of theological insights and principles, living contact with concrete Asian realities is necessary, and thus the collaboration of the entire local church, in dialogic process, is called for.[7]

The bishops were firm in their resolve. Their final Taiwan statement virtually became an FABC strategic plan. They wrote: To preach the gospel means making the message of Christ "truly incarnate in the minds and hearts of our peoples." The means of achieving this, they decided, is to build "incarnate," "indigenous," and "inculturated" local churches. These churches, to be one with Asia, have to be "in continuous, humble and loving dialogue" with the living traditions, cultures, and religions of Asia. In the same breath, the bishops noted they have to be in dialogue with the Asian people. Above all, this means being in dialogue with the poor—because the vast majority of the peoples of Asia are poor. Remarkably, the leadership of the FABC would continue to uphold these goals, despite considerable challenges and opposition, for at least the next three decades. The vision statement that came out of Taiwan has set the direction for the FABC and, through it, the local Asian churches, into the twenty-first century.

The bishops, in committing themselves to "the total development of our peoples," had linked evangelization and human development. Father Peter Phan of Catholic University of America, a native Vietnamese and president of the Catholic Theological Society of America in 2001, points to the special significance of this linkage. Reaffirming Catholic social teachings and echoing words that first emerged at the 1971 Synod on Justice in the World, Phan states that for the Asian bishops human development was not "merely an ethical injunction but a strict imperative and constitutive dimension of the church's evangelizing mission."[8] The idea that work on behalf of justice as "a constitutive dimension" of the preaching of the gospel would appear again and again in FABC statements over the years. In the words of the Asian bishops at FABC, "action on behalf of justice and participation in the transformation of the world fully appears to us as a constitutive dimension of the preaching of the gospel." "We affirm this teaching again," they stated, "for we believe that this, in our time, is part and parcel of the 'preaching the Good News to the poor'" (Matt. 11:5; Luke 4:18). They went on to recommend that the 1971 Synod on Justice statement be incorporated into their instructions and preaching at all levels of society.[9]

Consider, then, the enormous commitments the Asian bishops made at FABC I as well as the insights they were to take back to their local churches. They embraced:

- *Inductive theology:* They decided to seek out how to live and to proclaim the gospel in the new circumstances of the Asian context.

- *Local church:* They made their local churches the cornerstones for their reflections, saying each will communicate God's saving love when it ceases to be structured, governed, and symbolized in a foreign way and speaks to people in language and ways of being that a particular people understands. They added that this "radical particularity" does not mean isolation from other communities of faith; on the contrary, the more one is immersed in the reality of culture, time, and place, the more one needs to be in communion with other local churches—both for the good of one's own community and for the good of the others.

- *Inculturation:* The Asian bishops were the first to use the term in an ecclesial setting.[10]

- *Interreligious dialogue:* They stressed that being church means nothing less than being in dialogue with local culture and religion.

- *Preferential option for the poor:* They concluded that they had to participate in what they called a "dialogue of life" with the poor. This requires a genuine experience and understanding of the poverty, deprivation, and oppression of many of the Asian peoples (FABC I, art. 20).

Should one be surprised by these conclusions? Going in, few might have anticipated such strong affirmations. But there were hints that momentum had been building. Four years earlier, the Manila bishops' document called for "an open, sincere, and continuing dialogue with our brothers of the other great religions of Asia that we may learn from one another how to enrich ourselves spiritually and how to work more effectively together on our common task of total human development." The ideas of interreligious dialogue and human development, as essential components of the new commitments, were already visible in the Manila mix. In Taiwan, FABC I went forward, putting meat on the Manila bones. It can be said that it was the Taiwan meeting that gave birth to the uniquely Asian Catholic mission contained in the "triple dialogue," the dialogue with culture, religion, and the poor.

The bishops at FABC I actually issued two statements, a larger one and an abridged version. The latter was more specific. In it the bishops summarized the key elements crucial to successful evangelization in Asia. They listed them as inculturation, dialogue, and service of the poor—being grounded locally, being in the mix of culture and religion, and being in solidarity with the poor. Indeed, Taiwan launched the Asian Catholic leadership as few might ever have imagined. Yet much core work remained to be done. The bishops knew their journey would not go forward unless they took ownership of their Catholic spirituality. As with their approach to church mission, developing an approach to an Asian Catholic spirituality would require entering into a process of transformation. It would require identifying, as never before, their Asian spiritual character. Be it out of the East or out of the West, or out of both, it had to become their own. Their challenge was to seek the Spirit as authentically as they could believe possible.

CHAPTER 3

Spirituality of Harmony

Those who want to know the truth
of the universe should practice . . .
reverence for all life. This manifests
as unconditional love and respect for
oneself and all other beings.
                                    —*Lao Tzu*

I do not wish to dye my clothes saffron,
the color of a holy order; I want to dye
my heart with divine love.
                                    —*Kabir,*
                        fifteenth-century Indian poet

In the years that followed the Second Vatican Council, the Asian leadership faced many challenges, not the least having to do with rediscovering their Asian identity. Most Asian clergy and religious until then had spent much of their lives in Western settings, attending schools run by Westerners or overseas seminaries. Now it was time for these same Asians to reassert their Eastern character. The Vatican Council decision to use the vernacular in liturgies was an enabling one. It both reaffirmed the importance of the local church and touched off a flurry of church discussions and activities aimed at enhancing inculturation. Implicit in the decision was the value the church was placing on language—in the case of Asians, *Asian* languages. If the Vatican Council was about anything at all, it was about renewal. It was about generating new life in the local churches. It was not by accident that the first Vatican Council document to be published was the Constitution on the Sacred Liturgy (*Sacrosanctum Concilium*), signed by Pope Paul VI on December 4, 1963. In the spirit of renewal, the Constitution on the Sacred Liturgy called for the use of the "mother language." That document commissioned years of work for bishops, theologians, pastoral planners, and linguists. It stated that "provisions shall also be made, when revising the liturgical books, for legitimate variations and adaptations to different groups, regions, and peoples, especially in mission lands, provided that the substantial unity of the Roman rite is preserved." Much work had to be done and there would be much discussion as to what the fathers meant when they wrote the words "legitimate variations." Fortunately, it was a period of high energy and excitement throughout the church. The very thought of praying *as a community* in one's own Asian language was still novel.

The languages of Asia, of course, are more distant from Latin than are the major languages of Europe and the Americas. Since language and culture are intimately tied, the dramatic move to the vernacular was an even more significant step in Asia toward inculturation. Presenting translations from Latin into the Asian languages would only be the first step in a long journey. Once the essential value of praying as community in one's native tongue had been accepted by the universal church, it would not be long before the needs for more substantial inculturation would become apparent. At least that was the hope of many Asian pastoral planners. In retrospect it might be argued that it was a misplaced hope. Or, more properly, a misplaced expectation. The path ahead both for those advocating greater inculturation and for those resisting it would be painful and arduous. The council unleashed enormous energy throughout the churches of Asia. Quickly new theological, liturgical, and biblical centers sprang up. Visionaries stepped forward. Asian pride grew, while in the West the church witnessed a postconciliar letdown. It led to the departure of tens of thousands of clergy and religious. In Asia there was no such letdown—or exodus. Some have suggested that this was because the novelty of the postconciliar experiment in Asia outshined nagging questions of celibacy and obedience, more common in the West.[1]

Before the council, Asian Catholicism was almost entirely a European transplant. For centuries missionaries had come to Asia with the aim of conquering souls for Christ. They built churches, hospitals, and schools, loyally obeying their superiors in Rome. Then missionary work focused less on teaching the gospel than on teaching the catechism and the prayers of the liturgy. What gave potential converts and the faithful hope was not so much belief in Jesus Christ and his teachings as it was belief in a church that claimed to be the sole means of salvation. Catholicism was seen as having power and authority on its side. Once converted and among the ranks of the faithful, Catholics lived in a defensive posture, often cut off from their Asian brothers and sisters. In the wake of the council, this defensive posture began to crumble. Facing the continued pressures of the postcolonial period and a growing appreciation for the importance of culture in the lives of all peoples, European bishops began to turn their dioceses over to newly ordained indigenous bishops. The goal of inculturation—defined as "a deep and mutually enriching encounter between the Gospel and a people with its particular culture and tradition"[2]—was placed on every Asian chancery table. Yet there were more questions than answers. Yes to local culture, but which Indian culture? India alone has thousands. How specific? And yes to dialogue with other religions, but how? Yes to breaking out of the old defensive attitudes, but by what means? And how fast? Yes to the whole notion of inculturation, but using what guiding principles, values, and spirituality? Language, while important, is only a *means* to an enriched spiritual life. Something deeper was called for, something internal that would integrate and direct the wider pursuits. As part of the broader quest for inculturation, the Asian bishops were beginning to ask what an authentic Asian Catholic spirituality might look like. How would it differ from the Western spirituality they had inherited? And what might be discarded if they took the new course? These were critically important questions and each seemed to lack a clear answer. But it was important and notable that prayer and spirituality had come to the surface on the Asian agenda.

Answers would be found to many of these questions in the years that followed. Developing a more authentic Asian Catholic spirituality could be seen as an endless process. As important as any answer was the fact that new questions were being asked. The Asian church leadership was being called to greater discernment. As they increasingly felt the freedom to break out of old habits, they found themselves entering into deeper introspection. It was a time for challenge, but it also was a time for new growth, new maturity, and new responsibility.

It came as little surprise, then, that the choice of the theme for the second FABC plenary, held in Calcutta in 1978, was "Prayer—the Life of the Church in Asia." By then many local religious, priests, and bishops had involved themselves in a wide variety of Asian prayer forms. They had gained both knowledge and confidence in the process. Embracing the subject of prayer, as they were to do in Calcutta, they knew they had rich resources to draw on. Calcutta, in fact, was to be only a single step in a much longer journey into spiritual inculturation—but it would be an important one. It would be a time when the Asian bishops once again would empower each other by sharing ideas, stories, and experiences. Confident and seeing themselves as *Asian* spiritual leaders, they felt free to draw on their rich Asian spiritual trove: breathing techniques, mantras, yoga exercises, mindfulness, meditation practices, all woven together in a unique Asian sense of unity, of oneness, of sacredness, of total harmony. It is difficult to say there is any one "Asian" response to prayer. If pressed, one might say many Asian Catholics feel more comfortable praying in silence and practicing meditation techniques. The Asian Catholic bishops, during their most recent FABC plenary session in 2000, gathered each afternoon for Taize chants in front of a sanctuary filled with scores of votive candles. Following the prayer service, which also focused on scriptural recitations, many bishops sat in silence, meditating for a half-hour or longer.

Asian prayer in some ways reflects Asian thought itself. Within it one finds a longing for wholeness. Asians are not as quick to divide large metaphysical concepts in two as traditional Western Aristotelian thought has done for millennia. Asians prefer to unite, not divide. Good and evil are less two sides of a coin than places on a larger prism. While Westerners might talk of an examination of conscience, Easterners are more prone to speak of seeking greater awareness. Awareness of spirit comes with a quieting of mind and body. In the East how one relates to the outside world is not necessarily the fundamental question. In Asia how one integrates oneself, and in the process becomes more fully aware, is more likely to lead to proper behavior. Again, the emphasis here is on achieving wholeness, mystical unity, Oneness. Achieving harmony is simply finding something that has always been there waiting to be found—if only one stopped to make the effort.

Even the Western notion of nonviolence, a value and state highly prized by many Western Christians, is defined through its opposite, violence. Holistic Asian thought might share the same "nonviolent" spiritual state, but it prefers to get there through different constructs. Most traditional Asians don't live in the Western "either/or" world. With world cultures mixing as never before, however, some of these differences may, in some instances, be blurring.

VIETNAMESE GARDEN

Switch for a few moments to a woman religious in Vietnam—one of many Asian Catholics who have lived and taught harmony all their lives. To Thi Anh, a Sister of Saint Augustine, is a mystic who, nearing eighty, remains actively engaged in the world. She has made spiritual enlightenment—seeking her Tao, she says—a lifelong pursuit. Steeped in Eastern philosophy and spirituality, Anh practices psychology she learned in the West. Her thinking, like that of many other Catholics of her generation, is a product of East and West. She is at peace with both. When she is not meditating, she is counseling battered women in Ho Chi Minh City.

My wife and I found her in her garden behind her home when we visited Vietnam early in 2000. She has been a friend for decades and we wanted to visit again, if only briefly. Anh was eager to reassure us that she was in good health, although she looked frail. We talked about old times, about family, and about how Vietnamese were bearing up after the country had opened up once again to the West. The pace of life in Vietnam began to change in the early 1990s after the Vietnamese Communist leadership began to seek foreign investments. Vietnam, after decades of war and decades more of Communist rule, seemed to be trying to balance its hard-won independence with the need for foreign capital. By the turn of the century, the city streets were buzzing with commercial activity, gaps between rich and poor were once again growing, and the Communists looked very much like the old capitalists. We shared our thoughts and perceptions on the changes occurring throughout the country. But that day I came with other questions in mind as well.

"Pray? How do I pray? How do I not pray?" She responded breaking into a broad grin. Turning to the flowers in her garden, she said: "In every flower I see the smiling face of God. They make me smile." Standing beneath an overhanging branch of a small tree, Anh reached up and picked a star fruit, a favorite Vietnamese delight. Minutes later we were drinking tea and eating the cut fruit at her kitchen table. Vietnamese spirituality, Anh told us, is the product of several religious and philosophical traditions: Confucianism, with its stress on social responsibility and a moral code; Taoism, with its notion of allowing nature to take its course; and Buddhism, with its understanding of the centrality of human suffering, one of Buddhism's four Noble Truths. These three paths, she said, converge to make up the Vietnamese soul. They live in harmony in Vietnam, she added.

"The longing for harmony is essential to the Asian makeup," she went on. We see it at work in Asian politeness, courtesy, and tactfulness. We see it at work in the Asian desire to stay on good terms with family and relatives and neighbors. We see it in the humility Asians have when they place themselves within their environment. Anh continued, saying that there can be a downside in the Asian tendency to blend in. It can cause repressed feelings and withdrawal. Left unchecked it can lead to negative energies.

"Are the East and the West in essential conflict?" I asked, opening a topic Anh loves to talk about. Some years ago she authored a study that attempted to answer these questions. Her answers are influenced by the Chinese philosopher Lao Tzu.

"Yin and Yang," she says, "complete each other. So, too, must East and West."[3] "The East has spiritual answers for the West," she said. "The West has answers for the East, especially as we face our hunger and poverty." East and West can hold each other in balance.

The notion of harmony shows up in various ways in Asia, for example, in medicine and the belief in the need to maintain a healthy balance of body, mind, and spirit. Yoga teaches that a healthy body, mind, and spirit are one. In Asian symbols, the Yin and Yang teach endless interdependence and larger ineffable unity. In ancient China, harmonious family relationships were viewed as requirements for harmonious feudal relationships. When these existed there was peace in the kingdom, and the emperor, the Son of Heaven, could claim the mandate of heaven. Discord in the kingdom brought his rule into question.

This need for harmony might, in part, be the result of Asian diversity. Across nations so diverse in identity how does one find unity? When I studied Southeast Asia in graduate school I encountered the history of Indonesia—a nation of approximately 13,000 islands, 300 ethnic groups and 250 languages—and the challenges it faced after independence from nearly 350 years of Dutch rule. It was in 1945 that Indonesia's first president, Sukarno, helped develop his new nation's state philosophy. It was called "Pancasila" in Sanskrit, meaning five principles. Pancasila comprises five interrelated principles, all aimed at establishing peace and harmony: belief in God, a just society, national unity, democracy, and social justice.

This sense of spiritual order, this harmony, this desire for oneness are, of course, not limited to Asian spirituality. They go to the heart of mysticism worldwide. One need only recall Franciscan spirituality or Christian mystics such as Bonaventure, John of the Cross, Catherine of Siena, Meister Eckhart, or Hildegard of Bingen. While Christian mysticism shares much with the East, unlike the Eastern mysticism, it has not integrated into mainstream Western religious practice. Of course there is not a single spiritual path in the East, just as there is no single spiritual path in the West. There are many paths within each. In the West, the Greek and Hebrew paths were very different. In the East, the Brahminic and the Buddhist, the Confucian and the Taoist, and the Hindu and the Islamic each took a separate path.

It is frequently suggested that religious belief in the West is more reasoned, less intuitive. The Western mind tends to separate, analyze, and clarify. In the West we sometimes speak disparagingly about "blind faith," meaning a faith devoid of reason. Western philosophy, indebted to the Greeks, stresses reason. It shows up in the development of Catholic dogma.

On the other hand, Eastern spiritual thinkers, while not necessarily rejecting reason, have used other disciplines to explain life. The Asian mind tends to synthesize and unify, seeking wholeness. For Asians, the basis or criterion for moral discernment is drawn not from universally accepted moral norms but from what their cultures say. Asian thought is taught through stories, poetry, dance, and even puppet shows. Asian cultures are generally known as "shame cultures," because moral standards are based on honor and shame, which is quite different from Western cultures, known as "guilt cultures."

Eastern religions employ art and intuition to make moral points. The thoughts of the Asian poet Lao Tzu were recorded in poetry. His writings are full of imagery and are intuitive. Traditional Western religious belief is deductive, emerging from abstract truths. Eastern belief is more inductive, stemming often from texts or human experiences. "If it can be contained it hasn't been touched," Lao Tzu wrote. Again he wrote: "The Way is always still, at rest / And yet does everything that's done." Still again: "The Way begot one, / And the one, two; / Then the two begot three / And three, all else."[4] Illogical? Maybe. Yet his impact on Eastern thought has been profound.

The Eastern desire for balance emerges as well from a respect for nature. To understand the difference between East and West, one need only visit an art gallery and compare the works of the European masters with those of Asian artists during the same periods. In classical Western art the human figure often played the central role. In Eastern art this is rarely the case. In Asian art, if the human had any place at all, it was unobtrusive. Eastern art attempts to evoke a sense of peace and tranquillity, reflecting the importance given to these spiritual values. Here again we see the Asian mind-body-soul seeking harmony and balance.

With logic and reason has come the Western idea of progress. It is a linear idea. We see ourselves as moving forward and this makes sense to us. The Eastern mind is more likely to think in a circular manner. Reincarnation is the prime example. The Western mind, meanwhile, lives within and chooses between opposites—good and evil, body and soul. The Western mind has been heavily influenced by dualistic thought patterns found in the Greek Stoics and early Christian Gnostics. We grew up to view our bodies as sinful but containing a potentially grace-filled soul. The Eastern mind is less apt to see this division. It is more apt to think holistically. It embraces both as one. The Eastern mind prefers to avoid traditional dualisms. To the West's yes-or-no question, the East responds with "neither" or "both/and."

The Asian bishops, having committed themselves to the triple dialogue at the first FABC plenary—dialogue with culture (inculturation), religions (interreligious dialogue), and the poor—were now in Calcutta seeking something more, something distinctly Asian to help move them forward. They had left their earlier gatherings—Manila in 1970 and Taipei in 1974—elated. Out of the first came a commitment to structuring an organization, out of the second came directions for their evangelization efforts. Now they were seeking spiritual fuel. More correctly, they were seeking greater authenticity in their prayer lives. The choice of prayer as the theme for the second FABC plenary was on the mark.

RETURNING HOME IN CALCUTTA

As had been the case in Taipei, the bishops in Calcutta met for more than a week, discussing and experiencing prayer, including Asian meditative techniques. Afterwards they outlined their thoughts in a loose statement that was largely a summary of various ideas that had come to them during their time together.

They prefaced their remarks by saying that their focus on prayer should not be misconstrued as a withdrawal from the urgent pastoral tasks they had earlier put on their agenda. Rather what they intended to do, they explained, was to ground those pastoral initiatives in a spiritual realm. Looking for guidance, the bishops wrote, they had turned to "that source from which the light and energy of the Lord comes."[5] They looked to the Holy Spirit. Working with their theologians, they noted that they had drawn energies not only from traditional European prayers but also from Eastern prayers. Calcutta marked the first time an international body of Catholic bishops had come together and "baptized" Asian spirituality, *viewed only a few years before with great suspicion and hostility within the church.* In a way, the step they took was quite ordinary, extending from the notion of being in dialogue, as they had promised in Taipei, with Asian culture and religion. In another way, it was quite extraordinary, as they were acknowledging the work of the Holy Spirit in the other religions of Asia, acknowledging that they had something to learn from these religions. One can only imagine that many of the bishops were simply sharing publicly some of the Asian prayer practices they had been developing for years. It was akin to coming out of the proverbial closet with their Asian souls. It was a liberating and proud moment.

As they had done at FABC I and as they would do at subsequent FABC plenary gatherings, the bishops began their FABC II closing statement by describing the context in which they found themselves. They wrote that their churches faced the growing threat of secularism and, beneath its weight, the disintegration of traditional communities. These changes were leading to a loss of an Asian sense of belonging and to the breakdown in personal relationships. In their next breath, with characteristic optimism, they also said the moment presented new opportunities. They linked challenge and opportunity, pointing to Chinese ideograms that combine to spell out the word "crisis." One is the ideogram for "danger," the other for "opportunity." Yes, they said, there were real dangers for their churches, but these perils also provided opportunities. In the midst of turmoil, they wrote, many Catholics were turning to God for help and forming deeper spiritual relationships.[6] In turn, this was strengthening their churches and helping them to become true communities of prayer.

After focusing on prayer for more than a week, the bishops at FABC II believed they were better prepared to move ahead. They were ready to face the future believing they had examined carefully the signs of the times.[7] These signs, in turn, were pushing them yet further into a process of inculturation of faith. They knew they wanted to make the experience of prayer more meaningful to their people. "We are daily more convinced," they wrote, "that the Spirit is leading us in our time, not to some dubious syncretism (which we all rightly reject), but to an integration—profound and organic in character—of all that is best in our traditional ways of prayer and worship into the treasury of our Christian heritage."[8] The "our" referred to their *Asian* heritages. Challenging their imaginations, they decided they had to wed Eastern and Western spirituality and prayer. The process of inculturation was now a two-way street: it meant both "Christianizing" Asia and "Asianizing" Christianity. To better bring the liberating message of Jesus to their peoples they wanted to reach into their Asian cultures to "fertilize" the Word of God.

Clearly the Asian bishops were gaining confidence. A measure of that confidence is found in the suggestion that the Asian trove of spiritual richness they wanted to spread among their peoples need not be limited to people living in Asia. If it would be good for Asians, they reasoned, these same treasures would be good for the universal church. Indeed, it was time to begin to share their proud Asian heritage wherever receptive believers could be found. They wrote:

> We have already dwelt on what Christian prayer has to give to Asia. But Asian prayer has much also to offer to authentic Christian spirituality: a richly developed prayer of the whole person in unity of body-psyche-spirit; contemplation of deep interiority and immanence; venerable sacred books and writings; traditions of asceticism and renunciation; techniques of contemplation found in the ancient eastern religions; simplified prayer-forms and other popular expressions of faith and piety easily available even to simpler folk.[9]

In these words we see the linkage of inculturation and interreligious dialogue. It would be a connection that would grow stronger in the years ahead. If the process of inculturation requires a deeper respect and knowledge for the spiritual traditions of Asia, as the Asian bishops postulated, then conversing with and learning from the stewards of those traditions make perfect sense. The bishops were doing more than admitting that the religions of Asia have spiritual treasures to offer. By extension, they were telling the world that God, the source of those treasures, has been active in those religions through history. In speaking as they did, the bishops at Calcutta were building a positive climate for interreligious dialogue. They wrote:

> The spirituality characteristic of the religions of our continent stresses a deeper awareness of God and the whole self in recollection, silence and prayer, flowering in openness to others, in compassion, non-violence, generosity. Through these and other gifts it can contribute much to our spirituality which, while remaining truly Christian, can yet be greatly enriched. Sustained and reflective dialogue with them in prayer (as shall be found possible, helpful and wise in different situations) reveals to us what the Holy Spirit has taught others to express in a marvelous variety of ways.[10]

Proud men wrote these words. In the process they were reclaiming their Asian heritages and placing these at the service of the church. They were also setting the groundwork for a continuing process of spiritual discovery and engagement that would further shape their imaginations. The significance of this new departure would only grow in the years ahead. What at first seemed like a simple move driven by pastoral concerns—making prayer life more meaningful—would turn out to have important theological and evangelical implications for the entire church. The bishops started with the premise that the prayer forms of other Asian religions had merits. By implication the religions that had fostered those prayer forms must also be pleasing to God, the source of all goodness. And if those religions were pleasing to God, then would it not make sense that they are part of God's divine plan? If this is the case, then is religious pluralism also part of God's plan? What role, then, should evangelization take? Where do efforts aimed at conversion fit in? These were not easy questions to answer. Consider, for example, how the Indian theologian Jesuit Samuel Rayan pondered the work of the Spirit in other religions. He wrote:

> God speaks to every group and age, and communicates with them in a variety of sounds and symbols. Divine gifts and graces are not concentrated and heaped up in any one place or time or in a single human group or spiritual experience or religious tradition. None of these exhausts the truth of God, nor the truth of the relationship God builds with us, nor the truth of the human predicament, nor of the human heart, nor of the dreams God has lodged in it. Every religious tradition is partial and imperfect, and has a share in distorting God's message and disfiguring God's face, and wrecking God's work in history. God speaks to each through the rest. God

places in many hands and hearts gifts needed by and meant for all. God sends each to its neighbor to learn its own name. For no religion is meant to be an island, separate and self-sufficient. All the religious and spiritual traditions need each other's word of revelation, reassurance, challenge, correction, promise and assistance. The achievements of each tradition, its symbols, saints, scriptures, art and insights belong to all to the extent they are life-promoting and liberating. They must be respectfully sought, offered, received, assimilated, integrated and lived for the benefit of the human family and its earth-home.[11]

The broader point here is that the process of meeting pastoral needs was leading the Asian bishops deeper into theological and ecclesial questions. The primarily pastoral course the Asian bishops set out on can be viewed in a number of ways. Certainly what they were doing came as an extension of Vatican II renewal. It can also be seen as early stages of a "post-Western" Catholicism, an Asian Catholicism that was now drawing on Eastern cultures. It can finally be seen as helping the church become a truly global religion, a truly catholic Catholicism. In this context local churches, networked together to make up the universal church, borrow and share to better understand Christian revelation. Will such a Catholicism emerge in the twenty-first century? No one can know. What Calcutta indicated, however, is the difficulty of containing Catholicism in its largely Western template. When Catholic history is recorded decades or even a century hence, the late twentieth century could well be seen as the beginning of a momentous transformation period in which Catholicism shed its primarily European template and became a global reality. If this happens, the bishops of Asia will be viewed as apostles who spoke the Christian message, using new languages to meet the needs of the new times.

The Asian bishops are and are not "revolutionaries." They may be helping to change the way the church views its mission, but they are also cautious, even conservative men. Yet they are fundamentally Asian! And, given the chance, they think and act as Asians. They know how to minister to Asians. It has been their commitment to ministry—knowing what is required to keep the faith alive and growing in Asia—that has pressed them to move forward, even at times reluctantly. In the process some have acted against their conservative natures.

Asians carry a sense of history deep within them. The Asian bishops are not exceptions. From young adulthood, each Asian Catholic must confront potentially troubling questions: How was God active in Asian history *before* the arrival of Christianity in Asia? Was the Creator of all that is good and glorious present or absent in Asia *before* the name "Jesus" had been spoken on Asian lips? What is God's providential plan for the lives of billions of Asians, including family members, who happen to be Buddhists, Hindus, or Muslims, many never having heard the name of Jesus? The Asian bishops have answered with an emphatic affirmation that God has been active in Asia through Asian history—both in Asian cultures and in the great religions of Asia.

Of course, Calcutta was not the first time the Catholic Church had wrestled with these questions. "Could there be salvation outside the church?" the bishops asked at the Vatican Council. Yes, they answered. The Spirit does work outside the Catholic Church.[12] Salvation is possible. The Asian bishops were now advancing that view, making it more emphatic. They spoke more specifically and more personally, recognizing the hand of God in *not just the lives of men and women of good will, but also in the religions of Asia*. Not many years earlier, these religions were considered threats to Christian faith, their followers, heathens and infidels. The bishops in Calcutta further opened the doors for Asian Catholics to accept as they never were able to before not only their own heritage but also the people, often family members, with whom they shared villages, towns, and cities. The ramparts had come down. Whole new attitudes and relationships could now develop. It was a monumental step forward. While the words of the Asian bishops were not "binding," they were setting their local churches of Asia on radically new paths.

The bishops' consideration of prayer had led them to embrace both inculturation and interreligious dialogue more deeply. It was also moving them forward in their thinking about the third element of the triple dialogue—their need to live in solidarity with the poor of Asia, most of whom are quite young. (Half of Asia today is under the age of twenty-five.) After Calcutta, the prayer life of the local church would be understood in a larger social context. "Authentic Christian spirituality," the bishops wrote, means having "a richly developed prayer of the whole person in unity of body-psyche-spirit."[13] Stressing their own version of the "seamless garment," they linked the spiritual and material orders. By this the bishops meant that greater efforts had to be made to overcome pietistic or egocentric mysticism. They were calling for an engaged spirituality of harmony, one that comes out of an understanding of extensive relationships and a commitment to the greater well-being of the human family. As the Asian bishops wrote, "harmony embodies the realities of order, well-being, justice and love as seen in human interaction. . . . Harmony is not simply the absence of strife. . . . The test of true harmony lies in acceptance of diversity and richness."[14] Harmony begins with the Trinity and is found among all peoples and throughout the whole universe. The notion of harmony has another dimension, implying a blending of social and spiritual. In this sense the Asian bishops' notion of harmony avoids the trap of traditional dualism. Rayan again puts it this way:

> The word [spirituality] is problematic, even dangerous. It seems to exclude material realities, and activities connected with them. It is suggestive of the immaterial, the non-bodily, the non-social, the a-historical, the interior, the otherworldly. It smacks of the dualism and docetism which bedeviled certain religious traditions, even Christian ones, in the past. . . . [It identifies] with piety, devotion, prayer, dogmas, rites, cults and the organization of these, or with matters pertaining to the individual soul and its salvation as distinct from matters that concern the body or the human community.[15]

Rayan offers another way to look at spirituality. He writes:

> All creation . . . is radically spiritual: the earth and the sky, birds and beasts, women and men are all spiritual from their foundations and in their essential openness to the Spirit's influence. This perception is vital for all authentic and holistic understanding of spirituality, which would avoid all dualist and docetist pitfalls. . . . To be spiritual is to be open to reality and responding to it relevantly and as adequately as possible. . . . To be spiritual is to be open . . . to all further possibilities, rejecting none, shutting out nothing. Openness means listening to the other, to the depth and the silence of things and events, refusing to close the door to possibilities however unfamiliar, unpalatable, challenging and disturbing. Openness means being ready for the surprise of history and of the cosmos.[16]

Years later, in 1995, the FABC's theological advisory commission looked back over a quarter century of FABC development and credited the bishops at Calcutta for beginning a process that would foster an Asian Christian "integrated spirituality." Calcutta had been, the commission stated, a key moment in church life. There the bishops began to weave together the spiritual and pastoral missions of church life. Drawing on that Asian bishops' reflection, the commission concluded: "Christians are to be motivated about their right place in the cosmos and about their respect for God's creation of the human person and nature, to practice a spirituality that promotes social harmony by concrete action."

In the years that followed Calcutta the Asian bishops worked to fill out their vision of spiritual and pastoral harmony. Their point of departure was a belief that they were modeling a new vision of Catholicism. "A new world [is] being born" in Asia in the wake of the colonial period, they wrote.[17] Their enthusiasm did not stem from some abstract idea. Rather it was growing out of their personal convictions that Asia would change if religious leaders of all faiths could come together and make it happen.[18]

So what would the outline of the Judeo-Christian story look like through an Asian lens that stresses a spirituality of harmony? One long-time Asian observer outlined the biblical story in these words:[19]

In the beginning God created the heavens and earth and all was in harmony. Human beings became the stewards of the Creator and creation. They lived in harmony with creation. But the sin of Adam and Eve introduced discord into creation. Yet God's love and grace never faltered. The history of God's salvific work of restoring harmony in Christ begins at the moment when disharmony was introduced into creation. Restoration of harmony in Christ was fulfilled through the history of a people of God. The Exodus event and God's covenant with Moses, with the accompanying obligation of fidelity to the Lord, though confined to Israel, was a preparation and paradigm for the liberation of the whole of humankind from sin and its restoration to harmony. The historical coming of Jesus Christ is for the New Testament the salvific event that fulfilled the Old Testament expectation of God's reign. The life of Jesus ushered in a new harmony among people and in the cosmos. Jesus fulfilled the Old Testament expectation of the coming reign of God by being the person of harmony. It is through Jesus that God saves the whole human race and the entire cosmos. It is through Christ's self-emptying, becoming obedient unto death on the cross, that he identified himself in love with all of humanity, especially the rejected, the weakest and the poorest of all. The reign of God comes upon us through the Christ of harmony. Through Jesus' ministry we learn the path of harmony. The mystery of the reign of God, the God of harmony, becomes operative in and revealed through the life of the whole human race and in the order and workings of the cosmos, especially through the paschal events of Jesus' passion, death and resurrection. Pentecost was the culmination of Christ's redemptive work of restoring harmony. The apostles, filled with the Holy Spirit, with the bond of unity and harmony, began to speak in many languages, as the Spirit gave them ability. The church is the community of those who have experienced Christ and have appropriated the life manifested in Jesus Christ. Therefore, the church is the sacrament of harmony for all humankind. In this capacity, it is called to transcend all distinctions of race, caste and sex. It is called to become the sign and instrument of peace on earth among all peoples. The church fulfills its mission as sacrament of peace and harmony through its commitment to justice and by listening to the

Word of God who gives peace and by being open to the Spirit who constantly weaves among human beings solid harmonious bonds. When sin is understood as the disturbance of the original harmony of creation and Jesus Christ as the One who was sent to reconcile and reestablish the harmony, attention is drawn to his central message and act, namely, the proclamation of the values of the Reign of God and his Paschal Mystery of life through death. For the values he proclaimed—love, truth, justice and the dignity of the human being—he gave his life, died for them.

This short narrative helps one see how an appreciation of culture, of a different mind-set, can enhance the Christian faith story without compromising it.

It is not Asians alone who are being called on to "inculturate" the faith, to tell the Christian story using words and ideas that are meaningful and alive within their culture. The same challenges exist in the West and other parts of the world where the cosmic story, the story of our fourteen-billion-year-old universe, provides a new dynamic scientific context for the Judeo-Christian story. It is said that the world's collective imagination shifted when humanity first saw photographs of planet Earth taken from the moon. No longer was there an up and down—just the planet Earth suspended, without borders, without nations, so precious and vulnerable, in space. When imagination enters a new paradigm so too do we, and so too do we retell those stories that give us meaning. This was precisely what the Asian bishops had set out to do in Calcutta: introduce the symbols, sounds, prayer forms, and stories that would ignite the deeper faith story, grounded in the life, death, and resurrection of Jesus Christ.

As the Asian Christian story developed through the collective work of Asian theologians and bishops, it began to emphasize the notions of the Cosmic Christ, Creator, and Spirit who live beyond time and place, infusing all creation with love and liberation. The Asian Christian story offers the incarnate Jesus who entered history and preached harmony, liberation, and just relationships. The Asian Christian story speaks of church as sacred sacrament, as a communion of relationships, perpetuating harmony by reclaiming justice and the protection of the poor.

No serious change comes without hard work, even pain. The Asian bishops, setting out on their new course, knew they had a great distance to travel. The gap between their vision and the reality they hoped to achieve has been significant—and remains so today. All knew the journey would be long and arduous. They knew it would require decades, perhaps even centuries, to make a substantial difference. What they began to see as important was their commitment to the vision itself. Further, despite

their very own modest resources, each of the Asian churches had to figure out how to best become an advocate for the rights of the poor, for justice and equality—and still preach harmony and understanding and
respect for the culture.[20] Under the best of circumstances, it would be a
gigantic undertaking, one that would require much wisdom and patience.
The good news is that these are virtues seemingly in abundance in the
good-willed men and women who have entered leadership positions in
the Asian churches.

Thus the Asian bishops further integrated their spiritual lives with the
mission of the church. It is said that theology happens when people analyze their life experiences in the light of their relationships to God. This
was precisely what was happening in Calcutta and in the years that followed. Asian theology was emerging with greater clarity, coming out of
countless gatherings and reflection papers. The bishops had good reason
to be pleased.

CHAPTER 4

Tasting Poverty

Whatever you do to the least of my
brothers and sisters, you do to me.
                        —Matthew 25:31

For those with faith,
every action,
every breath,
derives its meaning
as part of
a larger plan.

                        —Janina Gomes

Easier said than done—or so the saying goes. That was precisely the situation in which the Asian bishops found themselves as they entered the decade of the 1980s. They had embraced some lofty pastoral ideals, including "the triple dialogue" and the transformation of their spiritual vision. Now they faced many questions. What form, for example, would these dialogues with cultures, religions, and the poor take? Who would do the work? How would they develop? How would they integrate their social, religious, and spiritual visions? In brief, how would they move from word to deed? Their roadmaps were still very sketchy.

Some matters were clear in their minds. The bishops knew they could count on each other's support, and they knew their theologians were working with them on the journey. Importantly, they felt grounded in the context out of which they had to further develop their reflections. With 80 percent of their people hungry and poor, they knew their priorities. With more than 50 percent of their people under the age of twenty-five, they knew they had to pay special attention to both defending and forming the young emerging generations. Many of the bishops were still young enough to know first-hand the humiliation of the colonial experience. They very much wanted to avoid slipping into the new forms of economic slavery that were gaining a foothold in Asia.

Guidance? Their new commitments were telling them to listen to the poor and the oppressed. The poor, then, were no longer *objects* of Christian concern, but the very *subjects* of Christian salvation. This change represented a monumental shift in their pastoral approach. It had simplified matters, giving them a yardstick against which to measure every decision they would have to make. It was a case in which the Word was visibly bringing to life before their very eyes "the new way of being church" that they had begun talking and writing about in the preceding decade. Further, the very simplicity of the profound ideas contained in "the triple dialogue" made agreement and planning all the easier. Clearly, their commitment was to Jesus Christ, Savior to the World. The means of expressing that commitment, however, was to be the steadfast approach of witness and dialogue. Looking back to Manila after a decade, observers could see the growth in the pastoral vision, and that was encouraging. What started as a simple desire to create an entity to share pastoral concerns across national borders had grown into a living and breathing organization that was spawning profound ideas and new pastoral programs. Furthermore, the FABC's accomplishments were energizing Asia's theologians, who could see their ideas moving off the pages of theological publications into local, national, and transnational FABC programs.

Liberation theology, with its "preferential option for the poor," was very much alive in the late 1970s in Asia. It took various forms. *Dalit* theology, for example, surfaced and grew in India. The *dalits* (from the root word *dal* in Marathi language, which means to crack open and split), among the lowest in the Indian caste system, had been discriminated against in society and even in the church itself. In rural areas throughout India, even today the *dalits* are barred from using common wells, roads, and other common facilities. The Catholic Church has become a home to many of these marginalized peoples. Nearly three-quarters of all Indian Catholics are *dalit* or tribal converts. Yet for complex reasons, some going back centuries to when Catholic missionaries attempted to convert the Hindu upper classes as a mission strategy, *dalits* have felt the burdens of caste distinctions within local churches. Catholic communities in India have at times had separate seats in churches and separate cemeteries for the *dalits*. For its part, *dalit* theology has provided a vivid description of these exploited outcasts within the Hindu caste system while it has articulated the hope and struggles of the *dalits* for liberation.

Another Asian liberation theology, *Minjung* theology, arose in Korea. The Korean *Minjung* theologians became convinced that Jesus Christ is first and foremost present among the poor and the disinherited *Minjung* (people). This theology grew in large part as a reaction to the military dictatorships of Korea in the 1970s and 1980s, a time when workers, farmers, and fisherfolk were oppressed and exploited in efforts to boost the

economy. Its Christology drew from the messianism found in the biblical tradition as well as from the messianic traditions found in Korean
Buddhism. In the Philippines, other theologically based liberation movements developed. The most acknowledged was the nonviolent movement—the Peoples' Power movement—that eventually swept Ferdinand
Marcos from power.

In each of these instances along with a number of others, the focus for
theological reflection was on the oppressed. In each instance the reflections were coupled with and energized by a wider interest in culture and
religion that was sweeping through the academic world in the 1960s and
1970s. The notion of culture and its importance had only recently begun
to seep out of academic circles and into the mainstream. As these ideas
became more popular they were affecting the ways religions, including
Catholicism, approached their mission work. Suddenly, the world wanted
to preserve ethnic identities, which were seen, much like endangered
species and plant life, as something precious and irreplaceable. On the
other side of the coin, long-held notions of European cultural superiority were being called into question as never before.

Meanwhile, interest in culture stimulated interest in religion, seen as
part of its essential fabric.[1] All this meant that the bishops and theologians of Asia had much fresh material to draw from at the very time they
were making their own case for greater inculturation within the church.
For their part, the Asian leaders had much to ponder and were painfully
aware of their minority status in most Asian nations. They knew how vulnerable their local churches were. It made enormous sense for them to
express ethnic and national pride—and it came quite naturally. These
expressions had a secondary impact. They opened up channels of communication with others within their countries, including other religious
leaders. The Asian Catholics in the past thirty years have been conscious
of the need to build bridges. The process has not been easy, especially
when they have had to choose between serving the interests of the poor
and those of the powers that be. The Asian Catholic leadership early on,
however, came to understand that meaningful change could take place in
Asia only if it found allies who believed in the same ideals. This meant
coalition building was becoming part of the mission of the church.

All this represented a 180-degree turn for Asian Catholic leadership
from that period before the Vatican Council when Christian communities lived defensively in Asia, largely cut off from their neighbors—and
certainly from leaders of other religions then still viewed as "hostile" and
practicing forms of paganism. The post–Vatican Council change in Catholic attitudes was not simply theoretical. It had an immediate impact on
Catholic families and communities. One's Buddhist aunt or Islamic
cousin or Hindu sister-in-law was no longer to be viewed as hostile, no

longer seen as damned for failing to embrace Christianity. Families and friends who were not members of the church—*98 out of 100 Asians!*—could now be accepted and embraced as good and loving people, not unlike other Catholics. Consider the power of the imagery: members of different Asian religions, Catholics among them, forged together in common purpose, walking forward, hand in hand. Together on a journey. Unprecedented.

Many factors played into this new spirit of cooperation. One stands out. It was the insight—indeed, the affirmation—that God has been active in Asian history over the millennia. Thus, the Spirit lives in the other religions of Asia. Proud Asians could hardly be expected to think otherwise. An all-loving Being had to have been there all along. Whatever else one might think, the religions of Asia somehow fit into God's infinitely wise and loving plan for humanity. Of course the Asian bishops wanted to share the Christian message of mercy, forgiveness, and salvation. That's a given. What was new was the idea that Christianity would find its way into the future through dialogue, and that through this dialogue Christians would be better positioned to live out the gospel. Not everything demanded immediate clarity. Not all truth had been revealed. The Asian Catholic leadership had a new sense of purpose and were being driven by their belief that if they trusted the Spirit, if they stayed faithful to their mission as best they could understand it, the rest would simply have to be left in God's hands.

Whatever else might happen as the bishops pondered their future, one thing was clear. The old evangelization days of simple catechetical answers were over. The church had entered into a new era, one that required more give and take. The Word of God was no longer traveling down a one-way street. New evangelical insights along with new social, political, and religious realities were forcing change. Additionally, most Asian nations, including, for example, India, Malaysia, Indonesia, Vietnam, Laos, and Burma/Myanmar, were starting to limit the number of foreign priests who were allowed to live in these countries as missionaries. Meanwhile, indigenous priests were growing in numbers. National pride translated into the need for Asians to make decisions that affected Asians. Paradoxically, their pride enhanced their faith to sustain a more humble Catholicism, one that did not have all the answers and that felt the need to reach out to other religious communities. How far the Asian bishops were willing to go in their retreat from triumphalism was not always clear. Choan-Seng Song, a Taiwanese-born Protestant theologian, heavily influenced by Confucianist and Taoist ideas, is one of a number of Asian theologians who argue that Christianity must go far indeed. He and some other theologians say it must give up totally its exclusive claims on salvation history.

From the mid-1970s through the 1980s, the Federation of Asian Bishops' Conferences put words into practice. It was a time of new initiatives, a time when the FABC unveiled its initial programs. Diocesan and national pastoral commissions began their work too, as did countless social, missionary, religious, and lay leaders. Each was animated by the forces of renewal. Unlike the old days when instructions came from the top down, these initiatives were being carried out on a regional or national basis. The FABC was making its mark as well, especially the newly formed offices of Human Development and Ecumenical and Inter-religious Affairs. For centuries, the churches of Asia had expressed concern for the poor primarily through charitable works and development projects. This began to change after the Vatican Council, a change that accelerated after the creation of the FABC.

ENERGY AND GOOD WILL PREVAIL

During the late 1960s and 1970s the Asian churches were especially receptive to change. There was much work to be done. The sixteen council documents had to be translated into local languages, taught to the people, and implemented. In the wake of the council, nationalism, cultural pride, and fresh theological thought combined to bring unparalleled energy to the young churches of Asia. Social action in the Catholic church in Asia began to emerge at two levels. At the grass-roots level, movements of Catholic activists became more discernible. These movements were made up of workers, university and school students, intellectuals, priests, sisters, and religious orders of men and women. It was in 1965, the council's final year, that 150 Catholic priests met in Hong Kong, bringing with them a new, radical consciousness. They met under the banner of the Priests' Institute of Social Action (PISA). Their aim was to bring new directions to the social action apostolate for the Asian churches. To live out the council's ideals and to be credible voices in Asia, they felt their churches needed to undergo radical change. "Cut the ties with the colonial past! Identify with the poor!" These were their cries. At another level, the level of the hierarchy, social action was also emerging under the FABC banner. In June 1969, as a follow-up to the Hong Kong meeting, forty bishops, priests, and laymen met, this time at the Jesuit House in Baguio, Philippines, 150 miles north of Manila. There they discussed the idea of creating an Asia-wide social action office. While the Hong Kong meeting had been primarily a training seminar, the Baguio meeting, organized by social action veterans, carried more clout.[2] The group searched for ways to work across national boundaries. During the meeting, the nine attending bishops met informally and decided to keep lines of communication open. Moreover, they decided to create a secretariat with a chairman and full-time secretary and set up an office in Manila. Their choices: Philippine Carmelite Bishop Julio Xavier Labayen, the well-known activist, as chairman and Philippine Jesuit Horacio de la Costa as secretary. This group became the nucleus of a social justice lobby group among the Asian bishops and played an important role in the history of the FABC development. The group moved into full gear on the second day of Pope Paul VI's visit to Manila, when Cardinal Justinus Darmojuwono of Indonesia, Bishop Hsu of Hong Kong, Bishop Labayen, and Father de la Costa met to consider how the Asian office they had planned at Baguio might be integrated into whatever episcopal structure might emerge after Manila. The men decided to be patient and watch developments. Their patience eventually paid off, and the newly formed FABC decided to make the Baguio vision its own. The secretariat would become the Office for Human Development. It would carry a social mandate—and eventually help spell out what the bishops meant when they talked about their "new way of being church."

The OHD was to play a significant role in the formation of the bishops' emerging social justice vision. With Labayen chosen as its first executive chairman, the office had a committed visionary as a leader, a man who believed in grass-roots organizing, and a bishop who was solidly committed to the notions of solidarity with the poor and the formation of small Christian communities. The OHD saw its first task as radicalizing the bishops. This would be done, they thought, through training programs, "exposure-immersion" experiences aimed at allowing the bishops to witness poverty as they had never witnessed it before. The program called for them to live, at least for a few days, in contact with the poorest of the poor: slum dwellers, bonded laborers, subsistence laborers, political prisoners, and others. These seminars would last roughly two weeks at a time, providing the bishops with plenty of time to discuss what they were learning. As they finished each seminar, they put their experiences and discussions into words. Episcopal traditions in Asia, often in distinctly hierarchical cultural settings, had kept most bishops among the elite. It was unheard of that they should mingle with "ordinary" people, let alone learn from them. These programs marked a radical shift in church thinking. While many of their hearts had been in the right places, most Asian bishops had been largely shielded by years of seminary and rectory life from the harsher realities of poverty. The actual taste of poverty up close would be new for many and shocking for some. It was a radicalizing experience, as can be seen in the statements the bishops wrote after the sessions. The seminars began to be called institutes and took the formal name "Bishops' Institutes for Social Action," or BISA. They went on for more than a dozen years from 1974 through 1987.

Following their first BISA seminar, the bishops wrote: "The over-

whelming majority of our people are poor, but let it be clearly understood what we mean by *poor*. Our people are *not* poor as far as cultural
tradition, human values, and religious insights are concerned. In these
things of the spirit, they are immensely rich."[3] BISA I had some sobering
moments as they cautiously decided to enter into deeper solidarity with
the poor. They knew the choice could have serious consequences in Asia.
In BISA I, written in March 1974 in Novaliches, Philippines, the bishops
wrote their report almost with a sense of trepidation:

> Thus opting to be with the poor involves the risk of conflict with
> vested interests or "establishments," religious, economic, social,
> political. It also involves, for leaders of the church especially, *loss of
> security,* and that not only material but spiritual. For it means tak-
> ing the unfamiliar course of looking for guidelines of policy and
> action not to ready-made theological, legal and sociological systems
> developed principally in the West, but to a discernment of the his-
> torical process taking place among our own people. . . . We end with
> a word of hope. Our problems are great, but the human potential of
> our people is also great. If only they can liberate themselves from
> the outer and inner constraints that bind them, they will themselves
> take up and bring about their own integral human development. To
> this task of liberation we dedicate ourselves.[4]

The new focus on poverty soon spawned larger structural questions. Central to these was, Why are so many Asians poor? It was not long before
they found themselves searching for answers, moving deeper into social
analysis.[5] If anything, succeeding BISA seminars only further convinced
the bishops that they were on the right path. They felt encouraged by the
Synod on Justice in 1971 and its famous proclamation that "the work for
social justice is a constituent element of preaching the Gospel."[6]

BISA II followed BISA I by only a year, taking place in April 1975 in
Tokyo, Japan. At the conclusion of this second seminar the bishops wrote
they could see clearly "the importance of the *social* dimension of sin and
grace."[7] Poverty speaks loudly when given a human face. The Asian bishops found themselves on the same road their Latin American episcopal
brothers had traveled a few years earlier. In nations where the poor suffer
much oppression, an active "preferential option for the poor" leads trav-
elers into a confrontation with unjust structures.

Social analysis was not entirely new for the bishops. FABC documents
from the start attempted some form of analysis.[8] What changed as the
BISA gatherings progressed was the intensity and depth of the analysis.
Moreover, the bishops were taking ownership of the process, and they
wanted to avoid using entirely Western tools for their analysis. Instead
they sought out techniques suited for their roles as *religious* leaders. The

bishops at BISA I through III attempted to interpret the social dimensions of the gospel within the context of Asian poverty. In the process they were being drawn more deeply into the staggering dimensions of Asian poverty. Eventually they concluded that working for the poor would be an altogether inadequate response. Instead, what they needed to do was to enter into solidarity with the poor. In other words, they had to become poor themselves. Their churches could no longer exist as privileged oases. They had to leave their secure dwellings to live *among* the poor. Additionally, the BISA seminars, under Labayen's influence, stressed the need to build base communities of peoples who could help support each other. The new wine they were seeking needed new wineskins. In fact, what the bishops were coming to realize was that many of their church institutions and programs, designed initially to help the poor, were at times working against their best interests. Many programs, supported generously with funds from the West, were too large and too expensive—and often too elite—to be maintained within the new model of a humbler church living in solidarity with the poor.

BISA IV through VI stressed the need for interfaith cooperation with the aim of affecting social change. There were practical reasons here too. The social challenges were viewed as daunting and the ranks of Catholics were few. Real change could come only if networks of people committed to change could work together. What was happening during the BISA gatherings was not only the evolution of a vision but also the growth of a process of decision making: the consensus model of leadership. The Asian bishops have used this model to their advantage for decades. It takes time, respect, and shared values, and the Asian bishops were ready to invest all three. The approach is also very Asian. For one thing, it is non-confrontational; for another, it attempts to avoid dividing the group into "winners" and "losers." It takes a lot of give and take. When it works, however, it is a powerful model because everything from workshop statements to seminar programs and plenary assembly papers emerges with many parents. The "consensus" model of leadership has been one of the most important achievements in the FABC's three-decade history. It has also kept the Asian bishops from some of the debilitating divisions that European and Latin American bishops conferences have experienced in recent years. Thus, the BISA gatherings can be credited with both putting a personal face on poverty and helping the bishops discover a methodology to move them forward over the years.

DRAWN DEEPER INTO ANALYSIS

BISA VII in Hua Hin, Thailand, in January 1986 gathered sixty-eight participants, among them forty-three bishops representing each of the

FABC's twelve bishops' conferences—Pakistan, India-Nepal, Sri Lanka, Bangladesh, Thailand, Malaysia-Singapore-Bunei, Indonesia, Philippines, Japan, Korea, Taiwan, and Hong Kong. The stated purpose of BISA VII was "to discover a liberative spirituality for social action among the poor and by the poor." It followed the challenge laid out at BISA VI, when the bishops concluded they needed to delve deeper into the spiritual dimensions of their work. They wrote then:

> A new spirituality that will suffuse evangelization and embrace the plan of God for the whole creation is imperative. Mere individual salvation is not enough; salvation must be for the whole person, all people and even the cosmos. This spirituality must not be inward looking but must place the church at the service of the whole human race.

In this light the bishops chose "Asia's Religio-Cultural Heritage and Human Development" as the theme for BISA VII. The bishops, with the help of their theologians, were coming to new pastoral insights and needed the precise words to describe them. They were searching for answers. BISA VII, by all accounts, represented a very important breakthrough. In the final document, they spelled out the way, for the first time, to bind together the elements of Asian culture, religion, society, politics, and poverty—and how they might respond to these as spiritual leaders. They wrote:

> Culture, religion and society are interdependent, interacting and mutually transforming. In our Asian continent, which is the cradle for all the great world religions, culture and religion are integrated. Religion is the dynamic element of culture. Together they form the religio-cultural system, which interacts with the socio-economic-political system of society, permeating every sphere of human life. Asian poverty is not a purely economic concept, neither is its religiosity merely cultural. Poverty and religiosity are interwoven in the Asian ethos, in such a way that at a certain point they seem to coalesce in order to procreate the specific character of Asia. Within the fabric of this rich and varied religio-cultural heritage of Asia, but especially in the lives of the poor, the bishops sought to discern the creative impulses of God's liberating Spirit as the poor struggle to free themselves from deprivation and oppression and strive for genuine communion among people and nations.[9]

The bishops had come to a new level of understanding. It was their peoples' religions and cultural heritages that were the sources of dignity and meaning in hard times. This was a simple yet profound insight, and it proved to be a liberating moment, providing much new energy. During BISA VII the bishops also tried to assess the work of their earlier BISA seminars. Exposure *to poverty* had brought them closer to the stark reality, but immersion *in poverty* allowed them to experience the perspective of the poor themselves. "Exposure," they wrote, "is like a doctor's visit for diagnosis; immersion is like the visit of a genuine friend entering into a dialogue-of-life. . . . [Exposure-immersion] follows the basic principle of the Incarnation."

It awaited BISA VII for the bishops to take ownership of a specific method of social analysis that would propel them forward. These are the steps that emerged: Step 1, "exposure-immersion," requires coming face to face with the harsh realities of life in Asia, tasting its suffering, poverty, and exploitation. Step 2, "social analysis," requires studying the widest context of the religio-cultural reality, or, as some would say, "the signs of the times." Step 3, "contemplation," requires becoming present to an awareness of God and divine activity within the social reality. While strict social analysis is necessary in identifying the social, political, and economic factors that lead to poverty, the bishops stated that it alone is not enough. They needed another element, a spiritual element. They needed to take time for contemplation. This step, in the words of the Sri Lankan Jesuit theologian Aloysius Pieris, who has long been associated with the call for "spiritual introspection" within the context of social analysis, requires a "sympathetic and respectful dialogue with Asia's great religions and the religiosity of the poor."[10] Step 4, "pastoral planning," seeks to translate the previous three stages into concrete plans carried out with an emphasis on dialogue. The bishops stressed nonconfrontational problem solving, an approach that fits with their core spiritual vision for Asia, a continent returning to harmony in all aspects of life.[11] This was no small accomplishment. The four-step method would allow the bishops to assess countless perplexing social-justice issues from a deeply Christian point of view, one that values the social sciences but sees them as incomplete without placing God within the broader picture.

Meanwhile, the cornerstone of the Asian bishops' commitment to dialogue was the insight that peoples of other Asian cultures and faiths are not to be regarded as "objects of Christian mission," but rather as "partners in the Asian community." Out of this partnership was to come mutual witness.[12] The bishops saw their pastoral cycle as open to continual renewal, following further evaluation and reflection.

The BISA gatherings had been highly motivating and very personal events. One OHD staff member recalled hearing stories of how the BISA gatherings affected the participants in personal ways. Said one bishop: "I have been in my diocese thirteen years and never realized squatters lived just three hundred meters from my house. My host family was Protestant. The August heat was unbearable. After three days living in their small house, the family went out, leaving me alone so I could bathe." Said another bishop: "I went to live with a poor Muslim family who welcomed me whole-heartedly. They were very happy to have a Catholic bishop in their house and told me that their leaders had never come to stay with them." Still another: "Arriving in a small farming village, I realized I left my wallet in my car. For the first time in many years I had to experience not having even a small coin with me. I felt insecure and uncomfortable. The experience of being poor even for a few days helped me have a new insight."[13] Decades later, the impact of these immersion experiences would stand out in the minds of many bishops as having had a fundamental impact on the way they began to approach their ministries.

The BISA statements became bolder with each passing seminar. They seemed to build from one to another. If there was a problem with this radicalizing process it was the challenge to live up to lofty declarations. It is said that for something to happen it first must be imagined. The BISA series represented some of the first visible evidence that what had been imagined was taking shape in the lives of the bishops and their churches. Yet it would be a long journey, a very long journey, for some from the relatively privileged states in which many Asian Catholic bishops had lived for years. In the 1970s and 1980s, the Asian bishops were motivated by the needs of their peoples, chief among these the needs for food and livelihood. Their writings, coming out of countless meetings, institutes, assemblies, consultations, congresses, colloquia, and FABC plenary sessions, came to reflect these basic needs and eventually led into analyses aimed at explaining why so many were being denied the basics.

When the immersion programs were introduced in the local churches across Asia, the reflections became less abstract, more experiential, and therefore more understanding of the situations. The experience of meditation and contemplation with people of other faiths helped the bishops to develop a new spirituality through silence and meditation in the context of Asia. The spiral approach enhanced the realization that growth in faith is not a linear process, but comes through human experience of reality, prayer reflection and action, and then again experience.[14]

Later the BISA programs were replaced with a second phase of programs, still run by OHD, called the Asian Institutes for Social Action, or AISA. As a result of greater contact and links among episcopal commissions, the BISA process was translated into AISAs. The difference was that the program identified a bishop with a particular pastoral need in his diocese. For example, the bishop of a diocese in the Philippines brought his priests and laity together with bishops from other countries. They then went through the Pastoral Spiral experience. At the end of the process, the diocese had a concrete pastoral program for itself.[15] The subjects of AISA immersion included industrial workers, immigrant workers, slum dwellers, victims of tourism, fishermen, farmers, and women workers.

The OHD also coordinated the justice and peace network of the FABC from 1979, out of which emerged Hotline, a human rights network to meet urgent appeals, and the now autonomous Committee of Asian Women, an Asian women workers' network. Both have their secretariats in Hong Kong.

In retrospect, it is clear that these were times when words, actions, and spirit came together in remarkable ways, and not without some painful introspection. It was not uncommon, watching the events unfold, for observers and participants to say they could feel the hand of the Holy Spirit in the willingness to go forward in the face of great risk. A number of prominent Asian theologians, after studying the collection of Asian episcopal writings over the years, collaborated to distill what they found to be "the most salient features" in the evolving bishops' statements. In the essay "What the Spirit Says to the Churches," a handful of theologians offered the following list of commitments:[16]

1. To enter into solidarity with the people, especially the poor

2. To Jesus, his values and teachings and the belief that through the incarnation Jesus entered into solidarity with the suffering of the world

3. To Jesus' vision of the reign of God

4. To the belief that God is present and encountered in the social and secular realities of society

5. To the proposition that working on behalf of the poor is an essential element of evangelization

6. To transformation of the churches of Asia into churches of the poor

7. To the continued analysis of the causes of poverty

8. To a more rigorous defense of the poor through a commitment to human rights—not only individual but also communal and collective rights

9. To the use of Asian resources to solve Asian problems

10. To answer social and economic problems by being animated by a spiritual vision.[17]

The list shows the extent to which the bishops of Asia had wedded themselves to the poor and to a mission of working for social justice.

They also spoke of the commitments in terms of placing their churches at the "service to life." "We Asians are searching not simply for the meaning of life but for life itself," they said. "We envision a life with integrity and dignity, a life of compassion for the multitudes, especially for the poor and needy. It is a life of solidarity with every form of life and of sensitive care for the earth."[18] Underlying these commitments was the conviction that God is fully present in the suffering and struggles of the marginalized of the world. Curiously, their commitment to poverty made them all the more hopeful. They wrote that they found hope in a general awakening among the poor to unjust structures and to the longing of so many Asians for lasting peace and harmony.

From the viewpoint of the Asian theologians, the insights they had developed from their experiences very much belonged within the body of Catholic social teachings. Yet these insights were not being recognized by the wider church. At a symposium in Hong Kong in March 1992 involving thirty-one theologians and social activists, theologians complained that the universal church had not been influenced by their Asian experiences. Father Aloysius Pieris noted that Catholic social teaching comes from the West's socioeconomic history and uses paradigms not easily applicable to Asia. "Rome has not been touched by the significant historical movements that have penetrated Christians in the Third World," the Sri Lankan theologian said. Particularly absent is "an openness to the prophetic voices that emerge from movements like the basic human communities of Asia," he said.[19]

REACHING OUT IN DIALOGUE

As noted earlier, the bishops knew that tackling the numbing issues of poverty and injustice in Asia could not be done in isolation. Rather their work called for cooperation with other religions sharing the same values and concerns. Thus, a dialogue with poverty went hand in hand with a dialogue with other religions. The task of this dialogue fell to the FABC's Office of Ecumenical and Interreligious Affairs. As OHD had done, the Interreligious Affairs office decided to begin the dialogue with a series of seminars to help educate the bishops. The first Bishops' Institute for Interreligious Affairs, or BIRA I, took place in October 1979 in Sam Phran, Thailand, outside of Bangkok. This BIRA seminar gathered bishops from Japan, Korea, Taiwan, Sri Lanka, Hong Kong, Macao, and Thailand, all countries with significant Buddhist populations, to deepen their understanding and commitment to dialogue with Buddhists. BIRA I posed two questions: What should be the pastoral position of the Catholic Church for dialogue in each particular country? What concrete steps should be taken for the near future to advance dialogue? The bishops studied the issues and found that relations with Buddhists were improving in their various countries. They said they were experiencing greater openness and more contacts with more opportunities for dialogue. They also found common concerns as religious leaders called out for more just and humane societies, for better education, and for wider information, as well as a desire to deepen cultural identities and cultural roots. "We feel the urgency for dialogue," the bishops wrote, "because of the promptings of the Spirit of Christ, moving us in love to open ourselves to Buddhists in new ways, respecting them so that we may help one another to grow together in the fullness of our total reality."[20]

BIRA II took place the following month in Kuala Lumpur, Malaysia. This time the bishops came from Bangladesh, India, Indonesia, Malaysia, Philippines, and Thailand. The purpose was "to deepen our understanding of and commitment to dialogue with Muslims." Again the bishops said they found improved relations between the religions. However, they also found factors "inhibiting dialogue," such as triumphalist attitudes "on both sides" as well as certain political conditions in some countries. "In spite of these obstacles," the bishops wrote, "there is a growing awareness on the part of Christians of the necessity for dialogue as an activity intrinsic to the Christian response to God's message."[21]

BIRA III, held in Madras, India, in November 1982 drew bishops from Bangladesh, India, Indonesia, Malaysia, Thailand, and Sri Lanka. As with BIRA I and II, it called for greater dialogue, understanding, and "the common promotion of integral values like freedom, equality, fellowship and justice." This time the bishops wrote that dialogue is "a crucial challenge to the churches of Asia in their growing commitment to the building of the kingdom."

The BIRA series strengthened a realization that the Spirit is alive in all religions. Dialogue, they wrote, is the means for uncovering the mystery of God's divine plan. It goes along with evangelization, the bishops argued over the years. It was both necessary and complementary, they said. However, for dialogue and evangelization to be effective they would require a new spirit of humility. Participants reported that discussions went beyond the traditional view of evangelization as bringing people to the Catholic Church, and instead gave attention to the mandate of bringing the Good News to people. The latter sees evangelization as an open-ended process that views conversion as a matter between the individual and God, in contrast to a more traditional approach which defines baptism as the goal. In this light conversion is not so much a person changing from one religion to another as a person turning toward the Spirit and moving away from selfishness and sin to love and justice.[22]

The BIRA statements made references to the need for self-emptying, a full turn from the triumphal spirit that characterized many of the Asian churches in decades past. In the end, the BIRA series were small but significant steps into the future. The statements were also beginning to force further reflections on how Catholics should present themselves to the wider world in order to be effective witnesses of the faith. With a growing spirit of openness, humility, and dialogue, the bishops were seeding Asian gardens in the hope of bringing greater peace and harmony to their nations. The tone set by these initiatives rippled through the Asian churches. Christian–Muslim dialogue grew slowly in a number of countries. A dialogue commission was established by the Catholic bishops of Pakistan in 1985. Small dialogue groups met regularly in various cities, such as Lahore, Multan, and Karachi. It was seldom easy. From the Muslim side, the World Muslim Congress invited Christians to its ninth assembly, held in Karachi in March 1986. It even invited Pope John Paul II. The pope did not attend, but sent a message and a delegate.[23]

From a theological perspective, the BIRA statements did not go much beyond similar calls for dialogue at the Vatican Council. These new calls, however, were coming from Asia and calling out for Asian dialogue. While pastoral in intent, they also had theological implications. Importantly, the bishops' primary focus was no longer the institutional church itself but rather the larger *mission* of the church. The bishops were intent to bring physical and spiritual liberation to the peoples of their lands; they were intent to work to end poverty, to work for justice. They were focused on building the reign of God. In this sense, their efforts were part of a wider transformation, first within their hearts and later within their approaches to church life itself.

CHAPTER 5

Reign of God

*If language is not correct, that which
is said is not understood, if that which
is said is not understood, what ought to
be done is not done. If what should be done
is not done, morals and art deteriorate. If
morals and art deteriorate, justice goes
astray. If justice goes astray, the people
stand in confusion. Therefore, there must
be not arbitrariness in what is said.*
—Confucius

*The spirit of God is upon me, because God
has anointed me and has sent me to bring
glad tidings to the lowly, to heal the
brokenhearted, to proclaim liberty to the
captives and release to the prisoners.*
—Isaiah 61:1-2

The Catholic Church's approach to mission turned upside down in the years that followed the Vatican Council, in no small part because of changes in attitudes among the Asian Catholic leadership. Most involved in the mission work would say that the era was marked by a new state of maturity and that it was characterized by a healthy return to basic gospel values. However, these changes were not universally accepted, especially by some of the more tradition-minded clerics in Rome. The traditional mission approach viewed Asia and the Asian people primarily as potential converts to the church. Missionaries came to Asia to save souls, to draw them away from the perils of pagan religions—from godlessness. In the process, these missionaries would build the ranks of their churches, which were usually replicas of churches they had left behind in their native lands. These "mission" churches would use the same canons, the same liturgies, and the same theologies as their European brothers and sisters of faith.[1] Often the very architecture of these churches was modeled after the churches and cathedrals of Europe. Pictures of saints that hung on the walls of European churches were brought to the mission churches to hang there. In the old missionary order—some have referred to it as the "cookie-cutter" missionary world—the primary emphasis was on moral and spiritual welfare of the potential Christians. The urgent need was to save them from the fires of hell by bringing them into the fold. In the old missionary scheme, the Catholic Church was the sole channel to salvation. This view of mission, of course, assumed that God was absent from the other religions of the world. It also assumed, at least from the Asian perspective, the superiority of Western culture and civilization. This approach to missionary activity falls under the common heading of "salvation theology." The primary focus of salvation theology is on the church—the instrument of salvation.

The newer missionary world order finds its modern Catholic roots in the council documents of *Lumen Gentium*, the Dogmatic Constitution on the Church; *Ad Gentes*, the Decree on the Missionary Activity of the Church; and *Gaudium et Spes,* the Pastoral Constitution on the Church in the Modern World. The latter was fundamental in reorienting the church. Essentially it argues that the church exists to serve the world and that Christians must commit themselves to living out the gospel call to work on behalf of human dignity and to build a more just and peaceful world. For many Catholics, the council marked the long-overdue end of the defensive posture that grew in the wake of the Reformation. For the churches in Asia, the council also marked the beginning of a new era of a more inclusive Catholicism, a less Eurocentric church. In the eyes of many Asian Catholic leaders, Vatican II ushered in a much more welcoming vision of church, one that placed Catholics and cultures everywhere on equal footing. Some Asians saw this shift as so monumental that they likened it to the breakthrough experienced at the Council of Jerusalem described in the Acts of the Apostles. Before Jerusalem I, the early disciples of Jesus were pretty much what Jesus expected them to be— good Jews. After Jerusalem I, these disciples had a new evangelical sense of purpose. They wanted to take their new message of love and hope beyond the Jews, to the Gentiles. That shift of mission, of course, changed the history of much of the world.

The Vietnamese theologian Father Peter C. Phan of the Catholic University of America explains that before the Vatican Council, Catholic missionary theology placed its primary emphasis on building up the church. This was done through proclaiming the church's role as the means to divine reward. Witnessing to the Gospels and working to meet the physical needs of the locals were secondary concerns. Thus, the order of priorities were church, proclamation, mission, and reign of God. The top priority, of course, was the physical extension of Catholicism, "implant-ing the church." After Vatican II, the approach to Catholic mission main-tained the same values but flipped them upside down. After the council, according to Phan, the mission priorities became working to build a more just world, witnessing to the Gospels, and through this witness, proclaiming Christianity's salvific role and, finally, building new churches. Thus, the new order is reversed: reign of God, mission, proc-lamation, and church.[2] Missionaries today are, then, less "church-centered." Their work is directed outward into the world: building the reign Jesus came to announce—peace, justice, and solidarity among peo-ples. In this setting, religious conversion is not irrelevant, but it comes as a possible fruit of a deeper sense of purpose. The Asian bishops have essentially endorsed this approach as one that is compatible with the spirit and needs of the Asian peoples. Most Western missionaries in Asia and Africa today see themselves as Christian emissaries working to alle-viate suffering and pain and to build better lives for the people with whom they come into contact. This approach is referred to as "mission theology," in contrast to the older "salvation theology."

The Latin American bishops endorsed the same approach in the late 1960s when they embraced the cause of social justice and their "prefer-ential option for the poor." In a broader sense, the Asian bishops were among those influenced by the Latin American bishops and liberation theology, first unveiled in the landmark work of the Peruvian priest Gus-tavo Gutiérrez, *A Theology of Liberation: History, Politics and Salvation*. Mission theology shares similarities with liberation theology. Both are worldly; that is, their concern is with the total well-being of their peoples. Both are contextual; that is, they claim to respond to the specific condi-tions in which they find themselves. Both are infused with gospel values and see as their end purpose the building of the reign of God on earth. The Asian theologians, influenced by liberation theology, have seen themselves responding to their own Asian contexts. The starting point for Asian theological reflections has been the specific context of the specific Asian church, be it India, the Philippines, Sri Lanka, or Korea. These responses—these theological reflections—have been the engines of the pastoral responses of the Asian churches during the past three decades, and together they have laid out the broad outlines for the overall pastoral vision of the FABC.

These new approaches to doing theology have come largely in the wake of Vatican II. Contextual theology is inductive. It starts with cir-cumstance and "induces" larger conclusions about the order of society as well as the challenges and responsibilities facing the human family. Tra-ditional theology is deductive. It begins with abstract concepts about God and the natural order and from these moves to specific rules or principles of conduct. This reversal in theological approach has been much more pervasive among theologians working in the poor nations of the world. In this sense, its energies have been coming from the "peripheries" of the church. These same ideas often show up among theologians in the West who work among and derive their ideas from Hispanics, African-Americans, and Native Americans.

However, even these dramatic shifts in the way the Catholic Church began to approach its missionary work in the postconciliar period were further influenced by changes occurring in Europe and elsewhere where forces of secularization were gaining and forcing many to reevaluate the very notions of mission and mission territory. Before the council, it was customary to speak of the missions as places in which the church had yet to be firmly established. At the council, instead of speaking of "missions" as such, the bishops opted for the word "mission," rooted in the Trinity. The council fathers wrote the following in *Ad Gentes,* or the Decree on Missionary Activity of the Church: "The pilgrim Church is missionary by her very nature, since it is from the mission of the Son and the mission of the Holy Spirit that she draws her origin, in accordance with the decree of God the Father." Thus, the council began to view the entire church as on mission everywhere, even though special tasks vary according to circumstances and need. Meanwhile, *Ad Gentes* states that the "seeds of the Word" are already present in other religions. In a similar vein, *Gaudium et Spes,* the Pastoral Constitution on the Church in the Modern World, states that the salvific action of God reaches out to all people in ways unknown to us. In other words, people can be saved outside the church. *Lumen Gentium,* the Dogmatic Constitution on the Church, defined the church as the sacrament of the unity of all peoples and the beginning of the reign of God. It affirms: "The obligation of spreading the faith is imposed on every disciple of Christ, according to his or her state." Hence, it would be misleading to speak about "mission" as only meaning "foreign mission." Similarly it would be inappropriate to say that only an elite few, declared "missionaries," are called to live out this call to mission work. The council was saying that all Christians are called to be missionaries. The council was also saying that the purpose of mission was no longer seen as "saving souls" as such, but rather living out the life of a Christian—that is, living by the Gospels and celebrating life by making the world a better place in which to live.

This work is not carried out in isolation. It is done in cooperation with others of good will. The Vatican Council document *Nostra Aetate*, the Declaration on the Relationship of the Church to Non-Christian Religions, refers to God as the common origin and end of all people of the earth. It states that truth can be found in the other religions of the world. These words helped change the Catholic view toward non-Christian religions. No longer were the non-Christian religions of the world to be viewed as "godless." Indeed, each contained truths that called out for greater examination and understanding. These shifts, combined with changing notions regarding culture and language coming out of academic centers, also played major roles in toppling a centuries-old Catholic consensus on church mission.[3]

The council documents touched off far-reaching discussions on mission through many publications and church gatherings, each seeming to push older ideas of mission farther from center stage. Missionaries were arguing for the more Gospel-based approach to missionary work. So, too, they argued that the Catholic Church needed to pay much more attention to local culture. In effect, they endorsed the model of dialogue, a two-way interaction of sharing between the Christian and the non-Christian. The geography of mission had changed. The frontiers that once separated Christian from non-Christian lands, the "saved" from the "heathens," were no longer as clear. Additionally, many in the West lived in increasingly secular societies. Christians in the West and elsewhere were rubbing shoulders with Buddhists, Hindus, and Muslims. The major religions of the world had expanded to a point that they now butted up against each other. Phan writes: "The danger of extinction threatening the old theology of mission became an opportunity for a new theology of mission to be born, in which a quiet Copernican revolution took place."[4]

Pope Paul VI helped with the revolution with his 1975 apostolic exhortation entitled *Evangelii nuntiandi*. The document came to be viewed as the Magna Carta for the new mission theology. In the document Paul VI described the process of "evangelization" as a rich, complex, and dynamic one. "For the church, evangelizing means bringing the Good News into all the strata of humanity, and through its influence transforming humanity from within and making it new," he wrote. In his mind, evangelization was an all-embracing activity done in a variety of ways. The document gave greater prominence to thought about the reign of God. Mission work came to be seen as involving entire cultures. While it was not necessarily Paul VI's intention, some Catholic writers even began to question the continued feasibility of speaking about individual conversion. *Evangelii nuntiandi* seemed to raise as many questions as it tried to settle. For Catholics involved in mission work these were healthy discussions. The church was wrestling with fundamental issues. It was assessing how it would relate to the modern world. It was examining nothing less than how Christians should take their religious beliefs into the world in order to transform it. Change does not come easily; ideas held for centuries do not give way to new ideas without certain strife and unsettlement.

Against this background, Pope John Paul II began to insert his own thinking about mission. He began to speak widely about evangelization, or more specifically, "the new evangelization." It was fifteen years after Pope Paul's letter that Pope John Paul, in 1990, wrote the encyclical *Redemptoris missio*. His panorama for evangelization was not as subtle or as comprehensive as was Paul's. John Paul II's encyclical seemed to try to go back to basics and to remind Catholics of the urgent task to proclaim the Good News to those who had not yet heard it. While affirming that the Spirit is active in creation and in other religions, John Paul said that the Spirit cannot be separated from the Spirit's particular activity within the Catholic Church. In other words, dialogue with cultures and other religions, while good and necessary, should be viewed only *as a means* to the more important work of proclaiming Jesus as the One and unique Savior of the World. To the consternation of some and the relief of others, the pope's words appeared to be a step backward into the area of the older theology of salvation. Working to build the reign of God on earth, to promote social, political, and spiritual liberation is well and good, the pope was saying. It is to be the work of Christians everywhere. However, this work cannot ever be separated from, or come at the expense of the Catholic Church itself. This is because the church is the unique instrument of salvation and Christians are called by the Gospels to proclaim Jesus as the Savior of the World.

To those wondering if conversion among non-Christians was still relevant or whether it had simply been replaced by interreligious dialogue, the pope's emphatic answer was "yes, it is relevant and central to the mission of the church." Respect for conscience and the belief that salvation is possible in any religion do not in any way negate the need to proclaim that Jesus is Savior, the pope insisted. *Redemptoris missio* was not necessarily directed at Asia; however, it was heard in Asia. Some Asian Catholics, while agreeing with its essentials, disagreed with the methods of evangelization the pope seemed to have in mind. For years the Asian bishops have argued that their emphasis on dialogue has not diminished the central importance of evangelization, including the need to proclaim Jesus as Savior. Yet they have stressed that the methods and languages of Europe cannot and should not simply be transplanted into Asia. Cultural and social differences, the Asian leadership has said, need to be given serious thought. At a minimum, in some nations publicly "proclaiming" Jesus as Savior could lead to a death sentence.

Meanwhile, the Asian bishops' own views on mission cannot be divorced from all these wider discussions on the subject that have continued in the church over the years. There was no mention of the kingdom or reign of God in the first FABC plenary assembly in 1974. Gradually, however, in the years that followed references to it began to show up in FABC documents.[5] Maryknoll Missionary Father James H. Kroeger, professor of theology at the Loyola School of Theology in Manila, and Phan have both traced the evolution of mission in Asian thought. The first reference to the "kingdom" appeared at BISA III in 1975. The bishops spoke about the work of the local church as "building God's Kingdom on earth" by fostering gospel values together with followers of other religions and other people of good will. Again the bishops made a similar reference to the building of the kingdom of God at BISA IV in 1978 and BISA VI in 1983, where they stated that by becoming a "church of the poor," the church in Asia would be "sign and sacrament of the Kingdom of God."[6]

The interreligious dialogues held during the BIRA IV series, a seven-year series, also helped the bishops formulate their mission theology. At BIRA IV/1 in 1984, the bishops called for "clarification" in the understanding of the relationship between the church and the kingdom. An emphatic response came the following year in the statement the bishops wrote at BIRA IV/2:

> The Reign of God is the very reason for the being of the Church. The Church exists in and for the Kingdom. The Kingdom, God's gift and initiative, is already begun and is continually being realized, and made present through the Spirit. Where God is accepted, when the Gospel values are lived, where man is respected, there is the Kingdom. It is far wider than the Church's boundaries. This already-present reality is oriented towards the final manifestation and full perfection of the Reign of God.
>
> The Church is an instrument for the actualization of the Kingdom. In this process of continual renewal and actualization, she empties herself and dies like her Master (cf. Phil 2:7), through transforming and suffering, and even persecution, so that she may rise to a new life which approaches the reality of the Kingdom.[7]

In the eyes of the Asian bishops, Catholics were no longer to be viewed as the sole possessors of the kingdom, which went well beyond the church. FABC plenary assemblies also supported this notion of kingdom. At the third FABC plenary assembly, in Bangkok in 1982, the bishops wrote:

> Our Christian communities in Asia must listen to the Spirit at work in the many communities of believers who live and experience their own faith . . . and they . . . must accompany these others "in a common pilgrimage toward the ultimate goal, in relentless quest for the Absolute."[8]

Continuing, they stated: "The church constantly moves forward in mission as it accompanies all humankind in its pilgrimage to the Kingdom of the Father."

At FABC IV in 1986, the bishops concluded that the "seeds of the kingdom" are present in the youth of Asia, as well as in diverse cultures and religions. Within this plurality of cultures the church's task consists, on the one hand, of infusing gospel values and, on the other, of "drawing out more explicitly" the "seeds of the kingdom" already present. They wrote:

> Seeking the Kingdom that Jesus proclaimed is really to build it in the concrete experiences of the social, political, economic, religious and cultural world of Asia. In Jesus the Reign of God began; he came that we might have life to the full. The struggle for fullness of life in Asia is a seeking of the Kingdom. Discipleship then is not at all a withdrawal from the world, but an immersion into the wellspring of Asian reality so that it might have life. Communion, solidarity, compassion, justice, love are keynotes of a spirituality of discipleship.

At FABC V in 1990 the bishops wrote that "a renewal of our sense of mission means, first of all, renewal of our faith that . . . filled with the Spirit, he [Jesus] preached the Good News of the Kingdom of God, and commanded his disciples to do the same. Lifted up from the earth, he draws all peoples to himself through his church, and through other ways unknown to us." The statement concludes:

> And finally, we evangelize because the Gospel is *leaven* for liberation and for the transformation of society. Our Asian world needs the values of the Kingdom and of Christ in order to bring about the human development, justice, peace and harmony with God, among peoples and with all creation that the peoples of Asia long for.[9]

At FABC VI in 1995, the bishops depicted the mission of Jesus as "announcing and inaugurating the Kingdom of God (Mk 1:15). . . . Jesus teaches what life in the Kingdom consists in," namely "communion with Abba . . . [and] liberating and recreating communion among neighbors."[10]

Depictions of the kingdom are not without their own cultural ambiguities. One cannot immediately expect ideas accepted in the West to be understood in precisely the same fashion in the East. Nevertheless, many Asian theologians have embraced the reign of God as the end point in their theological writings. Tissa Balasuriya, a Sri Lankan Oblate, makes the reign of God the central symbol of his "planetary theology." Aloysius Pieris writes that those addressed in kingdom of God references are not only the economically and sociologically poor but also "the poor that are religious and the religious that are poor." He speaks about the "poor monk," meaning that a society characterized by obedience to God attempts both to feed the poor and to avoid excessive materialism.[11] The kingdom, then, is both within and beyond.

From where does the theological focus of kingdom originate? The idea of God's rule is affirmed in various ways in the Old Testament and reached its high point in the New Testament. The expression "reign of God" or "reign of heaven" occurs more than 150 times in the New Testament. The reign of God became the central focus of Jesus' preaching.[12] Phan describes what Jesus meant by his vision of the kingdom, saying that it is characterized by "gratuitous forgiveness and reconciliation" and by "universal justice and peace."

Little did the Asian bishops imagine that their reign of God vision of church, driven by commitments to the poor, to inculturation and to interreligious dialogue, two decades in the making, was headed for more serious trouble. That is because on the other side of the globe, in November 1989, the Berlin Wall was falling.

CHAPTER 6

New Openings

*We can hold back neither the coming
of the flowers nor the downward rush
of the stream; sooner or later, everything
comes to its fruition.*
—*Loy Ching-Yuen*

Look at this flower.
—*To Kim Hoa*

During the years that the Asian bishops were developing their pastoral programs, one group of bishops was conspicuously absent—the bishops of China. The world's most populous nation was cut off from the rest of Asia during the 1950s, 1960s, and 1970s. Only slowly did it begin to open to the rest of the world in the 1980s and 1990s. Beijing suspicions linger. Even today the Chinese bishops, with the exception of those in Hong Kong, have no formal ties with the Federation of Asian Bishops' Conferences.

One and a quarter billion people lived in China at the outset of the twenty-first century. One out of three Asians is Chinese; one out of five persons on the planet is Chinese. At the time of the Communist Revolution in 1949 Catholics in China numbered about four million. Estimates today run from ten million to twelve million. While the figure is small relative to the population of China, the Catholic growth rate is well ahead of other Asian nations. Meanwhile, the best estimate of the number of Protestants in China is from twenty to twenty-five million.

Not much is known about the Catholic Church in China. Some of what is known is not shared widely outside of China for fear of making life more difficult for those who practice the faith. The church in China suffered enormously in the 1950s and then again in the 1960s during the Cultural Revolution. Part of that suffering involves the split of Catholics into two factions, sometimes referred to as the "official" and the "underground" churches. In some ways, these splits are painful and apparent; in other ways, they are complex and not easily understood by outsiders.

My first personal encounter with a Chinese Catholic bishop came in 1987 during a trip to Hong Kong. I was visiting several Maryknoll priests, including Fathers Bob Astorino and Ron Saucci, who together were working to shape the Asian Catholic news agency, UCA News. They introduced me to Bishop Aloysius Jin Luxian of Shanghai, who was visiting Hong Kong at the time. Saucci was working with Jin to help him set up a Catholic publishing house in Shanghai, one that would be able to print catechetical literature. The soft-spoken Jin is a Jesuit and is widely regarded as one of the leading pastors and intellectuals among Catholics in China. A bishop in the "official" church, he was already in his late sixties at the time I met him.

Jin's personal story reflects the pain, passion, and rock-solid faith one finds in many of the personal stories one encounters in China. Educated by Jesuits in Italy in the 1940s, Jin returned to China after the Chinese Communist Party came to power in 1949. He was arrested in 1955.

"The authorities wondered how it was possible that while others tried to get visas to leave, I was doing the opposite," he said. "Hence, they thought I had a mission to subvert the newly established government." Jin spent the next twenty-seven years in confinement, eighteen years in jail—of which four were in solitary confinement, and nine under house arrest. It was dire, he said. However he found it a time of deep, silent prayer. Without a Bible or prayer book, and forbidden even to speak of God, he was thrown back on his inner resources until his release in 1982. The afternoon I spent with Jin he showed no bitterness toward his captors and spoke with much hope for the future of the church in China.

Twelve years later I visited his diocese and spent time in his chancery. Although he was traveling at the time, he requested his aides to receive us and speak to us about the work being done in his diocese. It was in 1999 that my wife and I traveled throughout China interviewing Catholics in six cities. We traveled by plane, train, and bus, visiting as part of a delegation under the auspices of the U.S. China Bureau, headed by Maryknoll Sister Janet Carroll.

Catholics are relatively free to practice their faith in Shanghai. Even in remote areas, known for more open persecution, there has been a growth of freedom in recent years, according to Jin. He tells visitors that Chinese Catholics, in matters of faith and morals, are absolutely faithful to the pope's directives. However, as regards politics, the absence of diplomatic relations between the Vatican and China continues to create difficulties. "Clearly, the Chinese church," he told a reporter, "cannot support Taiwan as the Holy See does officially."[1] The bishop of Shanghai (there are no archdioceses in the official church) says the exchange of information between the bishops of the Chinese church and the Vatican is quite open. "We receive his [the pope's] encyclicals and apostolic letters regularly. Moreover, today there is television and electronic mail that enable us to maintain direct contact with the Vatican every day."

Our first day in China in November 1999 turned out to be unusually warm. It was a Sunday, so we headed off to Mass in Beijing. Our group went by bus to the Immaculate Conception Cathedral, locally called South Church and located at the rear of a tree-studded courtyard. At ten minutes before Mass was to begin the church was packed. Immaculate Conception was one of only five Catholic churches in Beijing; fourteen churches serve the diocese's forty thousand Catholics. I estimated that there were between six hundred and eight hundred worshipers, mostly elderly but with a smattering of young faces, jammed into the pews. Before Mass the congregation chanted continuously in a monosyllabic, high-pitched tone. Most were kneeling, many with rosaries in their hands.

I spotted a number of old paintings on the walls. They were mostly European saints. Later I learned that the older Chinese Catholics are attached to these Western figures. These are the faces of the Catholicism they grew up with. These are the faces on the holy cards they smuggled into the prisons and labor camps. These are the symbols of faith that connected them with everything they had come to love and hold dear. As I knelt with them I kept trying to imagine the terror these Catholics once experienced. The older ones had lived through the Cultural Revolution from the mid-1960s to the mid-1970s, a period when Chairman Mao turned the vengeance of a nation against all things considered elite or foreign—and Catholicism was considered both. From 1966 to 1979, institutional Christianity was completely eradicated in China. Bibles were burned and many pastors, religious, and converts were sent to prison. However, a few Christians continued to meet secretly in their homes. Through Deng Xiaoping's open-door policy, churches began to reopen in 1979.

This Sunday, inside the church just before Mass several priests were on the altar in the final minutes of a benediction service. One held a monstrance as he formed the sign of the cross. Incense filled the cathedral. At the back of the church several old priests, looking as if they were well into their eighties, moved about. One sat down behind a wooden board to hear confessions. All the worshipers looked over sixty or under thirty. No one in between. I was later to learn that nearly an entire generation was lost to the bloodshed that followed the Communist takeover.

The chief celebrant at the Mass was Bishop Michael Fu Tieshan, the bishop of Beijing. The liturgy followed Vatican II norms. Yet I was surprised to see women lectors who approached the altar wearing white surplices over red cassocks. Despite the many rosaries, some worshipers followed along, saying the prayers of the day. The choir sang enthusiastically, led by an animated young priest in his late twenties dressed in black suit and Roman collar. Later, this priest handed me his card, which read: "Fr. Francis Xavier Zhang, bishop's secretary for overseas friendship."

Before Communion, a mitered Bishop Fu conferred the minor orders of lector and acolyte on twenty-one young seminarians, all in their early twenties.

Though the liturgy was familiar, the words were foreign to me—until the Communion service. That's when the choir burst out with "Amazing Grace." After several verses in Chinese, Father Zhang sang a solo verse in English, his way of welcoming our group.

After Mass, we were invited to meet Bishop Fu. We sat on wooden chairs arranged in a rectangle, just outside his office. The head of our delegation, Sister Carroll, sat next to the bishop. Aides appeared and filled small cups or glasses with tea. They placed dishes of fruits—bananas and tangerines—on the tables and invited us to drink and eat. Ritual plays an important role in building friendships and communities in Asia. The tea ritual is common throughout Asia. It is a sign of warmth, a kind of handshake extended into pleasantries and conversation.

The Catholic Church and government in China have ritualized their own ties. The forced marriage pleases neither, but neither can opt out. How these relationships work out depends a lot on local circumstance and local personalities. Catholics in southern China and along the coast experience more freedom than others do. The Chinese living in these areas have had more contacts with outsiders than those living inland and in rural areas. Official regulations, one learns, can be bent if you know the right people. Some call it corruption; others, accommodation; others simply call it the Asian way. "There's a kind of I know you know I know attitude, but let's agree not to talk about it," said Carroll.

This Chinese approach has led some priests with a pastoral focus to decide they get more of what they want if they compromise and try to get along. Meanwhile, it has been precisely the willingness to compromise and work within the system that has offended other Catholics who strenuously hold that to compromise on matters of religion is to sell one's soul and betray one's faith. In China, the gulf between Catholic pragmatists and Catholic idealists seems at times virtually unbridgeable. Many Chinese, including Catholics, agree they have greater freedom of expression than they did a decade or more ago. As one young man sarcastically put it, China has moved from being a totalitarian nation to being an authoritarian one. Yet he agreed that this is a substantial step forward. On the surface, Catholics worship freely, but appearances can be deceptive. Churches operate with many restrictions. No foreign missionaries are allowed, for example. Catholics must register and are ineligible for Communist Party membership (meaning social advancement). Churches are built only with government approval. No private Catholic schools are allowed. No official contact with the Vatican is allowed. Life may not be easy, but it lacks the stark terror Catholics experienced in the 1960s and 1970s when bishops, nuns, priests, and lay leaders were imprisoned or ridiculed or both. Today, Catholic leaders can still be arrested for breaking the rules, but detainment, not long-term imprisonment, is more often the punishment.

Bishop Fu, a typically tall northern Chinese, has been the focus of much controversy. Consecrated bishop of Beijing in 1979, he is also chairman of the Chinese Catholic Patriotic Association, which links the government and the church. During the Cultural Revolution, Fu came under heavy attack, as did other priests. And, like other priests at the time, it is said he compromised by getting married. Years later, this cloud still hangs over his head. Chinese Catholics never warmed to the marriages, forced or not, of their priests. The marriages, it turns out, played a role in dividing Catholics and left many dispirited.

Fu greeted us warmly and searched for ways to reach out. He recalled visiting Maryknoll's New York headquarters years ago. The Chinese architectural style of Maryknoll's seminary overlooking the Hudson River north of New York City is iconic of the importance China once held for Maryknoll. For more than three decades, China was its principal mission. That ended when the Communists expelled all missionaries in the early 1950s. Maryknollers began to return quietly to China more than fifteen years ago. Since then, several dozen Maryknoll priests and sisters have worked there.

Sister of St. Joseph Catherine McNamee, a member of our group, recalled visiting China in 1981 as a member of the first U.S. Catholic college presidents' delegation to China. Back then, only a few people gathered in the church on a Sunday morning, she said. The Mass then was still in Latin and priests kept their backs to the worshipers, nearly all of whom were elderly.

Bishop Fu offered statistics, making the point that the Catholic Church in China is alive and growing. There are now 115 dioceses. In the past twenty years, the church has welcomed more than one thousand new priests and more than three thousand new nuns. However, this growth brings new challenges as well. At the top of Fu's list of needs is better formation for the nation's nuns and priests. For more than thirty years the church saw virtually no new ordinations. Only in 1979 was Catholicism allowed to begin to revive itself. Today there are almost no priests or nuns between the ages of thirty-five and seventy; healthy religious formation in seminaries and convents has become a high priority.

SEMINARY LIFE

Throughout our visit, we sought out young seminarians and candidates for religious life in at least four different cities. We found them all eager to serve the church. They study in buildings that can best be described as rudimentary. They have access to few books, get by on little food, and live in crowded dormitories with little or no hot water. Yet they are enthusiastic and full of hope. It is difficult to determine what drives these young people to the religious life. We did hear much talk in post-Marxist China about the search for meaning among the young.

In each seminary our group was welcomed warmly. We saw in these young Catholics a longing to be tied to the universal church. Making connections became critically important to us too. I toured seminaries and found meager libraries. Most of the books had been published in the 1950s and 1960s. I remember thinking at the time that Catholicism in China is coming up through the ashes more by the power of faith than by contemporary theology. There seems to be no shortage of candidates for the priesthood. Local, regional, and national seminaries are full. One member of our group, Father Michael Farano, director of the Society for the Propagation of the Faith in Albany, exclaimed as he walked into a packed seminary hall in Xi'an: "I haven't seen this many seminarians in one place since I was seventeen years old."

Formation, not numbers, is at the heart of the clerical challenge. We met the vice-rector of the Shanghai seminary. He was in charge of formation. He was a twenty-eight-year-old priest at the time. Officially, there were some sixteen hundred seminarians and fifteen hundred women in various stages of formation in China in 1999. This figure, however, does not take into account those seeking religious formation outside official, government-sponsored seminaries and religious houses. We heard that the "underground church" was training another eight hundred seminarians and one thousand young women for religious communities.

The National Seminary in Beijing housed forty-four students when we visited it. Bishop Joseph Liu Yuanren met us at the front gate. He was an unassuming man dressed in an old gray suit and open collar and was at the time president of the Chinese Bishops' Conference. During a tour of the building he told us 1,070 new priests had been ordained for the official church since 1982. This included, he noted proudly, more than eighty from the National Seminary.

The age of Chinese church leaders, of course, is a major concern. Elderly bishops, many over eighty, continue to set church policy. Their passing in this decade will cause radical changes for the church, quickly lowering the leadership ages by some thirty to forty years. Generation gaps are difficult enough, but this upcoming two-generation jump will be unprecedented in recent church history. When a younger generation of church leaders comes to power, Catholicism will spring forward with a vengeance into some uncertain future. The national seminary is located in an old cement-block building. Unlike other seminaries, it is located inside the city. It looked like a run-down boarding school. Liu eagerly unveiled for us a miniature model of the new national seminary planned to be built in the next few years with the help of government and foreign funds. Catholic seminaries, like other schools, receive modest government stipends for each student who studies in them.

To upgrade the educational standards, China's bishops have been sending seminarians abroad: some to Australia, Hong Kong, and the Philippines, others to Europe and to the United States, since 1992. However, the transitions have not been easy. While traveling in China, I heard stories of some who returned with fresh ideas and post–Vatican II theology only to be shut out by their bishops. "Try again in ten more years," one bishop told a returning student. "By that time I will be dead."

We also heard stories of stellar leadership candidates, who, after studying abroad and being rejected back home, simply gave up. More care needs to be given, it seems, to the problems of culture shock. Going overseas for training—which many Chinese church observers support—has slowed to a trickle. Both the passport and visa application processes have tightened up in recent years, restricting the numbers coming to the United States.

It was getting dark when we finished our visit to the National Seminary. Liu walked us down a narrow street to a nearby restaurant, where we dined and he answered questions. Many seminarians are coming from rural areas, he said, and lack proper study habits. To combat this, he said he planned to borrow disciplinary ideas from the Chinese army. It was not clear exactly what he meant by those words.

We came away with a generally positive impression of the students, who were both prayerful and attentive. A Chinese Catholic woman who has studied in the United States told us that seminarians are generally sensitive young men, but once they become priests many become quite autocratic.

The Chinese government forbids Catholic schools. It does, however, encourage Catholic medical and social work. In recent years growing numbers of young Catholic nuns have been responding, providing one of the more hopeful initiatives in government and church cooperation. Official Catholic education meanwhile, is forbidden outside the physical boundaries of official Catholic properties. Foreign proselytizing is strictly outlawed. Religious training is officially allowed to take place only on church grounds. All this has limited the roles many women religious play. In Shanghai, perhaps the most progressive diocese, some women religious act as diocesan administrators. In other locations, they do pastoral and medical work.

Women interested in religious life begin with a lengthy period of candidacy during which their religious and education backgrounds are assessed. Their first temporary vows follow a two-year novitiate. These vows are renewed annually for five consecutive years before final vows.

LESSONS OF HISTORY

China proclaims a five-thousand-year-old story. In every city we visited we saw monuments and artifacts hundreds or often thousands of years old. The Great Wall was built 220 years before Christ. We walked through the Heavenly Temple and the Forbidden City in Beijing, where emperors offered prayers to the God of Heaven for centuries. We went to the tombs of seventeenth-century Catholic missionaries, saw Christian crosses etched on Nestorian tablets thirteen hundred years old. It is easy to understand why church life, like other aspects of Chinese life, is not prone to change quickly. The people cling to whatever they can during unsettling times.

Consider what the people of China endured during the twentieth century: a long and bloody civil war, the fight to end colonialism and Japanese imperial rule, the founding of a republic, Communism, the Cultural Revolution, and, most recently, moves to a state-directed capitalist economy. Touring China I began to understand better the significance of traditional Confucian thought and its hierarchical worldview. Emperors ruled with absolute authority for thousands of years. China has had little or no experience of political or social pluralism. The emperor's will has always been the law. Why would it not remain so today? Now, however, it is in the guise of the leadership of the ruling Communist Party. Today the Beijing government controls newspapers, television, much of the economy, and even family life. The government's one-child-per-couple rule is still enforced in many parts of China. Beijing demands respect. As wide as the United States, China has one time zone, Beijing time. On the surface, people have the right to do as they please—as long as they don't buck national authority.

Like other Asians, the Chinese are still emerging from colonialism. Hong Kong was returned in 1997; Macao in 1999. There is bound to be suspicion of the West as well as an eagerness to show the world they can manage their own nation without outside interference. This same pride spills over into religion. Many Catholics respect Rome and admire the pope, but feel comfortable being able to run their own church.

Places as well as people spoke to us. Beijing's South Church is a fascinating example. It traces its origins to a chapel built in 1605 by Matteo Ricci, the esteemed Italian Jesuit missioner. In 1610 the chapel was replaced by a church and became known as the Hall of the Lord of Heaven. Wise missionaries sought favor with the court. The church compound housed a conservatory and a library, which drew the attention and respect of the royal family. In 1775, two earthquakes and a fire destroyed the church, but an emperor donated twenty thousand pieces of silver to have it rebuilt. In 1900, the church was burned to the ground during the Boxer Rebellion, a peasant-led revolt against foreigners. In 1904, the church was rebuilt again, only to be closed during the Cultural Revolution, when it became a shoe factory. Finally reopened as a church for foreigners and local diplomats in 1971, it became a place of worship for local Chinese in 1979.

The ebb and flow of fear and fortune in Chinese history contain many lessons. The very stones of South Church speak of China's precarious social order. Over the centuries the stability of Christian life, like all else in China, has depended on the good will of the "emperor." Today that emperor is the Beijing government.

It is a matter of fact, however, that China's Catholics are divided. To understand Chinese Catholicism's divisions, one needs to recall the early and chaotic 1950s, when the Communist Party solidified its control by aligning itself with majority factions within various social and ethnic groups. It became official policy to divide groups in order to conquer them. The Chinese Communists infiltrated groups, then singled out "enemies" in their midst. After purging a "principal enemy" it would find a new "principal enemy." In the Catholic context, the Communists, in the name of nationalism, at first attacked foreign bishops and missionaries, then "unpatriotic" Chinese bishops and priests, and finally lay leaders. With each move, it further divided Catholics and sowed suspicion.

The approach worked brilliantly, soon forging two camps: those who accommodated to the regime, often to meet urgent pastoral needs, and those who simply refused. The former began to operate as the "official," government-sanctioned church; the latter went underground.

This policy of divide and conquer found as its primary vehicle the "three-self" movement, which began in 1950 when a Chinese priest published a declaration in which he proposed a total break with all imperialistic powers and a church that would be "self-administering, self-supporting, and self-propagating." This, in turn, gave birth to the Three-self Patriotic Movement and led to the formation, in 1957, of the Chinese Catholic Patriotic Association. It would be the governing vehicle for the official church in the decades that followed. The Communists suc-ceeded in turning Catholic against Catholic. In a brutal twist, even those Catholics who chose to "cooperate" in the 1950s eventually ended up in prison and labor camps in the 1960s during the second wave of massive oppression, the Cultural Revolution.

Pondering all this, at one point I somewhat facetiously concluded that the decades-long feud among China's Catholics is between those who spent ten years in prison for their faith and those who spent twenty years in prison for the same faith.

China was completely closed to outside contact during the 1950s and 1960s. The mid-1960s were especially crucial years to be out of touch. That was when the world's bishops met in Rome for the Second Vatican Council. Anthony S. K. Lam, executive secretary of the Holy Spirit Study Center, a research institute established in 1980 in Hong Kong, points out that while the bishops in Rome were developing the theology of the local church during the council, Chinese Catholics were already implementing it, that is, learning to live entirely on their local resources. After a decade of horror and the death of Mao Tse-Tung, Catholicism in China began to come out of hiding. To many it looked like the old church, but it had been purified, Lam writes, "emerging from the fires of persecution and very conscious of its own identity."

A few years back I attended a talk by Bishop John Tong of the diocese of Hong Kong.[2] He offered a Chinese perspective on the divisions among Catholics in China. To understand these divisions, Tong said, it is first necessary to understand the national patriotic sentiment that brought the Communists to power on October 1, 1949. "The Chinese people have finally stood up!" Tong quoted Mao as saying that day. Everything for-eign was quickly purged. In 1949 foreign bishops were still in charge of 120 of 140 existing Chinese dioceses or apostolic prefectures. Tong praised the work of missionaries in China, but added that they had been "remiss" in not turning more of the leadership over to local Chinese before the Communist takeover. It was a costly mistake for the church.

He spoke of the formation of the government-approved Chinese Catholic Patriotic Association in 1957, the first illicit ordinations of two Chinese bishops without Rome's approval in 1958, and fifty-two such ordinations in all by 1962. He called these priests "good and intelligent" men, said some were forced to marry under political pressure, but that their marriages were never really accepted by Chinese Catholics. He spoke of the unfathomable hardships of the Cultural Revolution between 1966 and 1976 and how virtually all Catholic leaders, members of the official church included, ended up in prison camps. (It is estimated that some thirty million Chinese died as a result of the "great leap forward.") Tong spoke about the new beginnings in the late 1970s and the subsequent elevation of eighty-one more priests to the rank of bishop without Rome's approval. One of these was Bishop Fu, consecrated bishop of Beijing in 1979. These new bishops, Tong said, were "motivated by pastoral concern." We must affirm, he said, that their problems are matters not of faith but rather of law.

Tong spoke of the underground church and how its bishops began consecrating more bishops who recognized Rome. Bishop Fan Xueyan of Baoding diocese, who died in 1992, consecrated three bishops as soon as he was released from prison following the Cultural Revolution. Only afterward did he tell Rome. The pope, in turn, legitimated Fan Xueyan's appointments and granted them special use of their faculties to consecrate successors as well. They were also given authority to ordain priests as bishops in neighboring dioceses when the need arose. Tong said these actions led to the indiscriminate ordination of more underground bishops. Today there are as many as fifty bishops who have been consecrated secretly. Some dioceses have as many as three bishop ordinaries. Tong called these "men of strong faith," adding that many "have not received adequate training."

Underground bishops, meanwhile, have established their own seminaries, sometimes meeting in rural homes. In 1990, when a rumor circulated that the Vatican was on the verge of establishing diplomatic relations with Beijing, Tong said, some underground bishops, fearing that they would be overlooked, called a secret meeting to set up their own episcopal conference. The open church had set up its episcopal conference in 1980. So now there are two.

Although underground Catholics remain faithful and loyal, Tong added, their isolation has fostered a "closed mentality," where rumors flourish and misinformation leads to further divisions and separations. "The hardening of conflicting positions results in serious obstacles to eventual unity within the whole church," he said.

During the 1980s and 1990s, the severity of punishment for "unpatriotic" behavior among Catholics significantly diminished. However, many Catholics—some say half or more—continue to worship clandestinely in their homes rather than cooperate with those Catholics believed to be government "collaborators." Meanwhile, many underground Catholics continue to be harassed by government authorities. Some still go to jail for practicing their faith.

Many Catholics in the underground church, Tong noted, play a prophetic role by refusing to participate in a government-sanctioned organization. They challenge government policy from a Catholic standpoint regarding human rights and religious freedom. At the same time, many Catholics in the official church play a priestly role, working within the system to minister to the spiritual and sacramental needs of Catholics.

Tong was evenhanded in his remarks and referred to the situation as "complex." In some locations, bishops in the open and underground churches have reconciled and now cooperate. In others, bitterness and rivalry remain the norm. Most underground priests refuse to set foot in the open churches, yet are often protected, fed, and clothed by members of these churches. When asked what outsiders might do to help, Tong recommended, "Pray for us." We heard the same response to the same question wherever we went in China. The answer had as its intended message: "Don't take sides. You will only make matters worse."

For its part, Beijing maintains that it would be willing to improve relations with the Vatican, reiterating two preconditions: that Rome sever ties with Taiwan and not interfere in China's internal affairs. Beijing holds that any Vatican appointment of a Catholic bishop constitutes meddling. The Vatican, of course, maintains that appointments are an ecclesial, not a political, matter. In China's defense, it holds that the pope, as a head of state, cannot solely be a religious leader. Beijing has stressed the need to solve a Sino-Vatican diplomatic matter—the Taiwan issue—before going further in negotiations on religious matters. The Vatican would prefer to deal with religious matters first.

I learned of priests and lay leaders in the underground church who have continued to resist and have continued to be arrested, especially in rural areas. Churches built without government approval remain potential targets. In many areas, to avoid police detection, Catholics gather for Mass in private homes. Every few months a report surfaces of the harassment and arrest of such Catholics. In March 1998, for example, Amnesty International reported that about two hundred Catholics were detained for up to three months in late 1997 in the eastern province of Jian Xi. A frequent chronicler of church persecution is the U.S.-based Cardinal Kung Foundation, which has contacts with the underground church, especially in the Shanghai region.

While any religious harassment is unacceptable, there is irony in the Catholic situation in China. Some in the underground church, acting out of loyalty to the pope, appear to let personal fervor blind them to repeated papal pleas for reconciliation. This unwillingness to follow the pope's lead reportedly has been justified with statements such as "the Holy Father simply does not understand." Meanwhile, adding to the irony, by far the great majority of bishops in the official church, who were appointed without Rome's permission, have quietly been reconciled with Rome. These ordinations are now considered both valid and licit.

Beijing seems to have softened its hard-line stances in recent years. In February 1989 it began permitting Chinese Catholics to acknowledge the pope as their spiritual leader. So Chinese Catholics now pray for him at Mass. In Shanghai, a prayer for the Holy Father after Mass lasted several minutes. Yet Catholic bishops cannot have any official dealings with the Vatican.

In August 1997, Archbishop Claudio Celli, the papal delegate who handles relations between the Holy See and the Chinese government, passed through Beijing, according to Tong, holding brief discussions with the Chinese Foreign Ministry about allowing local appointments of bishops— provided the pope had the final say. That visit to Beijing was followed by the visit of the senior Vatican official, Cardinal Roger Etchegaray.

There have been several waves of missionary activity in China, the first in the seventh century, when Nestorian Christians came to the western frontier; the second in the thirteenth century, when Franciscans entered; and the third in the late sixteenth century involving Italian Jesuits. This third wave was the most important. It was led by Father Matteo Ricci, who gained influence among the Chinese political and intellectual elites of the Ming dynasty. The Jesuits achieved this by accommodating Catholic teaching to the ideology of state Confucianism.[3] In effect, they said that Catholicism was consistent with ritual practices that linked family hierarchy to the hierarchical order centered upon the emperor, the Son of Heaven. Thus, Catholic hierarchy could be seen as intertwined with and reinforcing the imperial hierarchy. This was inculturation before the word had been coined and turned out to be a high road to conversion. Ricci once said, "To win the Chinese, bring mathematicians and astronomers—and forget the theologians."

The early Jesuits, led by Ricci, were fabulously successful in making inroads into the imperial court, but it was not to last. Their success soon drew other religious orders to China, including Dominicans in 1631 and Franciscans in 1633. These new missionaries, fresh from Europe, looked with suspicion on the efforts of the Jesuits. They viewed the Jesuits as having been in China too long and having lost touch with the one true faith. This view, perhaps involving jealousy as well, led to what is called the "Chinese rites" controversy, which centered on three divisive issues: the Chinese name for God, ancestor worship, and the honor paid to Confucius.

For nearly fifty years the Jesuits defended their positions until, in 1709, Pope Clement XI officially condemned the Jesuits' efforts. It was a tragic mistake. Persecutions almost immediately broke out, and for the next one hundred years Christianity was viewed as a hostile and alien force. It took centuries for the church to admit its mistake. Only in 1939 did Pope Pius XII finally rescind the decision, but by then the window of opportunity had long been closed. One noted China historian,

G. Thompson Brown, has written that "if the Jesuits would have been left to themselves, the Christian mission in China would have continued its remarkable growth with the possibility that China would have become a Roman Catholic nation."[4]

Two hours south of Xi'an by jet is the beautiful and restful city of Guilin in southern China, where our group visited the tiny church of St. Thérèse of Lisieux—now really a temporary chapel since the roof caved in two years ago. We arrived a day before local Catholics would gather to dedicate a cornerstone for a new church. It was a proud moment. A young layman insisted we examine blueprints. We also watched as several laborers, digging with shovels, cleared rubble from where the new church would be built. These were Catholics of modest means but immodest ambitions. Although it is no longer unusual for Catholic churches to open or reopen in China—we were told that six thousand churches have been built or restored in the past ten years with government permission—we also heard of newly constructed churches torn down because they had been built without permission. Securing permits can consume a lot of time and energy in China.

Catholics also told us that government authorities had requested that these Catholics build a larger church in downtown Guilin, reasoning it would help the city's booming tourist trade centered on boat cruises down the spectacular Li River. The Guilin Catholics rejected that plan, however, choosing to build near the site of their former church. Funds are coming mostly from Germany.

Bishop Benedict Cai, age eighty-one, arrived by bus for the dedication ceremony after an eight-hour trip. Cai, a stick-thin man, was all smiles as he greeted us. The church project is a testimony to cooperation and sheer determination. It will be built one brick at a time, on a foundation of sheer faith like churches of old.

But can the spirit hold out against consumerism, especially when consumer instincts, so long repressed, are now exposed to so many blandishments? Bishop Jin of Shanghai has been outspoken on the subject. He has called consumerism the greatest current threat to the Chinese soul. "We feel very weak and powerless against the tide of modernization that brings a lot of products, including corruption, idolatry of money and a spiritual vacuum," he has said.

Shanghai was the last stop of our trip. It has one of China's best organized dioceses with a rapidly expanding flock of 106,000 souls and eighty-two churches. The Shanghai diocese runs a major and a minor seminary, a convent, a publishing house, and a press. The printing press, run by women religious, is limited by law and tax regulation in what it can publish. Its focus is attempting to inculturate Chinese thought into

Catholic prayer and spirituality. The actual printing press—mainland China's largest Catholic printing press—is the result of fund-raising efforts, mostly in Europe, with the help of Father Saucci.

We visited a Shanghai convent where the novice mistress could scarcely be past her thirtieth birthday. We also saw China's first—and only—retreat house, the Guangqi Spirituality Center, which opened in April 1999. The three-story building, managed by nuns of the Shanghai diocese, has fifty-one double-occupancy rooms, a chapel dedicated to St. Ignatius, prayer rooms, conference rooms, and a garden. It is being used to provide much needed meeting space for Catholic gatherings. Jesuits in Europe donated one-third of the $1.2 million needed to build the retreat compound. Other foreigners, mostly Europeans, covered the rest. Two bronze plaques of donor names indicated a great willingness among Europeans, including key members of the hierarchy, to fund China church projects.

We were told that U.S. bishops have resisted assisting China's Catholics because Rome does not recognize the official church's bishops' conference. On the last day of our trip, a local Catholic woman who spoke English handed me a note to better explain herself. It said: "Chinese Catholics are faithful to God, to the universal church and to the pope. . . . We are one church, although we are separated in two parts. We aim toward a goal, which is to bring us to reconciliation and unity. . . . We confess that we are loyal to the pope; we are members of the whole universal church." She was not the only person who stressed the theme of church unity during our visit. The theme came up again at our final Mass in China, in Christ the King Church in Shanghai. The closing hymn that Sunday morning moved us all deeply. It was the very recognizable "Ode to Joy," celebrating humanity, unity, and boundless spirit. It was then that it finally struck me. What we were witnessing in China was nothing less than a triumph of human spirit. None of us left doubting whether Catholicism had a future in China. We were less certain what shape that future would take.

PART 2

CHAPTER 7

East–West Bridges

*Even as people approach me, so do I
respond to them.*
—Bhagavad-Gita 4:11

The terrorist attacks on September 11, 2001, dramatically pointed out how religion can be abused. They were also a reminder of the importance that religion will certainly play in the twenty-first century—for better or worse. In a world that has become so much smaller with fast communication and air travel, interreligious dialogue and understanding have become even more vital. Despite many setbacks, the good news is that such dialogue and understanding have increased substantially in the past century. From the Catholic perspective, breakthroughs toward new openness can be traced to pleas by Pope Pius XII in 1957 and Pope John XXIII in 1960 to send missionaries into Africa, Asia, and Latin America. Many religious orders responded generously, and these missionaries often became Catholic "ambassadors" overseas, even as they went about their mission work. Eventually they returned as "reverse missionaries," lobbying for greater cultural awareness and for changing U.S. policies that create hardships and injustices overseas. Having once spread the gospel abroad, they saw their new role, in light of fresh insights gained overseas, as spreading it at home.

Furthermore, interreligious dialogue in the late 1960s got a major boost from Vatican II, with its emphasis on building stronger bonds with other Christian and non-Christian religions. Interreligious dialogue was not a priority in the Catholic Church until the time of the council. The change came in 1965 with the passage of the council's Declaration on the Relationship of the Church to Non-Christian Religions, *Nostra Aetate*. The document read: "The church, therefore, urges her [sons and daughters] to enter with prudence and charity into discussion and collaboration with members of other religions. Let Christians, while witnessing to their own faith and way of life, acknowledge, preserve and encourage the spiritual and moral truths found among non-Christians, also their social life and culture." One year earlier, Pope Paul VI had established the Secretariat for Non-Christians—since March 1, 1989, known as the Pontifical Council for Inter-religious Dialogue—to prepare Catholics for further interreligious dialogue. The creation of the secretariat and the Vatican document have provided the form and substance for the church to go forward.

Religious communities played especially important institutional roles in furthering cultural and religious awareness, all of these efforts subtly changing attitudes among the religious leaders of the world. After the papal calls to expand mission, a monastic-based organization, the AIM Secretariat (Aide a l'Implantation Monastique), was created in 1960 (AIM now stands for Alliance for International Monasticism). Missionaries initially viewed the work of the gospel as a kind of one-way process, taking the Word to the nonbelievers. It was not long, however, before their experiences had taught them mission work was more complicated and subtle, requiring a deeper appreciation of foreign cultures and a better understanding of foreign religions. Inculturation, at its most fruitful level, is a two-way street. One step in the advance of this insight took place in Bangkok in 1968, when Catholic monastic superiors purposely met in a Buddhist setting to deepen dialogue with monastics *of other religions.*

Pope Paul encouraged this effort. In October 1973, in Bangalore, India, Christian and non-Christian monastics met to talk with one another about their common experiences of God. The success of that meeting prompted Cardinal Pignedoli, then the Prefect of the Secretariat for Non-Christians, to ask then Benedictine Abbot Primate Rembert Weakland to encourage Benedictines to become more involved in interreligious dialogue, because, as he put it, "monasticism is the bridge between religions." These dialogues have continued and have helped broaden Catholic perspectives.

To get a sense of the progress that has been made since the council, some historical context is required. It is helpful to remember that centuries back our ancestors had no notions of "East" and "West." They lived in isolation, either in one of the shifting empires or changing nation-states of Europe, or in one of the kingdoms or emerging nations of Asia. The Far East had almost no fix in Western consciousness before the fourteenth century and the travels of Marco Polo. Concepts of East and West, as we tend to see them today, emerged along with the explorers of the fifteenth and sixteenth centuries. Columbus, Juan Ponce de Leon, Vasco da Gama, and Ferdinand Magellan charted the New World maps. The age of exploration quickly led to the age of commerce and, in turn, to the age of colonization. Centuries of Western domination of the East followed. In turn, these were followed by decades of Eastern resistance and finally postcolonial independence. It was only after World War II that Asia began to stand proud once again. It was only in the wake of the colonial period that the West seemed to awaken to the intrinsic value and beauty of the lands. With freedom and national independence arose fresh opportunities for true dialogue and sharing. Of course, there were exceptions to these wider patterns. Enlightened minds see the world through different eyes. Saints and sages have lived throughout history. Wise men and women—from East and West—have long sought to reach out, crossing cultures, in search for a deeper understanding. How are people alike? How are they different? What common aspirations and bonds do we all share? Do Asians think differently from Europeans? Many argue that they do. Although common sense would say that any vast assertion should be approached skeptically. At the same time I would argue that broad generalizations can help the imagination and can lead to an openness of mind and a willingness to learn from other cultures.

For example, Eastern thought is far less dualistic than Western thought, and this difference can affect one's view of reality. In the West, without much questioning, we divide reality into opposites and choose between them. We see the world as a struggle between good and evil. We say we have a body and a soul. We view God as divine, whereas we, on the other hand, are merely human. These basic dualities frame our thinking and, in turn, our approach to existence. They shape who we are and how we act. These dualities have shaped Western philosophy, science, and medicine.[1] We view the very notion of progress as a movement toward a positive future and away from the negative past.

Eastern thought is less prone to see life in these stark opposites. Without these basic dualistic divisions, a different pattern of history has emerged. Eastern thought has traditionally viewed opposites not so much in conflict as part of a larger whole. The image of the yin-yang is the prime example. The two blend together as one. This type of thinking has led to a cyclical rather than a linear view of history. This type of thinking enters into the marrow of Asian thought in its literature and poetry. Consider the words of the Chinese sage Lao Tzu:

> Is there a difference between yes and no?
> Is there a difference between good and evil?
> Must I fear what others fear? What nonsense!
> Having and not having arise together
> Difficult and easy complement each other
> Long and short contrast each other
> Front and back follow one another.

So does a line drawn in the sand divide or connect? Asian traditions affirm the basic goodness of humans and the world. They tend to view humans as free and capable of self-transformation. This positive view contrasts with the traditional way in which Christians look at themselves and the world. As a result of their understanding of original sin some cultures view humans as weak and sinful. The world is fallen. This pessimism is strengthened by the dichotomy that differentiates the creatures from the Creator. In the Asian tradition there is not such a radical dichotomy between the human and the divine. The Taoists and the Advaitic Hindus speak of the divine in the human.[2] In traditional Western spirituality, except in the thought of mystics, the spiritual seekers attempt to unite with God who is "out there." In some traditional Eastern spiritualities, such as Taoism and Buddhism, spiritual seekers find unity by attempting to empty themselves of all thought and passion. Some Eastern writers contrast the Asian spirit, with its emptiness and humility, with the traditional Western Christian mission, which they view as more aggressive and oppressive, even destructive.[3]

Asia has been the focus of much interreligious dialogue. The work in this area that went on there in the second half of the twentieth century was both unprecedented and revolutionary. That collective work can be seen as a bridge between the old attitudes and the new. Those involved in the work—far too many to mention here—can be seen as bridge-makers who first seriously connected Eastern and Western cultures and religions in ways that will undoubtedly help shape the history of this century. This chapter glances at a few of the better known of the early Catholic bridge-builders or, as some put it, "culture bearers."[4] Through experience and writings, each has helped define the meaning of interreligious dialogue. Each of those I have chosen to mention has touched my life personally. The most prominent were men, perhaps speaking to the traditional patriarchal nature of the major religions. However, this too has been changing. Religious women have increasingly become part of the dialogue. Several who jump to mind are:

- Sister Pascaline Coff, a Benedictine Sister of Perpetual Adoration and founder of Osage Monastery in Sand Springs, Oklahoma. She participated in many hospitality exchanges between Christian and Tibetan monastics in Asia and the United States. She is founder of the Monastic Inter-religious Dialogue board and has created and edited the East-West Intermonastic Bulletin. Osage Monastery, located in the diocese of Tulsa, Oklahoma, is a monastic ashram community whose aim is simplified living. It is open to those of all religions—or none.

- Teresita D'Silva, Benedictine abbess of Shanti Nilayam Abbey in India. Shanti Nilayam was originally founded from St. Cecilia's Abbey, Ryde, Isle of Wight, England. The first group of Indian sisters went to St. Cecilia's in 1963. Two years later, two pioneers, members of the Ryde community, went to India, where they purchased eleven acres of land near Bangalore. The Indian sisters returned to their homeland in 1969. By then the monastery was coming to life and was officially blessed in July 1970. A community of Benedictines has lived off the land since then and has been a center of much important interreligious dialogue.

• Sara Grant, Society of the Sacred Heart sister and founder of Christa Prema Seva Ashram in Pune, India. Grant traveled to India from England in 1956. Her mission was to head a newly formed department of philosophy at Sophia College in Bombay. In the years that followed she studied Hindu thought and Indian scholarship. In the wake of the Vatican Council she became active in furthering dialogue between the Christian and Hindu religions. In 1972, she was invited to join a small group of her own society and a group of Anglican Sisters of St. Mary of the Virgin in a venture to open the Christa Prema Seva Ashram. It was unique in that it was ecumenical and interreligious and became a meeting place for spiritual seekers from throughout India. Grant was a prolific writer, answering questions posed to her by first asking: "What do the Gospels say? What does the Spirit say?" Her Ashram experience—contemplative yet open to the vastness and complexity of life—moved her to ponder the needs of religious in India. In her last booklet, *Religious Life in a New Era,* she wrote that to preach the gospel in India religious need to be deeply spiritual men and women whose primary mission is seeking union with God. After years of declining health, she died at age seventy-seven in April 2000.

PIERRE TEILHARD DE CHARDIN

Pierre Teilhard de Chardin captured the collective imagination of a generation. He dabbled in what would become known as creation spirituality. I first encountered him in 1965 as a college junior when I read the *Divine Milieu,* published in 1927, a mystical interpretation of the universe.

Teilhard was born in 1881 in France and, after an education at a Jesuit boarding school, entered the Jesuit novitiate at age eighteen. His scientific interests had been initially stimulated by his father, who encouraged his children to collect fossils, stones, and other natural specimens. When the Jesuits were exiled from France, Teilhard continued his theological studies in the south of England, at Hastings/Sussex, where he was ordained in

1911. The French priest from an early age seemed to thrive on foreign cultures. Early on he had both a love for science and a passion for mystical theology. Teilhard, at twenty-four, found himself teaching at Holy Family College in Cairo, Egypt. The experience of living in Egypt offered him an opportunity to do research in both geology and paleontology, expanding his knowledge of earth history. It was in Cairo that he was first exposed to a multiplicity of cultures. The experience jarred him loose from his European roots. It was in 1938 that he wrote the last words of *The Phenomenon of Man,* which gave Charles Darwin a spiritual face. By then Teilhard's views were getting him into trouble with church authorities, and he was disgruntled, writing:

> I no longer have confidence in the exterior manifestations of the church. I believe that through it the divine influence will continue to reach me, but I no longer have much belief in the immediate and tangible value of official directions and decisions. Some people feel happy in the visible church; but for my own part I think I shall be happy to die in order to be free of it—and to find our Lord outside of it.[5]

After living in England for several years, he returned to his native France, where for nearly five years during World War I he served as a stretcher-bearer on the front lines. His spiritual reflections were always optimistic, surviving even the brutalities of war. Following the war, at forty-two, he was invited to be part of a scientific expedition to Inner Mongolia. The time there allowed him to become a specialist in Chinese geology. It was also there that he seemed to deepen his spiritual vision. Again returning to France, he found that his writings were getting him into deeper trouble with church authorities.

Throughout his life, Teilhard reflected with usual openness on the meaning of the Christian gospel in the light of modern science, especially in relation to evolution. He viewed the whole universe as converging on the Christ figure. He saw spiritual development as part of the evolutionary process. Teilhard's Christianity is inclusive. Christ is everywhere, a figure beyond church, beyond culture, beyond time itself. His views are hardly radical today, but a half-century ago they were viewed as revolutionary.

I encountered Teilhard just before I set out for Asia. That he did much of his writing in Asia made him more attractive to me. I could not help but wonder how much his personal experiences in Asia had opened his mind to his cosmic perspective on life and the church. Not long after I encountered Teilhard I purchased a silver chain and medal that I wore around my neck. The medal was etched with the Greek letters Chi and

Rho, together forming the early Christian monogram that symbolizes Jesus Christ. On the upper corners of this symbol were etched the first and last letters of the Greek alphabet, Alpha and Omega. The medal meant to proclaim: "Jesus Christ from beginning to end." But this was not just a proclamation about Jesus of Nazareth. This was even larger. This was an exclamation about the Christ of history, the Christ *beyond* history, the Christ of the cosmos!

Teilhard spent the last four years of his life in New York. His friends said he lived in depression during much of that time, his major work, *The Phenomenon of Man,* having been forbidden by his superiors to be published. On Easter Sunday, April 10, 1955, he died of a stroke in New York City. He was buried at Saint Andrew's on the Hudson in the cemetery of the Jesuit novitiate for the New York Province. By the fall of that year, the first edition of *The Phenomenon of Man* was finally published.

Teilhard presented Christianity within a new context, a scientific context. He saw science as a discipline and a spiritual instrument. Teilhard's spiritual vision placed the Jesus story within a far larger context. The more telling story, he was suggesting, is the Christ story within the unfolding cosmos. It is also noteworthy that Teilhard's imagery of God was not the traditional "God Above" but rather a "God Ahead." It is further noteworthy that at more or less the same time and quite independently, a Hindu philosopher named Sri Aurobindu was also toying with this idea. It might be imagined that spiritual consciousness is, indeed, expanding and that spiritual seekers, pondering and writing out of their own traditions, are moving to a new spiritual convergence, as Teilhard suggests. Is creation moving toward the Omega? If so, then humanity is moving toward the Omega as well. And if this is the case, how could there not be a convergence of spiritual insight despite vast differences among peoples in religious background, culture, and history?

It should be added that for most of the nearly twenty years that he lived in Asia his focus was on science. He was not there as a missionary, yet his attachment was to Christianity alone. He lived and worked at a time when Western criticism of Asian religions was the norm, and opportunities for communicating with Chinese scholars were limited. Language barriers and wartime considerations further limited interreligious dialogue.[6]

Today, many scientists would take issue with key elements of Teilhard's thinking—most importantly his view of the centrality of the human species. Many would also question his perpetual optimism and would not accept his directional interpretation of the evolving universe. The priest and cosmologist Thomas Berry, for example, while admitting to be heavily influenced by Teilhard's thought, is much less confident that humanity can survive its abuses of the planetary ecosystems. From

Teilhard, Berry derived an understanding of the psychophysical character of the unfolding universe. Matter for both Teilhard and Berry is not simply dead or inert, but rather a numinous reality consisting of both a physical and spiritual dimension. For Teilhard and Berry, the story of the universe is the primary context for understanding the immensity of cosmogenesis. They see consciousness as an intrinsic part of reality and a thread that links all life forms.[7] Berry first published "The New Story" as the initial booklet of the Teilhard Studies series in 1978. It was published nearly a decade later by *Cross Currents* and later revised slightly for its publication in *The Dream of the Earth* in 1988. In his writings, Berry seems to echo Teilhard's words: "We are not human beings on a spiritual journey; we are spiritual beings on a human journey."

THOMAS MERTON

When one speaks of spiritual beings on a human journey, Thomas Merton is a name that comes to mind. He has been a spiritual guide for decades. His Christian pacifism, his mix of contemplation and action, his sensitive social analyses, his appreciation for the written word, his eagerness to offer encouragement: these are just some of the engaging elements I have found in Merton's writings. When I was still in my impressionable twenties and the Vietnam War was raging, Merton, as much as any other person, became a soul-mate. During lonely or unsettling moments I would pick up a Merton book and open it to almost any page, and what I read seemed aimed directly at me. He had that ability. We bonded. We were both outraged by war, pacifist in heart, and drawn to Asia in ways we never fully understood. I first flew to Asia in June of 1963, from San Francisco to Tokyo. Five years later, in October of 1968, Merton flew the same route on his first and only Asian excursion. As he left the ground in San Francisco, he wrote:

> Joy. We left the ground—I with Christian mantras and a great sense of destiny, of being at last on my true way after years of waiting and wondering and fooling around. . . . May I not come back without having settled the great affair. And found also the great compassion, *mahakaruna*. . . . I am going home, to the home where I have never been in this body.[8]

Merton went "home" and took many of us with him on his journey as he shared his thoughts in his journals. Guided by his pursuit of the Truth, he set off for Asia confident that God's revelation is continual and reaches beyond the boundaries of his Catholic traditions. This Merton belief, this insight, is one he shared with other spiritual seekers who had traveled to Asia before him. Merton crossed the Pacific in the name of all believing and adventurous seekers. He spent fifty-six days on Asian soil before his accidental death on December 10. Yet during his life he had had personal exchanges with Asian gurus, most notably the Japanese Zen Buddhist scholar D. T. Suzuki and Thich Nhat Hanh, a Vietnamese Buddhist monk and poet. Merton elicited and shared truth. He felt that all spiritual treasures were worth finding, and much of his life was a search of both Eastern and Western traditions. In the process he fostered East–West spiritual bonds. It was not the extensiveness of his Asian writings as much as their popularity that built new bridges.

Having lived in Asia in the late 1960s and early 1970s, I felt a special kinship with Merton's Asian experiences. Once, in Bangkok, I tried to find the location of the conference center where he died by electrocution, only to learn it no longer exists. He enabled me, empowered me. His example encouraged many to take giant steps across traditional religious boundaries. Some wondered if, in his flirtation with the East, he was thinking of leaving his Catholic tradition—but not those who know him well. They say it was his faith, not his lack of faith, that compelled him to reach out.

Merton was born in France in 1915, but his parents moved to Long Island in 1916. He was sent to boarding schools in France and England. His father died of a brain tumor while he was still young. Reading Blake enkindled in Merton an interest in religion, which was fortified by a trip to Rome. After a year at Cambridge, Merton moved to New York in 1935 to enter Columbia University. He received his Bachelor of Arts degree in 1938 and was received into the Catholic Church that year. He obtained his Master of Arts degree in 1939 and was rejected as an applicant to the Franciscan order the following year. Some months later, he went for a retreat at the Abbey of Gethsemani in Trappist, Kentucky. There he finally found a home. On December 10, 1941, he officially entered the Abbey of Gethsemani.

Merton's Asia journey began decades before he actually set off for Asia. At age twenty-three he met a Hindu monk named Bramachari and asked him to teach him about Asian mysticism. The monk, to Merton's surprise, advised him not to venture into Asian scriptures until he had first become familiar with the mystics of his own tradition. He suggested that Merton read Augustine's *Confessions* and Thomas à Kempis's *The Imitation of Christ*.[9] That advice impressed Merton, who from then on took the Christian mystics more seriously. About the same time, Merton came across Aldous Huxley's book on mysticism, *Ends and Means*. It sowed in him a new attraction for apophatic mysticism, a spiritual path that seeks to find God through no created thing, not even through words or mental images. This discipline would later enable Merton to relate to Buddhist teachings about the void and emptiness.

In the 1950s Merton's fascination with mysticism and Asian religions surfaced again. He began to study Buddhism, focusing on the Zen tradition. In 1956 he read everything he could find by Suzuki. Three years later, Merton began a correspondence with him, confessing that he did not pretend to understand Zen but felt he owed a debt to Suzuki. "Time after time, as I read your pages, something in me says, 'That's it!' Don't ask me what. I have no desire to explain it to anybody. . . . So there it is, in all its beautiful purposelessness."[10] He took the occasion to send Suzuki a collection of sayings of the Desert Fathers, the Zen Masters of the early church. While Suzuki never came to Gethsemani, Merton's abbot allowed him a short trip to New York in 1964 to meet Suzuki, then age ninety-four. The men talked and drank green tea. The main thing for Merton was "to see and experience the fact that there really is a deep understanding between myself and this extraordinary and simple man whose books I have been reading now for about ten years with great attention." According to Merton's friend James Forest, Merton felt that when he was with Suzuki it was as if he was spending time with his own family."[11] The two men's correspondence eventually was published in a collection of essays known as *Zen and the Birds of Appetite*. Suzuki's essays revived Merton's interest in Chuang Tzu. In 1961 Merton enlisted the help of John Wu to prepare *The Way of Chuang Tzu*. He wrote in the book's preface in 1967, "I have enjoyed writing this more than any other book I can remember. . . . I simply like Chuang Tzu because of what he is."

The year 1967 was one of the bloodiest years of the Vietnam War. It was also the year Merton had a visit from Thich Nhat Hanh, the exiled Vietnamese Buddhist monk who had been living in France. For Merton it was like meeting Chuang Tzu in the flesh. As the two monks talked, the different religious systems in which they were formed did not seem to matter. "Thich (Venerable) Nhat Hanh is my brother," Merton said in a memorable preface to a book by Nhat Hanh. "He is more my brother than many who are nearer to me in race and nationality, because he and I see things exactly the same way." When Merton asked Nhat Hanh what the war was doing to Vietnam, the Buddhist said simply, "Everything is destroyed." This, Merton said to the monks of Gethsemani, was truly a monk's answer, revealing the essence without wasting a word.

Merton believed that religions have reached a stage in history where they can no longer exist in physical and spiritual isolation from other cultures and religions. He understood that spirituality that teaches religious superiority is incongruous. Another Asian, Mohandas Gandhi, also had a major influence upon Merton. Committed to nonviolence as Merton was, Gandhi looked beyond his own tradition to seek spiritual wisdom. He embraced the example of Jesus, although he could not accept the institutionalized Christianity of the West. For his part, Merton found in the Indian text the *Bhagavad-Gita,* with its ideal of *karma-yoga* (union with God in action), ideas that appealed to him, especially notions of an integrated life of contemplation and action.[12] Merton was impressed by the power of the *Gita* on Gandhi. He considered Gandhi a true example of the union of spiritual fervor and social action, "a healthy blending of the contemplative heritage of Hinduism with the principles of *karma-yoga* and the ethic of the Sermon on the Mount."[13]

In 1968, Merton finally received permission from his abbot to travel to Asia. His last Asian spiritual ventures were among the most intimate. In India he met with both Hindu and Buddhist contemplatives. The high point of his stay there, he wrote, was meetings with the Dalai Lama, the exiled leader of Tibetan Buddhism, at Dharamsala in the Himalayas. They met three times over several days and developed a warm relationship. After the initial meeting, Merton wrote in his Asian journal:

> The Dalai Lama is most impressive as a person. He is strong and alert . . . [a] very solid, energetic, generous, and warm person, very capably trying to handle enormous problems. . . . The whole conversation was about religion and philosophy and especially ways of meditation. . . . In general he advised me to get a good base in Madhyamika philosophy (Nagarjuna and other authentic Indian sources) and to consult qualified Tibetan scholars, uniting study and practice.[14]

For his part, the Dalai Lama would say he found Merton to be a truly humble and deeply spiritual man. He said he had never been struck so deeply by a feeling of spirituality in anyone who professed Christianity. Merton's visit seemed to change the Dalai Lama's own ideas about Christianity. The meeting, he said, had opened him to the truth that Tibetan Buddhism does not hold the world's only truth. Each time the men met their bonds seem to grow. The third and final meeting between the two men, Merton wrote, was the best of all:

> He asked a lot of questions about Western monastic life, particularly the vows, the rule of silence, the ascetic way, etc. . . . It was a very warm and cordial discussion and at the end I felt we had become very good friends and were somehow quite close to one another. I feel a great respect and fondness for him as a person and believe, too, that there is a real spiritual bond between us.[15]

A month later, Merton reflected on what it was like to be in Asia:

I am still not able fully to appreciate what this exposure to Asia has meant. There has been so much—and yet also so little. I have only been here a month! It seems a long time since Bangkok and even since Delhi and Dharamsala. Meeting the Dalai Lama and the various Tibetans, lamas or "enlightened" laymen, has been the most significant thing of all, especially in the way we were able to communicate with one another and share an essentially spiritual experience of Buddhism which is also somehow in harmony with Christianity.[16]

Before the final leg of his journey, the trip to Thailand for a monastic conference, he traveled to Sri Lanka (then Ceylon). There, along with another priest, he visited a famous Buddhist shrine at Polonnaruwa. Unlike the other priest who was with him, who did not enter the actual shrine complex because of its "paganism," Merton took off his shoes and walked barefoot toward the enormous Buddha statues. What happened to Merton was another impressionable moment in his life, a mystical moment for a Christian at an ancient Buddhist shrine.

After he arrived in Bangkok he gave a talk on December 10 on the subject of Marxism and monasticism. It was an auspicious day, the twenty-seventh anniversary of his entrance into the Trappist order. After the talk he was tired. The heat was oppressive. Since he planned to answer questions later in the evening, he went to his cabin to take a rest. He took a shower and put on a pair of shorts. Barefoot and still damp, he walked across the room and reached for a fan to turn it on before taking a nap. The current entered his body and he was thrown to the floor. When he was discovered later in the day he was already dead. Ironically, the pacifist monk's body was flown back to the United States with the dead bodies of young men, the latest casualties of the Vietnam War. Merton, one more body in a body bag on a U.S. Air Force plane.

BEDE GRIFFITHS

Bede Griffiths and Thomas Merton were two of the most significant Christian spiritual voices of the twentieth century. They were contemporaries. They knew each other's work. They met at Gethsemani in 1963—Merton then forty-eight, Griffiths fifty-seven. Both were English-speaking; both had some Anglican background; both had gone through a non-Christian period; and both loved poetry and literature. Griffiths had an

Oxford education, Merton a tumultuous period at Cambridge. Both became Catholics—Griffiths in 1931, Merton in 1938. Both became monks; both were fine writers; both attracted attention with their autobiographies, written soon after entering the monastery. Merton's was published in 1948, Griffiths' in 1954. Both became interested in interreligious dialogue; both pursued the East; both found their spiritual paths enriched by the discoveries they found in the East; both were contemplatives; and both were cross-cultural spiritual seekers to the last days of their lives.[17]

Born Alan Richard Griffiths on December 17, 1906, he came to be called the Thomas Merton of England, except that Griffiths delved much further into Eastern spirituality than Merton ever dreamed of doing. Griffiths' ascetic tendencies date back to his early experiments in communal living after graduating from Oxford. A staunch atheist at the time, he viewed himself as a pacifist and socialist. He was skeptical of moral absolutes. At the same time the romantic poets were influencing him, and this attraction to nature eventually opened him up to the presence of God in nature. At Oxford, Griffiths, like his professor and friend C. S. Lewis, after much soul searching, rediscovered the spiritual profundity of the Christian tradition. On Christmas Eve in 1931, Griffiths was received into the church. He entered Prinknash Abbey a few weeks later. It was on December 20, 1932, clothed as a Benedictine novice, that he received the name of Bede, which means prayer.

Years later, while prior of the Farnborough abbey in Scotland, Griffiths met Benedict Alapott, an Indian priest born in Europe who desired to start a foundation in India. Griffiths had been introduced to Eastern thought, yoga, and Indian scripture by a Jungian analyst, Tony Sussman. When Father Griffiths asked permission to go to India, he was refused by his abbot, who said, "there is too much of Bede Griffiths' will in this." Later, however, the abbot agreed to the move. Upon departing, his spirit was lighthearted. He wrote to a friend, "I am going to discover the other half of my soul."

In 1955, Griffiths traveled by ship to Bombay, and after pilgrimages through India his initial efforts to form a monastic community proved unsuccessful. During his travels, however, Griffiths gained two strong impressions: the pervasive "sense of the sacred" in Indian culture and the foreign appearance of the Christian churches, modeled upon European styles.[18] In 1958 he was provided a fresh start when he was invited by a Cistercian, Father Francis Mahieu, to help form a monastery in Kerala, a Kurisumala Ashram in the Syrian rite. In Kerala, Griffiths pursued the dialogue between Christianity and other religions. In his spiritual practice he integrated Christian prayer with yoga, both as a philosophy and as a physical discipline. This lasted until 1968, when Griffiths took off again, this time moving to neighboring Tamil Nadu, where he began a Hindu-Christian ashram in the Latin rite at Shantivanam.

Arriving at Shantivanam with two other monks, he again immersed himself in the study of Indian thought, attempting to relate it to Christian theology. He went on pilgrimages and studied Hinduism with the Indian Catholic scholar Raimon Panikkar. Under Griffiths' guidance Shantivanam became a center of contemplative life, of inculturation, and of interreligious dialogue. Meanwhile, Griffiths strove to promote his belief that true religion is beyond theology and churches and that the quest of God inevitably breaks through human-imposed barriers. Griffiths sought through the study of the sacred writings of the world's religions to find the one Source common to all religion. He delivered worldwide lectures on religion, drawing upon his readings in Hindu, Buddhist, and new age mystical literature. In January 1990, Griffiths suffered a stroke in his hut at Shantivanam. One month later, he recovered, saying it had been a struggle with death and divine love. He described this as an intense mystical experience. By then his heart was fluttering. He died on May 13, 1993, in his hut at Shantivanam surrounded by much tender loving care.

Griffiths was a man with a universal heart. He had no guile and saw no guile in others. He honored the sacredness of every person because he believed deeply that each person is a unique image of the divine. He was fascinated by the trinitarian mystery and even more so by the possibility that Christian theology can be found in Hindu doctrine. In *The Marriage of East and West*, published in 1982, Griffiths hailed the end of the age of Western domination and said that the world would find its future in Asia, Africa, and Latin America. Where the West went wrong, he wrote, was in allowing its "aggressive, masculine, rationalist mind" to take control. That was, he wrote, one of the fruits of the Renaissance, and it destroyed the harmony of the Middle Ages. What the East has to offer is the "feminine, intuitive, passive and receptive power" of creation. Meditation and contemplative prayer can help create the space where reason and intuition can unite, because without the other neither is whole and both are inadequate. Much of this sounds commonplace nowadays, but that is partly because Griffiths helped make it so.

Yet, as late as 1990, Griffiths was forced to defend Eastern spirituality against the Congregation for the Doctrine of the Faith's December 1989 response to the challenge of Buddhist and Hindu spirituality. Discussing Rome's warning that certain forms of Eastern prayer tempt people to try to overcome the necessary distance between Creator and creature, God and humankind, Griffiths wrote that "Jesus himself totally denies any such distance. 'I am the vine,' he says, 'you are the branches.' How can the branches be 'distant' from the vine?" We must "never in any way seek to place ourselves on the same level as the object of our contemplation," Rome insisted. "Of course, we don't seek to place ourselves on the same level," Griffiths countered. "It is God who has already placed us there. Jesus says, 'I have not called you servants, but friends.'" This kind of simplicity, of hard-won lucidity, had long become typical of the man. Undeterred, Griffiths pushed on. In a speech dictated after a stroke had paralyzed his left side, he said he saw a new world consciousness emerging, saw science as the altar upon which the marriage between East and West would be consecrated: "Science today recognizes that all order comes out of chaos. When the old structures break down and the traditional forms begin to disintegrate, precisely then in the chaos, a new form, a new structure, a new order of being and consciousness emerges."

ANTHONY DE MELLO

Anthony de Mello was a talented Indian Jesuit who captured the hearts and imaginations of countless Christians in East and West with his simplicity and pure heart. It is said that he lived a practical mysticism, becoming a guru of a whole generation through the 1970s, 1980s, and early 1990s. He reached his audiences through retreats, through books, and through his spirituality center in Lonavla, near Mumbai (Bombay). In his early years at the center he used Ignatian retreats for spiritual nourishment. Through his experiences as a retreat leader he came to realize, he said, that many people suffer from psychological hurts rather than from spiritual laziness. So he decided to enter the world of psychological healing. In the process, he emerged as a sage, a man of considerable wisdom, who used Eastern spiritual insights to bring healing in the West. He set about dismantling some of the gratuitous absolutes that popular religious traditions had set up to defend against possible lapses—images of hell, for instance. These images, he believed, might help keep people on the right track, but they also effectively prevent them from advancing along a healthy spiritual path because they bring heavy burdens of fear and guilt. He found a powerful aid in the Asian approach to truth, viewed as a journey and not as an endpoint.

He published a number of writings in the form of short stories or parables, full of humor but often critical of the many foibles of traditional religious people. His intention, he said, was to liberate his listeners from inherited constraints and prejudices. De Mello's most notable book, *Sadhana*, has seen more than two dozen reprintings, has sold more than 115,000 copies in English, and has been translated into three dozen languages. It was described by the Catholic Theological Society of America as "perhaps the best book available in English for Christians on how to pray, meditate and contemplate." Other books include *The Song of the Bird* (1982), *Wellsprings* (1984), *One Minute Wisdom* (1985), *The Prayer of the Frog* (2 vols.; 1988), *Contact with God: Retreat Conferences* (1990), *Called to Love* (1991), *One Minute Nonsense* (1992), and *Rooted in God: A Collection of Prayer Services* (1998).

De Mello died in 1987 at the age of fifty-six. He was living in New York at the time. What happened eleven years later, however, in the summer of 1998, took his friends and many followers by complete surprise. That was when the Vatican's Congregation for the Doctrine of the Faith condemned his works for "relativizing" the Catholic faith and thus leading his readers into what it called "religious indifferentism." Rome labeled de Mello's writings "incompatible with the Catholic faith," saying that within them it noted "a progressive distancing from the essential contents of the Christian faith." Congregation prefect Cardinal Joseph Ratzinger asked the world's bishops to try to withdraw de Mello's books from circulation or to ensure that they would be printed with a notice indicating they may cause "grave harm" to the faith.[19]

The U.S. bishops' response was lukewarm. Meanwhile, both the Jesuit Major Superiors of India and the Indian bishops defended de Mello. In India, theologians and friends expressed outright puzzlement at the Vatican action. Some friends suggested the Vatican might have been prompted by writings published *after* de Mello's death, writings that might not have fairly represented his thinking. Ratzinger's position was that Eastern spirituality, especially that of India, reinforces some of the worst tendencies in Western thought stemming from the Enlightenment. "The two philosophies are fundamentally different," he said in a 1996 address. "Nonetheless, they seem to mutually confirm one another in their metaphysical and religious relativism. . . . The areligious and pragmatic relativism of Europe and America can get a kind of religious consecration from India, which seems to give its renunciation of dogma the dignity of a greater respect before the mystery of God and man."

Some Americans familiar with de Mello's work rejected the claim that he has undercut church teaching. "It's extremely hard for me to believe that anyone would find anything de Mello says to be anything other than orthodox," said Jesuit Father Francis Stroud, who had collaborated with de Mello and ran a "De Mello Spirituality Center" from his residence at Fordham University in New York. "De Mello did emphasize that God is a mystery," Stroud explained. "But he would quote Thomas Aquinas saying the very same thing. . . . He never denied anything like a personal concept of God."[20] Jesuit Father Norris Clarke, a philosopher at Fordham who wrote about de Mello, said some of his statements were elliptical enough to support many interpretations. "He would talk about theology as pointing a finger at the moon, and we come to mistake the finger for the moon," Clarke said. "That doesn't have to mean anything unorthodox, although you could read it that way."[21] De Mello's superiors, under the umbrella of the South Asian Jesuit provincials, called on Rome "to be mindful of legitimate pluralism in theology" and said that decisions "taken unilaterally without a dialogue with the Asian churches" reflect a "lack of appreciation of differences and of proper procedures." They assured continued support and encouragement to their theologians "to go ahead, joyfully and in fidelity to God, to the gospel and to the church, with the difficult and challenging task of making the Word of God relevant to the situation in South Asia." They spoke about "the need for inculturation that considers the multireligious and multicultural South Asian milieu." Finally, their statement stressed the church's teaching that the universal church is a "communion of local churches" and that there is "legitimate pluralism in theology within the unity of faith."

De Mello wrote and spoke simply, not expecting his audiences to take him literally. Rather he wanted to point them to larger truths. "Nobody can be said to have attained the pinnacle of Truth," he once wrote, "until a thousand sincere people have denounced him for blasphemy." His purpose was to get people to think for themselves. What Rome seemed to fail to understand was that de Mello was not rejecting Catholic dogma, but was rather trying to find alternative expressions that would be faithful to the truth as well as intelligible to multitudes brought up in both East and West.

RAIMON PANIKKAR

Raimon Panikkar was born in 1918 in Barcelona, Spain, of a Hindu father and a Catholic Spanish mother. He grew up in the Catholic faith. An intelligent thinker, he earned doctorates in chemistry, philosophy, and theology. Eventually he studied for the priesthood and was ordained in 1946. In the early 1950s he moved to India, where he studied Indian thought in Varanasi, considered by Indians to be a holy city. Varanasi is the site of the famous Banaras Hindu University committed to preserving Hindu culture and thought. Panikkar eventually became a priest in the diocese of Varanasi, India. His writings grew in popularity and soon caught hold in the Western world. He became a much sought after speaker, lecturing at Harvard University. He was a professor of religious studies at the University of California, Santa Barbara, for some twenty years. He has retired and now lives in Spain.

Once he told an interviewer that while he was brought up in the Catholic faith by his mother he never stopped trying to be united "with the tolerant and generous religion of my father and of my Hindu ances-tors." "This does not make me a cultural or religious 'half-caste,'" he explained. "Christ was not half man and half God, but fully man and fully God. In the same way, I consider myself 100 percent Hindu and Indian, and 100 percent Catholic and Spanish. How is that possible? By living religion as an experience rather than as an ideology."[22]

Panikkar is the author of some forty books. One of the more impor-tant was *The Unknown Christ of Hinduism,* published in 1964, in which he argues that Christ exists in Hinduism, that Christ stands for all forms of God's self-revelation to humanity, that the divine Logos is perceived in various ways by different traditions. Panikkar studied Hindu Vedantic theodicy, which attempts to answer the question of evil. Hinduism, one of the oldest living religions, has gone through many changes in its 3,200-year history. Today it claims over five hundred million followers. The majority of Hindus live in India, while Nepal has the distinction of being the sole Hindu nation. Hinduism has no founder, no universal prophet, no common creed, and no institutionalized structure. It is more a culture than a set of doctrines. Hinduism is known for its inclusive, universalistic, and accommodative spirit.

Although in its first stage (1500 to 600 B.C.E.), Hinduism was primarily a polytheistic cultic religion, with priests and sacrifices to many gods, the second stage, the post-600 B.C.E. period, brought on what is called the Vedantic era, which was based on the monistic teachings of the *Upani-shads,* written by Indian sages. The *Upanishads* assert that the ultimate being *or* world-Soul (it would be improper to call this god since it is everything in the universe and beyond) is the very essence of the uni-verse, and that it pervades all of ultimate reality. Through a rereading of the second sutra of *Badarayana* Panikkar proposes a certain similarity between the concept of the Hindu source of creation and the Christ of the Christian tradition.

Another important book by Panikkar is *Intra-religious Dialogue,* which deals with the nature of dialogue. Dialogue, Panikkar argues, takes place first and foremost within the religious consciousness of the seeker. This dialogue is fed by encounters with other believers. He wrote in a classic statement: "I 'left' as a Christian, I 'found' myself a Hindu and I 'return' a Buddhist, without ever having ceased to be a Christian."

We must distinguish between inter-religious dialogue and intra-reli-gious dialogue. The first confronts already-established religions and deals with questions of doctrine and discipline. Intra-religious dia-logue is something else. It does not begin with doctrine, theology and diplomacy. It is "intra," which means that if I do not discover in myself the terrain where the Hindu, the Muslim, the Jew and the atheist may have a place—in my heart, in my intelligence, in my life—I will never be able to enter into a genuine dialogue with him.

As long as I do not open my heart and do not see that the other is not an other but a part of myself who enlarges and completes me, I will not arrive at dialogue. If I embrace you, then I understand you. All this is a way of saying that real intra-religious dialogue begins in myself, and that it is more an exchange of religious experiences than of doctrines. If one does not start out from this foundation, no religious dialogue is possible; it is just idle chatter.[23]

Panikkar taught what he titled the "Cosmotheandric Principle," arguing that the divine, the human, and the earthly are the three irreducible dimensions that constitute what is real. These three parts, he said, are not juxtaposed simply by chance, but are essentially related and together constitute the Whole. He is one of the few sages of whom it is truly said that he thinks pluralistically.

Panikkar lived and taught beyond theological circles, maintaining a passion for world justice. In an interview he once said: "Peace is not simply an ideal, it's a necessity, because the alternative would be a human and planetary catastrophe. Our competitive system, in which only things which can be given a financial value are considered to have any worth, cannot go much further."[24] He argued that the West unthinkingly imposes its value systems on other nations "as indispensable conditions for establishing a dialogue with other cultures." Yet, he reminded his audiences that 70 percent of the human family lives in conditions of utter inferiority and degradation, and, of course, "it's an affront to speak of dialogue if the conditions of equality are absent, if somebody is starving and has been deprived of all human dignity."[25]

Looking to the future, Panikkar has written that a new ecumenical council is needed, a second council of Jerusalem.

A council should be opened whose concerns would no longer be inter-ecclesial—dealing with priests, bishops, women's ordination and so forth—but would center on far more essential problems. Three quarters of the world's population live under inhuman conditions. Humanity is in such great distress and insecurity that its leaders believe they must keep 30 million men in arms! The church cannot be a stranger to such distress, to such institutionalized injustice. It cannot remain deaf to the cries of the people, especially of the humble and the poor. The council I propose would certainly not be exclusively Christian but ecumenical, in the sense that it would give a hearing to other cosmologies and religions. Its purpose would be to determine how the Spirit is inspiring humanity to live in peace, and to bear the joyous news of hope.[26]

Panikkar is an optimist. He sees the emergence of a new consciousness. He believes new revelations are part of reality, although the world does not always recognize these revelations. "Our incomprehension, however, does not excuse us from taking responsibility. Quite the contrary, we have to assume responsibility as we have never done before. It is a task of solidarity, but it will not be enough. We have to invoke higher help."[27]

While these prominent Catholic religious figures played key roles in bridging the East and West, they were not the only bridge-makers. In the long term, they might not be the ones to have the most lasting influences. The world shrank considerably in the late twentieth century, and as it did, all kinds of Catholic refugees and migrants moved about as never before. Economic and political forces were the chief motivating factors. Grounded in local beliefs and practices, these Catholics also began to bridge cultures—although many felt caught between old and new. It was never easy. Yet in a span of several decades, they began to help change the landscape of Catholicism in America, helping to move a once European-oriented church into a new multiethnic, multicultural Catholic age. They too were increasingly key figures in the coming of Catholicism's global age.

CHAPTER 8

Migrations and Settlements

Arise, awake, and having taken
possession of your gifts, realize them.
—Katha Upanishad

Asians were reported living in the United States as early as 1763, when a Filipino settlement was established at Saint Malo in the bayous of Louisiana. Known as "Manilamen," these settlers jumped ship to escape brutalities during the galleon trade between the Philippines and Mexico. They governed themselves and lived in peace.[1] The first major Asian settlements date back to the mid-1800s. Along with many others, Chinese were drawn to California by the gold rush. By 1852, more than twenty thousand Chinese had settled in California. Their numbers grew, in part because the Central Pacific Railroad needed laborers to complete its transcontinental railroad.

Racial prejudices surged as Chinese immigrants came to America. In 1860, section 69 of California's Civil Code prohibited the issuing of licenses for marriages between whites and "Mongolians, Negroes, mulattoes and persons of mixed blood."[2] In 1882, the United States Congress passed the Chinese Exclusion Law, which barred additional Chinese laborers from entering the country and prevented Chinese aliens from obtaining American citizenship. The move represented the first federal attempt to limit immigration to the United States by nationality. In 1909 the U.S. government passed a law denying citizenship to fifty thousand persons from Arabia because they were considered Asians. The Johnson-Reed Act of 1924, known as the "Japanese Exclusion Act," banned further immigration of Japanese laborers.

Life was never easy for early Asian immigrants. In addition to racial prejudices, many lived on scant incomes. Away from their lands and cultures, they also faced bouts of severe loneliness. The story is told of a young Japanese Catholic who lived in Los Angeles in 1912. Wanting to confess his sins, he wrote to his bishop in Hakodate, Japan, asking if it was possible to confess by registered mail and be pardoned in the same way. The U.S. church's pastoral care to West Coast Japanese, it is said, originated with this incident. Receiving the letter, the bishop of Hakodate requested assistance. The Maryknoll Catholic Foreign Mission Society responded, sending priests and women religious to Los Angeles in 1915, where they established Japanese schools and began to minister to Japanese immigrants. The Los Angeles Maryknoll initiative marked a chapter in a much wider story about Asian and Pacific Catholics in America.[3]

One of the more public acts of racial discrimination came in the form of Executive Order 9066 of 1942, which forced Japanese immigrants, including two-thirds who were American citizens, mainly from the West Coast, into internment camps under the guise of national security.[4] The Chinese Exclusion Law, meanwhile, was repealed in 1943. It was not until 1965, however, that an immigration law finally abolished "national origins" as the basis for allocating immigration quotas. In 1987 the U.S. House of Representatives voted 243 to 141 to apologize to Japanese Americans and to pay each surviving internee $20,000 in reparations.[5]

The largest waves of Asians to hit the shores of America occurred in the years that followed the Vietnam War, which ended in 1975. Fleeing political persecution, hundreds of thousands of Vietnamese, Cambodians, Laotians, and tribal peoples took to the seas, most ending up in refugee camps, eventually to be settled in America. By the time of the U.S. Census of 2000, the numbers of Vietnamese in the United States had swelled to 1,122,528, becoming the fourth largest Asian ethnic population in America after the Chinese, Filipinos, and Indians. Moreover, the 2000 census counted nearly twelve million Asian Americans in America, reflecting a growth of 48 percent since 1990. The census also found the Asian and Pacific American population to be the fastest-growing racial group in the country, one that is expected to double by 2010. The six largest Asian ethnic groups—Chinese, Filipino, Asian Indian, Vietnamese, Korean, and Japanese—account for 87.5 percent of Asian Americans. Other groups include Bangladeshi, Cambodian, Hmong, Indonesian, Laotian, Malaysian, Pakistani, Sri Lankan, Taiwanese and Thai. More than two-thirds of the Asian American population at the turn of the twenty-first century lived in six states: California, Hawaii, Illinois, Texas, New Jersey, and New York. These immigrants included significant numbers of Catholics, who, along with growing numbers of Hispanics, African Americans, and Native Americans, slowly began to change the complexion of the Catholic Church in America from its former European orientation to a more diverse, multiethnic orientation.

With the growth of the Asian Catholic populations have also come calls for change within the institutions serving those populations, including the Catholic Church. In response to these pressures, the U.S. bishops' Committee on Migration in the Office for the Pastoral Care of Migrants and Refugees, charged with providing care for the Asian Catholics, decided in 1999 to write a pastoral letter. Its purpose was to recognize the gifts that the new Asian immigrants were bringing to the church. The U.S. bishops approved the pastoral entitled, "Asian Pacific Presence: Harmony in Faith" at their annual meeting in November 2001. The pastoral estimated that there were 1,536,000 Filipino Catholics, 325,000 Vietnamese Catholics, 300,000 Chinese Catholics, 285,000 Indian Catholics, 74,000 Korean Catholics, and 32,000 Japanese Catholics living in the United States. The bishops listed the top ten dioceses showing the heaviest concentrations of Asian Americans as Los Angeles, Honolulu, Brooklyn, San Jose, Oakland, San Francisco, Orange, Seattle, New York, and Chicago.

The pastoral made the points that Asian American and Pacific American Catholics were not being either adequately recognized or served. One reason for the oversight, the pastoral suggested, has to do with the absence of Asian episcopal leadership in the U.S. Conference of Catholic Bishops. Despite years of talk about this shortcoming, not one Western rite Asian American bishop had been appointed by May 2002. "Today the Asian and Pacific communities in the United States . . . span several generations," the pastoral stated. "Yet Asian and Pacific peoples have remained, until very recently, nearly invisible in the church in the United States. Their absence in the episcopal leadership may be a factor." A modest exception to this oversight came in July 2001, when Rome appointed the first Eastern Syro-Malabar rite bishop of India to be the pastoral leader of the estimated 120,000 Syro-Malabar rite followers in the United States. It was widely believed that ethnic diplomacy had, in part, slowed the process. Some church observers said it would be inappropriate to appoint a Korean American bishop without appointing, say, a Filipino one or a Vietnamese one. Most Asian American Catholics saw no problem in appointing several Asian American bishops at the same time.

Veronica Leasiolagi Barber, a native Samoan and Director for Asian and Pacific American Affairs for the Seattle Archdiocese, said it was time "to recognize our presence in the United States," adding that Asian and Pacific American Catholics bring to the church needed "communal" values. "We are into doing things for others as community. This contrasts a bit with the more individualistic approach we see here." "I had one person say to me recently, 'We didn't know that Asians are Catholics. We thought they were Buddhists,'" she said. "Typical," she responded, adding she wanted to blurt back to the person that Jesus was an Asian!

GIFTS FROM ASIA

The pastoral letter made the point that America—and the Catholic Church in America—has been strengthened with each new wave of immigrants. It went on to list some of the "gifts" that the Asian Catholics were bringing to their new homes. The pastoral stated:

- Harmony Is Asian and Christian

    Harmony is central to the lives and cultures of Asian and Pacific communities. According to the bishops of Asia, "harmony embodies 'the realities of order, well-being, justice and love as seen in human interaction. . . . Harmony is not simply the absence of strife. . . . The test of true harmony lies in acceptance of diversity and richness.'"[6]

    Typically, harmony in the family binds generations together for the spiritual formation of the young. Culturally, the traditional arts of many Asian and Pacific societies link a person's actions with grace in society. Most of the time, harmony is characterized as well by a deep spirit of courtesy—a recognition that human solidarity derives from all persons' common relation to God, who is the source of all life.

    Harmony is authentically Christian and intrinsically Asian. Harmony draws its inspiration and strength from the harmonious relationship of the Trinity. Asians and Pacific Islanders teach a threefold harmony: (1) harmony with a personal God, the source of all genuine harmony; (2) harmony among all people; and (3) harmony with the whole universe.

- Family and Education Are Central

    For most peoples, the family is of the highest value. Asian and Pacific cultures place a particular emphasis on loyalty to one's family. Asian and Pacific families affirm many basic family values including love, integrity, honesty, thrift, and mutual support. Respect for elders and authority and sacrifice for children figure prominently in shaping their experiences. Harmony is crucial, along with the notion that the group predominates over the individual.

    Faith is an important element of life. Catholic identity among Asian and Pacific peoples is intimately connected with family and local community. Parents and grandparents are the primary teachers of gospel values and nurturers of the faith among the young. Special vocations to ministry are fostered in the family.

After the family, education is most valued by Asian and Pacific peoples. Thirty-eight percent of Asians in the United States have bachelor's degrees or higher education, compared with 20 percent of the total population. For example, among Asian Indian men, 66 percent have a bachelor's or higher degree.[7]

- Profound Spirituality and Religiosity

Asian and Pacific Catholic Americans and immigrants migrated with the experience and sensibilities of the great religions and spiritual traditions of the world—Buddhism, Confucianism, Hinduism, Islam, Jainism, Judaism, Shintoism, Sikhism, Taoism, and Zoroastrianism—together with Christianity. Their experience of the great religions and spiritual traditions teaches them to live with a profound sense of the sacred, a holistic approach to life and salvation, and a spirituality adapted to their needs and a life-giving vitality. Indeed the Holy Father said on April 19, 1998, "We want to listen to what the Spirit says to the churches of Asia that they may proclaim Christ in the context of Hinduism, Buddhism, Shintoism and all those currents of thought and life which were already rooted in Asia before the preaching of the Gospel arrived."[8]

Despite the fact that many Christian immigrants from Asia have suffered persecution in their homelands, we are mindful that their religiosity has roots in their Asian spiritual traditions. Their experience demonstrates the values of these religions and spiritual traditions, and how these values await their fulfillment in the revelation of Jesus Christ.

- A Long Tradition of Lay Leadership

Asians entering the church in their homelands before the Second Vatican Council were imbued with the understanding that the mission of the laity is crucial to the growth of the church. Partly because of their recent mission-based history, the Catholic Church in Asia and the Pacific Islands emphasizes the baptismal call to mission for all members of the church. Church leaders place great importance on lay leadership and the active role of women. Many Asian and Pacific Catholics who migrated to this country came with a rich experience of being active lay members and ministers of the church.

- The Contributions of Clergy and Religious

Many priests and religious sisters and brothers from Asia and the Pacific minister to the church in the United States. Most serve not only their ethnic groups, but also are pastors and associates in parishes, and teachers and principals of Catholic schools throughout the country. In many instances, Asian and Pacific priests and religious have established parish religious education programs in their native languages. Volunteer teachers in these programs are usually from particular ethnic groups; for instance, Hmong, Samoan-speaking, and Tongan priests, religious, and deacons often work with lay leaders in family evangelization programs.

Vocations are quite high in Asian and Pacific American communities both in number and in proportion to the current population. In 1999, 9 percent of those ordained to the priesthood in the United States were of Asian or Pacific heritage.

- The Heritage of the Eastern Churches

Many Asian and Pacific Islanders—native-born and immigrants—belong to the Eastern Catholic churches. These churches, principally of the Middle East and India, merit special attention. "From Apostolic times they have been the custodians of a precious spiritual, liturgical and theological heritage. Their traditions and rites, born of a deep inculturation of the faith in the soil of many Asian countries, deserve the greatest respect."[9]

Although their own priests served some of the Eastern Catholic faithful from Asia, the faithful were all subject to the local Latin bishops until the 1966 appointment of the Maronite and Melkite bishops. Bishops were later appointed to serve other communities. The appointment of bishops to serve the Armenian, Chaldean, Syrian, and, most recently, the Syro-Malabar churches followed.

The pastoral hailed the leaders among Asian and Pacific peoples in the United States, including governors, a U.S. senator, several U.S. representatives, cabinet members, as well as Nobel Prize winners, U.S. Olympic athletes, scholars, and scientists. Among these leaders have been prominent Catholic religious figures, including the mother general of the Sisters of Mercy, Sister Marie Chin, and Father Peter C. Phan, the first Asian American elected president of the Catholic Theological Society of America. Phan, who teaches at the Catholic University of America in Washington, D.C., has been developing a theological niche within Asian theology called Asian American theology. He is one of only about a dozen Asian American theologians. Although these theologians have been living and writing in the West, their roots are in Asia. According to Phan, they have worked to develop theology that places no culture or theological system ahead of another. Their aim is the development of a new global "intercultural theology." Meanwhile, being an Asian American can also mean not quite fitting into the norm, at least as most Americans see that norm. Phan likes to say that he lives and writes theology "betwixt-between." It can be a marginal and often lonely place, lacking the comfort of a single traditional identity. "Betwixt-between" means, he says, not being fully integrated into any one culture; being bilingual, but not achieving a mastery of one's native or adoptive tongue; speaking with a distinct accent; and having an inordinate desire to belong.[10] His "betwixt-between"cultural experience mirrors that of many other Asian immigrants.

The Asian American pastoral made a series of recommendations, including one that called for "an appropriate national structure" to coordinate Asian and Pacific Catholic matters. The recommendation fell short of asking for a "secretariat," such as those that coordinate African American and Hispanic affairs. The bishops created a Secretariat for African American Affairs in 1987; it opened in 1988. The U.S. Catholic Hispanic Affairs secretariat was officially created in 1972. The care of Asian and Pacific American Catholics has come under Migration and Refugee Services. However, with each passing decade the notion of maintaining the care for Asian American Catholics under Migration and Refugees has become more problematic.

"What we in the Asian and Pacific American Catholic communities are saying is that we are no longer newcomers," said Cecile Motus, coordinator for ethnic ministries in the U.S. bishops' Office for the Pastoral Care of Migrants and Refugees. "We are saying that many of us have been here five and six generations and that our pastoral needs are beyond the responsibility of the department of migrants and refugees." Motus, who worked on the pastoral letter, adds that the answer for the pastoral needs of Asians and Pacific Catholics might not rest in creating yet another secretariat.

"We have given the bishops wiggle room," she said. "What is needed is a whole new national restructuring, one that reflects the increasingly diverse multi-ethnic church we have become."[11]

The pastoral incorporates some of the themes that have been developed by the Federation of Asian Bishops' Conferences since the early 1970s, notably the notion of the triple dialogue with religions, cultures, and the poor. The pastoral represented the first time the motif was used in a Catholic episcopal utterance outside of Asia, indicating the spread of Asian Catholic thinking.

"Since the Second Vatican Council," the U.S. bishops' pastoral stated, "our brother bishops in Asia, who gather regularly as the Federation of Asian Bishops' Conferences, have developed a pastoral approach that emphasizes a threefold dialogue: with other religions, with cultures, and with the poor. Such dialogue can also be explored for its enriching fruit-fulness at all levels of the Church in the United States." The bishops concluded the pastoral with words of encouragement and hope. They also spoke of some of the lessons Asian American Catholics are teaching the wider church:

> By being authentically Christian and truly Asian in the footsteps of Christ, they have brought to us a more profound understanding of what it means to be truly Catholic. They have taught the Church in the United States the meaning of harmony; the necessity of dia-logue with their cultures, with other religions, and with the poor; a renewed sense of family loyalty; the unity between diverse cultures and diverse Catholic church communities; and the closeness of all God's creation.[12]

Their affirming words were another indication that Catholic ideas, for centuries having moved from West to East, had turned direction and were, at the outset of the twenty-first century, heading in the other direction.

PART 3

CHAPTER 9

Taking Notice

The temple bell stops
but the sound keeps coming
out of the flowers
　　—Zen Haiku Master Basho

My yoke is easy and my
burden light.
　　—Matthew 11:30

On November 10, 1989, the Berlin Wall fell, and with its collapse the Soviet empire came to a stunning end. The defeat of European Communism was greeted throughout much of the world with elation and relief, not least of all in the Holy See. Pope John Paul II, it is widely recognized, played an important role in its defeat, having galvanized the Polish worker's Solidarity movement during his visit to Poland in 1979. That movement became a catalyst for the antigovernment opposition forces in Poland in the years that followed, eventually unraveling Communism's grip there.

Pope John Paul beamed with satisfaction and pride as Poland emerged from the shadows of Communism and began to rebuild an economy with strong links to the West. Within the Catholic context, the pope saw Soviet Communism's demise as, among other things, the death of liberation theology, which, he felt, had been inspired by Marxist thought. During a flight to Guatemala in February 1996, for example, the pope offered his opinion that liberation theology essentially ended with the fall of the Berlin Wall. He characterized liberation theology as "somewhat a Marxist ideology."[1] John Paul's comments quickly made their way into the major Latin American newspapers, especially in countries such as Brazil, Peru, and the Central American countries, where proponents of liberation theology had been especially active. The Brazilian theologian Leonardo Boff, who left the active priestly ministry after being disciplined by the

Vatican in 1985, responded: "I'm sure the pope would be very happy to assert that liberation theology is dead, that all the poor are free, and they eat and live well, but this is an illusion that the church cannot hope to peddle to the oppressed."[2]

Liberation theology, spawned by class division and the abject poverty of Latin America, helped move the Latin American bishops to adopt their "preferential option for the poor," a theme they held to through the late 1960s and 1970s. As John Paul consolidated his grip on the papacy, however, he appointed more conservative bishops to key Latin American sees. These prelates eventually worked with Rome, hammering against the liberation theologians and diminishing their influence.[3] These same clerics felt more at home with the conservative governments of Latin America and did not like the church meddling in social and political affairs. For his part, the pope believed the fall of the Berlin Wall marked a critical turning point, the last nail in the coffin of liberation theology. But other factors also played roles in marginalizing the liberation theologians, including the pope's conservative appointments, the defeat of the progressive, liberation theology–inspired Sandinistas in Nicaragua in 1990, and the growth of evangelical Protestantism in the region.

Of course, siding with the poor, as the liberation theologians advocated, has long been part of the Judeo-Christian tradition. The "option for the poor" dates back to Hebrew Scriptures. Among the oldest biblical ordinances are laws designed to protect widows, orphans, and strangers. This biblical command is equated with what it means to know God (Jer. 22:13-16). In the New Testament, Jesus promises that the poor will inherit the kingdom (Luke 6:20); he identifies with the poor (Matt. 25:34). In more recent times, the "option for the poor" is found in Pope Leo XIII's landmark encyclical *Rerum Novarum*, which is viewed as foundational for Catholic social teaching. "The poor and helpless have a claim to special consideration," he wrote, noting the severe disparity in the possession and exercise of power as a factor contributing to poverty. The phrase "option for the poor" was reintroduced even more recently into the Catholic conversation at the first Latin American Episcopal Conference called after Vatican II, in 1968 in Medellín, Colombia. The times were ripe and the notion spread quickly throughout the church. At the second Latin American Episcopal Conference, in 1979, in Puebla, Mexico, the Latin American bishops strengthened their position yet again, writing: "We affirm the need for conversion on the part of the whole church to a preferential option for the poor, an option aimed at their eternal liberation."

Two years later, Pope John Paul II picked up the idea, using it in his Apostolic Exhortation on the Family. "The Christian family is called upon to offer everyone a witness of generous and disinterested dedication to social matters through a 'preferential option' for the poor and disadvantaged," he wrote. Yet John Paul has never really warmed up to the "option for the poor," at least as the Latin Americans had done. He does not like the notion of the church siding with one segment of society. On the theological level, Pope John Paul has never endorsed "contextual theology," a theology growing out of the conditions of a people or region. He has always viewed Catholic social teachings as universal, applicable to all in all circumstances. When the pontiff has used the phrase "option for the poor," he often reassures his listeners that Christ is present in *all* people, before adding, especially the poor. Further, the pontiff's option for the poor has had a distinctly spiritual ring. While he and many Third World theologians agreed that God speaks through the poor, they have disagreed on the specifics of the message and how people should respond to what the poor are saying. The pope's deep suspicions regarding liberation theology keep him distant from virtually all the contextual theologies that have been developed throughout the church, including those coming out of Asia.

Immediately after the collapse of the Soviet Union, the Vatican focused much of its attention on Eastern Europe, where churches were in desperate need. At the same time, with Soviet-styled Communism off the Vatican radar screen, it had more time to consider other threats to church orthodoxy. Vatican eyes turned East, where theologians and bishops had been writing for years about the need to inculturate the faith—make it less Western in appearance—and to work more closely with the Asian religions. This kind of talk frightened some in Rome. Their fear was that the Asian Catholics would "give up" too much Catholic content to befriend the other Asians. These concerns soon came to be lumped under an umbrella of concern called "religious pluralism." Curiously, Asian critics had a difficult time specifically identifying the advocates of this so-called "watered down" Catholic faith. Criticisms usually ended up being somewhat vague. The idea of the Catholic Church establishing better relations with other religions was not the issue. Everyone seemed to be in agreement that this was a good idea. From Rome's viewpoint, the fear was that these "better relations" might come at too high a cost—pulling back, for example, from a willingness to proclaim Jesus as the unique Savior to the World. Further, Rome feared that the new Asian thinking on mission, summarized in the triple dialogue, meant that the Asian Catholics would no longer be as eagerly seeking Catholic converts. Rome cited scripture, saying that Christians are all called to proclaim Jesus as Savior of all; the Asians responded that dialogue suited Asia better, and in the long run the approach would bear more fruit. In fact, by then the Asian leadership had come to believe it could learn more about the divine plan by establishing better ties with the other Asian religions. This was not being received well in Rome, which wanted little to do with Asian inculturation efforts, which were viewed as potentially diminishing Rome's own play in the local Asian churches. Additionally, many Roman clerics looked to Asia's contextual theologies as vestiges of liberation theology—and even, at times, errant.

In fact, there had been substantial communication and shared values between the Latin American and Asian theologians in the 1970s. Influenced by the common belief that theology grows out of local reflections, and responding to local injustices, both the Latin Americans and the Asians committed themselves to solidarity with the poor—the former, in Medellín in 1968; the latter in Manila in 1970. The Asians added a peculiarly Asian dimension to their theology: Asian spirituality. In other words, the prism of reflections was not simply "secular," not simply social or economic; it also had a religious connection. Bringing life to Christian communities in Asia meant putting an "Asian face" on Jesus, and this required a give and take with Asia, its peoples, religions, and cultures. Asian heritage is a spiritual heritage. It was this spiritual heritage that Catholicism had to connect with, relate to, learn from, and build upon. From the Asian Catholic perspective, God, the source of all that is good, has revealed and continues to reveal Him/Herself through the other religions of Asia. Did this mean that the Asian leadership was now saying that all religions are the same in the eyes of God? If you ask the Asian bishops you get an emphatic, "No!" To say that God is revealed in other religions does not mean to say that the fullness of God is revealed in them. The Asian bishops see the fullness of revelation in the person of Jesus Christ. Nevertheless, the Asian bishops tend to take a more humble role vis-à-vis the other Asian religions, especially in their writings, than many other bishops who concern themselves about these matters but who have not lived their lives in Asia. The theologies of Catholic Asia are certainly among the least triumphal in the church today. As far as many clerics in Rome are concerned this is a worrisome development, auguring a Catholicism that lacks traditional scholastic clarity and the energy or purpose to convert the world.

The various differences between the Vatican and Asian perspectives on matters of religious pluralism can get abstract and can defy easy understanding. Just as there is no single Asian perspective on these matters, there is no single Vatican critique. It is helpful to remember here that Asians feel more comfortable living with ambiguities in theological and spiritual matters than do most Westerners. Suspicions seem to grow with distance. The farther away, the more suspicion. I personally witnessed these dynamics play out at the Seventh Plenary Assembly of the Federation of Asian Bishops' Conferences outside of Bangkok in January 2000. Addressing the gathering the first day, Cardinal Joseph Tomko, prefect of the Congregation for the Evangelization of Peoples, warned the Asian bishops against allowing "weak Christology" to enter into their theological reflections. After his talk he was pressed by the bishops to give a specific example. He answered that a weak Christology would be one that portrayed Jesus as simply a wise person or prophet but not the Son of God. Again, he was pressed to offer an instance of such thinking in Asian Catholic theology. Finally, he replied that he had not found any. Exasperated, one bishop asked Tomko flat out if Rome would ever recognize an Asian Christ "if it saw one." The question brought widespread laughter from the assembly.

Pope John Paul II has been a strong supporter of interreligious dialogue—but within limits. At times gestures the pope has made contradict statements that have come out of the Vatican during his pontificate; prelates in the Roman curia have contradicted each other on matters pertaining to interreligious dialogue. It sometimes seems that Vatican prelates and Asian prelates both agree and disagree on these matters. In questions related to the issues of "religious pluralism," two things stand out: (1) nothing is simple; (2) nothing is settled. For example, Rome states unequivocally that "Jesus Christ is the unique savior for all humanity." The Asian bishops respond to this, essentially saying, "Yes . . . but"—Yes, true, but using those words in Asia do not make pastoral sense. Nevertheless, Rome does not like the Asian "but." The Vatican insists that it is essential to "proclaim" Jesus Christ as unique Savior. The Asian bishops again respond, saying proclamation is best done in Asia through dialogue. This is the approach the Asian bishops decided on in 1974 in Taipei, and it is the pastoral approach they have since followed.

The Asian Catholic leadership has felt for decades that Rome does not adequately support their efforts at inculturation and interreligious dialogue. Expressing a view commonly heard in Asia, Father S. J. Emmanuel insists that "interreligious dialogue . . . is not against the proclamatory mission of the church." Emmanuel, a former vicar general of the Jaffina diocese in Sri Lanka, was once an advisor to the Sri Lankan bishops. He explains: "In fact, dialogue and proclamation are integral but dialectical and complementary dimensions of the church's mission of new evangelization. Hence, inter-religious dialogue is an integral element of the process of building up authentic local churches in Asia."[4] Emmanuel goes on:

> Asian Christians had a Christian identity that was often suspected as diminishing, if not disloyal, to their national identity. Hence, Asians have the need to harmonize two identities into a single identity to live and act as Asian Christians. While Hindus, Buddhists, Confucians or Shintoists find themselves in their "natural habitat"

for their religious practices, it is Christians in Asia who are called to show their patriotism and nationality. This suspicion over their true loyalty to the nation and a consequent minority complex urge them to go further than mere adaptation limited to liturgical decorations and some *de-Westernization*. They want to follow the prompting of the Spirit as discerned by their Asian leaders for a genuine encounter with the cultures of the land. If culture is the God-given natural cradle of their birth and Christian faith too is a gift of God, why should we hinder the encounter urged by the Spirit?[5]

Listen to the Asian experience, Emmanuel and many other Asian Catholics insist. Nation matters. History matters. Language matters. Culture matters. All these, the Asians say, must be the starting points for their own Christian reflections and responses. This, in turn, raises a related issue that perhaps goes to the core of the Asian concern: Why should the Asian bishops have so little to say about the way they go about inculturating their churches? Why is it that Rome must give approval to pastoral matters regarding liturgies and translations? Why does the Vatican not *trust* the Asian bishops to know what is best for their own peoples? The Asian bishops are not alone in asking these questions. After a quarter century of unprecedented centralization of authority during the pontificate of Pope John Paul II, bishops around the world were asking the same questions. In Asia, however, so distant in culture and living with painful colonial memories, these questions take on greater urgency. Remember that the Asian bishops are mostly moderates, not prone to rash actions or anger. This does not mean, however, that they do not feel deep anguish and frustration.

The experience of the Indian bishops in the years preceding and following the Vatican Council is instructive. As far back as 1960, at the general meeting of the Indian bishops, Cardinal Valerian Gracias, the first Indian archbishop of Bombay, made the case for inculturation. Said Gracias: "Truth to be known and to be loved must be presented in a way adapted to the mentality of those to whom it is preached. [It] presupposes a personal respect and a sincere esteem for Indian and Hindu traditions, languages and ways of thought." Three years after the conclusion of Vatican II, the Indian bishops, responding to directives from the Vatican Sacred Congregation for Divine Worship, began work on inculturating their liturgies, including the Mass. The work went on for four years. Then at a meeting of the Indian bishops in Madras in 1972, sixty bishops voted to accept the text of an Indian eucharistic prayer; twenty voted against it. However, to the dismay of nearly all the bishops, Rome told the bishops to stop completely further attempts at liturgical inculturation—until first getting the approval of the Congregation of Divine Worship.[6] And the congregation was not high on the effort.

The church's dialogue with culture will continue to face serious problems as long as those responsible for the promotion of Christian life in the local churches are not permitted to decide what is good for their peoples. The Asian bishops in general, and the Indian bishops among them, have tried through the past three decades to settle their churches deeper into local cultures, and these efforts have often been frustrated by Rome. The history of these longings for inculturation can be found in the documents of the Asian bishops. Recently Jacob Parappally, an Indian scholar, wrote:

> The church's commitment to dialogue with the Asian reality of the plurality of cultures and religions finds expression in the documents of both the Catholic Bishops' Conference of India (CBCI) and the Federation of Asian Bishops' Conference (FABC). The statements of the CBCI and the FABC reveal the struggle of a church come of age to liberate herself from the burden of her links with the colonial powers in the past, her claims about possessing the monopoly of truth, her imported theology and forms of worship, her eurocentrism, her cultural alienation and her desire to become authentic local churches with an Asian face. The church becomes truly catholic when she is transformed by entering into dialogue with the cultures and religions of Asia and transforms them with the power of the Spirit who makes everything new.[7]

Frustrating the process of inculturation is harmful, believes Parappally and many others in Asia. He goes on: "If the role of the national bishops' conferences in promoting inculturation, which is not prejudicial to the faith of the universal church, be not recognized, it can create not only serious ecclesiological problems, but also prevent the effective and meaningful proclamation itself."[8] In the late 1980s, the Indian bishops once again approved an Indian eucharistic prayer and submitted it to Rome for approval. More than a decade later, they were still waiting a response.

The Indians, of course, have had large resources to work from, not the least of which have been the writings of their many theologians. Many of these theologians, in turn, have been influenced by other Third World theologians for decades. One of the most notable organizations that brought these theologians together has been the Ecumenical Association of Third World Theologians, or EATWOT, which came to life in Dar-es Salaam, Tanzania, in 1976, when twenty-two representatives from Africa, Asia, and Latin America, and one black theologian from the United States met for an Ecumenical Dialogue of Third World Theologians. Their purpose was to share their theological resources and support each other—Catholic, Protestant, and Orthodox. The decade before EATWOT's birth had been a time of explosive new theological energies coming from the poor nations of the world, mostly countries in Africa, Asia, and Latin America. During that time the national and international organizations were becoming more painfully conscious of the growing gulf between rich and poor. Much was being written exploring the reasons so many were so poor. The reasons for poverty, according to sociologists and theologians, had less to do with limited natural or human resources than with unjust international economic and political patterns. Development requires investments, but investors seek stability and return on those investments. Often the stability that was required meant more sacrifice and more oppression for those that were already poor.

Meanwhile, new political and theological movements addressing these inequities were gathering steam. Many bishops and theologians from the world's poor nations, encountering poverty close up, were finding that the traditional Catholic theologies they had inherited from the West simply did not address their peoples' conditions. They did not examine, for example, social structures, human interaction, trade patterns, or any of the host of forces that were oppressive to their peoples. Pressure grew among those Christians committed to bringing justice and life and liberation to the world to reformulate theologies so they would be more meaningful to people's daily lives, including the deepest struggles for a more just and egalitarian world. This was the backdrop for the founding of EATWOT. The EATWOT theologians, impassioned by the unjust suffering they found around them, felt compelled to make Christianity a truly liberating religion—and one that had something specific to say to the times. Christ viewed the world through the eyes of the poor and that is precisely what they believed they were doing as well.

BANDUNG CROSSROADS

It is not as if the Asian theologians had been hiding anything from Rome. Vatican representatives had come to every one of the plenary sessions of the FABC, and by all accounts they were always warmly received. Rome seemed pleased with the vitality of the Asian faith communities. However, this seemed to change somewhat at the Fifth Plenary meeting of the FABC in Bandung, Indonesia, in 1990. It was the first plenary meeting that Cardinal Joseph Tomko, Prefect of the Congregation for the Evangelization of Peoples, had attended. On July 18, Tomko delivered a keynote address that sent shivers down the spines of the Asian bishops and theologians in attendance. His comments that day were critical of the work of the bishops and, some thought, quite condescending. What bothered him, he said, was the lack of converts in Asia. He criticized the bishops for failing to bring enthusiasm and energy to the evangelical efforts. There was much more here than a question of zeal. The central issue was that his view, or Rome's view, of mission had been at odds with that of the Asian bishops for some time. It is said that Tomko's comments that day caused real hurt and resentment, but, while critical, they also had the effect of placing honest differences on the table. Here is what the cardinal had to say about the Asian view of mission:

> Let us be realistic. The church in Asia is almost everywhere a small minority, at times microscopic, hardly 2.5 percent of the entire population, and in some countries even less than 1 percent. Its growth has slowed down, for a number of external reasons, such as: the difficulties and obstacles of a political and cultural nature, the aggressiveness of the fundamentalist groups, the lessening of the number of missionaries as well as the obstacles that are being placed on their entrance or permanence, etc. But there are also internal reasons for the slowing down of its growth such as: current discussions on the very nature of "mission," different shifts—at times almost exclusive—in regard to the missionary effort, or concentrating on the economic and social development of the people, or on an interhuman dialogue rather than an interreligious one, the refusal to engage in conversions as if this were a kind of negative proselytism or a moral constriction placed on one's conscience, etc., all of these being theorized by some as a new and improved "missiology" or theology of mission! Moreover, the church in Asia, notwithstanding its promising fermentation of reactions, still runs the great risk of being either overcome by an inferiority complex rather than by its being a small minority, or of falling into a sort of stagnation renouncing the effort to grow, or even again of becoming a ghetto, or some sort of administrative and static church of one kind or another.[9]

The words were cutting. It was not exactly the kind of inspirational collegial address the Asian bishops imagined might fit the moment. Tomko's remarks took many Asian bishops by surprise because earlier Vatican envoys to the FABC had been more positive. Oakland bishop John S. Cummins, the U.S. bishops' FABC representative for many years, recalls, for example, that Cardinal Eduardo Pironio, the Argentinean from the Vatican Council on Laity, gave a "magnificent" ecclesiological presentation at FABC IV in Tokyo in 1986. Later the Vatican representative,

Cardinal Giovanni Cheli, was supportive at FABC VI in Manila in 1995. Tomko seemed rather to have come to scold the bishops, insisting that they had not been living up to the church mission, that they were failing in their first priority to proclaim Jesus Christ as universal Savior. "While all that the church does forms part of its evangelizing work," he said, "evangelization as proclamation of the death-resurrection of Jesus Christ, by which the gifts of repentance and forgiveness are offered to all by God through the Holy Spirit and sacraments, should receive priority in our planning, action, catechesis, preaching and teaching, allocation of personnel and in the distribution of resources." As if to be sure the bishops heard his point, Tomko repeated the word "proclaim" and "proclamation" no fewer than twenty-eight times in his address!

The Vatican's reservations seemed to grow more serious by the month, eventually leading to direct condemnations in the years that followed. Some of the major milestones in what came to be a new Vatican campaign to reassert orthodoxy, as Rome defined it, began around the time of the fall of the Berlin Wall and lasted up to and through the historic Synod on Asia, held in Rome in April 1998:

- October 1989: The Congregation for the Doctrine of the Faith issued a document titled "Some Aspects of Christian Meditation," in which it warned against placing Buddhist concepts on the same level as Christian revelation. The document cautioned against incorporating practices based on Eastern spirituality, such as yoga.

- July 1990: Tomko, Prefect of the Congregation for the Evangelization of Peoples, spoke at the Fifth FABC Plenary in Bandung, Indonesia, expressing serious reservations about the way the Asian bishops were viewing church mission work.

- 1991: Tomko, in an interview, referred to India as the "epicenter" of (certain theological) tendencies that do not uphold Jesus as the only Savior.[10] He claimed some Indian theologians had grown errant.

- March 1993: Cardinal Joseph Ratzinger, Prefect of the Congregation for the Doctrine of the Faith, in a speech in Hong Kong warned against growing "cultural relativism" in Asia. He singled out a tendency among some theologians working in inter-religious dialogue to emphasize the reign of God rather than Christ or the church.

- 1995: Tomko, speaking at the Sixth FABC Plenary in Manila, once again called upon the Asian bishops to make greater efforts to proclaim Jesus as the unique Savior of the World.

- May 1996: Ratzinger stated flatly that the "theology of religious pluralism" had come to be the gravest threat facing the church. He compared it to the threat of liberation theology in the 1980s. Said Ratzinger, comparing the two threats, "In some ways [religious pluralism] occupies today—with regard to the force of its problematic aspect and its presence in the different areas of culture—the place occupied by the theology of liberation in the preceding decade."[11]

- January 1997: The Vatican excommunicated Sri Lankan theologian Father Tissa Balasuriya after accusing him of theological aberrations, including assertions that Christianity is on the same level as other religions. A year later, under worldwide pressure, including from Asian bishops, the Vatican lifted the excommunication after Balasuriya signed a statement expressing regret for "perceptions of error" in his work and agreed to submit future writings to bishops for approval before publication.

- March 1997: Ratzinger described Buddhism in an interview with a French newspaper as "an auto-erotic spirituality." Ratzinger said, "In the 1950s someone said that the undoing of the Catholic Church in the twentieth century wouldn't come from Marxism but from Buddhism. They were right."[12]

- February 1998: German theologian Perry Schmidt-Leukel was denied permission by Cardinal Friedrich Wetter of Munich to teach Catholic theology. Schmidt-Leukel has written about religious pluralism and believes it is a topic that needs more discussion in the church. Schmidt-Leukel said he believed Ratzinger was consulted on the decision.

The attacks from Rome were dispiriting. It was clear that a rift between the Vatican prelates and the prelates of Asia needed to be addressed somehow. Many Asian Catholic leaders initially hoped these matters would blow over. Some in Asia tried to keep a lower profile as they went about their work. However, as the pontificate of Pope John Paul extended into its second decade it was clear that the matters would not simply go away. Meanwhile, the Asian Catholics were dealing with matters more immediate to their concerns. They were seeing the growth of social and economic malaise and a growing indifference among many younger Catholics, who felt their church was not going forward fast enough in addressing social and economic matters. Good words were one thing; acting upon them was another. By the 1990s the impact of globalization, with its demands for economic belt tightening and social disruption, was growing—and it was increasingly painful. By the 1990s, the optimism of the postcolonial era was giving way to new pessimism. Asian cultures were under serious attack with signs that some were cracking and growing more secular, and in virtually every Asian nation people were feeling the crushing weight of growing poverty.

CHAPTER 10

Asian Crossroads

The Spirit of the Lord is upon me,
because he has anointed me to bring
glad tidings to the poor. He has sent
me to proclaim liberty to captives and
recovery of sight to the blind, to let the
oppressed go free, and to proclaim a
year acceptable to the Lord.
                                    —Luke 4:18

The decades of the 1970s and 1980s witnessed much change across the continent of Asia, which was "modernizing," and in the process experiencing new and unsettling economic forces. These, in turn, generated large movements into cities in search of jobs. Towns were becoming cities and cities grew into mega-cities. Some Asian cities, such as Jakarta and Bombay (Mumbai), grew by several hundred thousand a year as people left their farms to seek employment in the expanding manufacturing and service industries. The search for work not only sparked massive population shifts but also shattered traditional cultural patterns, leaving many families broken and people feeling rootless and adrift. Experts say these movements into cities will continue and that Asia's urban population will double by 2025.[1] Meanwhile, between 1970 and 1990 Asia's population grew by an unprecedented 50 percent, from two to nearly three billion. The percentage of the population seeking work and shelter in urban areas grew from 20 to nearly 30 percent.[2]

Even a brief snapshot of those turbulent decades reminds the observer of the massive nature of the social and political convulsions the Asian peoples were experiencing:

- Vietnam: A brutal war ended, sending hundreds of thousands of refugees fleeing. Communists united the country, but eventually struggled to integrate a socialist and capitalist economy.

- China: Chairman Mao died, and with his passing the Cultural Revolution ended. China opened to the West and also entered the capitalist world while its attitudes toward human rights remained abysmal.

- Philippines: The dictator Ferdinand Marcos was thrown out through a Peoples' Power revolution, much of it involving the support of Catholic religious and lay leaders. President Corazon Aquino was ushered in on the wings of long-harnessed democratic sentiments. But these could not stop the country's generals from continuing to meddle in government politics.

- Cambodia: Pol Pot and the Khmer Rouge, spawned by a U.S.-inspired invasion, committed genocide against their people, killing an estimated two million before Vietnamese troops invaded the country and put an end to the misery.

- Hong Kong, Singapore, Taipei, Seoul, and Tokyo: These islands of prosperity enjoyed unprecedented new wealth—and population.

It was in the early 1970s that the Asian bishops first outlined their hopes for the future of their churches. Their blueprint was their triple dialogue, with the poor, with Asian cultures, and with Asian religions. Their plan was intended to integrate their churches deeper into the Asian psyche while moving them to focus beyond the churches to meet the pressing human needs, spiritual and physical, of their peoples. The point is that, for the moment and at least in theory, the Asian leadership had aligned their church visions with the real hopes and aspirations of their peoples, aspirations that involved both spiritual and physical needs. In the midst of the unsettling times, the bishops understood the need for both meaning and liberation, for grounding and for the fulfillment that comes from being an active subject in determining one's own destiny.

Through countless seminars, papers, pastoral centers, homilies, assessments, reevaluations, and outreach programs, the Asian leadership slowly gave life to their vision. Gains were slow but real, even as they were incremental and uneven. The 1970s and 1980s took their toll on most Asians. They were decades of historic social, economic, and cultural shifts. If a vast continent can be characterized as having a mood, then the Asian bishops probably reflected that mood over the years. In 1970, when they received Pope Paul VI in Manila, they were hopeful and optimistic. By 1990, the year the FABC met for its fifth time in a plenary assembly, in Bandung, Indonesia, the Asian bishops were still hopeful, as Christians are called to be, but they were less certain of the path ahead and seemingly less optimistic. There was just so much dislocation, so many unemployed, so much suffering—and the larger world seemed so indifferent. Contemplating Asia but failing to consider the gravity of human suffering caused by poverty is to miss a widespread human condition. Contemplating the Asian churches but failing to take into consideration the importance of the episcopal decision to enter into solidarity with the poor is to miss the wider Catholic Asian story.

Inspired through the 1960s, the international community was poised to take on Third World poverty in the 1970s. The words "international development" had become household words. Paul VI reflected this optimism in his 1967 encyclical *Populorum Progressio*. Peace, he wrote, "is something that is built up day after day in the pursuit of an order intended by God, which implies a more perfect form of justice among people." In 1970, the Asian bishops shared this assessment. Good work by good people would make the difference. The world's nations seemed committed to the task. By 1990 it was a different story. The promises of rich nations had gone largely unfulfilled, and the tasks seemed so much larger, so much more complex. The sense of initial optimism had disappeared and was being replaced by a new sense of resignation, a kind of acceptance that poverty was the inevitable by-product of change. From the perspective of the poor nations there was a sense of letdown, even betrayal.

This wider sense of pessimism found its way into international development gatherings, including the fortieth birthday celebration of the United Nations Development Program, held in October 1990 in Antalya, Turkey. The gathering's subdued mood was captured in the remark of a diplomat to a journalist: "Listen and don't quote me, because I am going to be very indiscreet. . . . The impression the world has been given for 20 years now is that the donor countries are opening a treasure chest for the poor, but it's nothing but trinkets, just well wrapped trinkets. The rich countries know it and so do the poor. . . . Aid fatigue has set in."[3] There was reason for pessimism. The economic figures coming out of the Antalya meeting that year were not good. During the 1980s, the group was told, resources from rich to poor nations actually reversed from a positive flow of $42.6 billion to a negative flow of $32.5 billion. Aid experts further reported that development funding would have to triple from its then $12 billion level simply to keep up with a 5 percent growth rate, and that food production for more than four hundred million people was failing to match population growth. United Nations figures also revealed that by 1990 the West's contribution to development aid had fallen to a miserable 0.09 percent of GDP (Gross Domestic Product)—and that 30 percent of that aid was going to service poor nation debts.

Other statistics began to fill out the grim global portrait, which only got worse in the 1990s.[4]

- 1.3 billion people, most of these in Asia, were surviving on $1 a day.

- 3 billion people were surviving on $2 a day.

- The income gap between the top fifth and lowest fifth of the world's people was getting wider: 7 to 1 in 1870, 11 to 1 in 1913, 30 to 1 in 1960, 60 to 1 in 1990, and 74 to 1 in 1997.

- The world's 225 richest individuals have a combined wealth of over $1 trillion—equal to the annual income of the poorest 47 percent of the entire world's population.

- Poor countries paid $270 billion in debt service in 1996—$60 per person, rising from $160 billion in 1990.

Additionally, by 1990, the fifth of the world's people that lived in the highest-income countries enjoyed:

- 86 percent of the world GDP

- 68 percent of all foreign direct investment

By 1990, the fifth of the world's people living in the lowest-income countries had:

- 1 percent of the world GDP

- 1 percent of all foreign direct investment

In 1990, assessing the state of world poverty, Maurice Strong, Secretary General of a United Nations Conference on Environment and Development held in 1992, attempted to shake the world awake to the dimensions of the problem, saying, "There is simply no future for the planet without a global war on poverty. It's just not feasible for the resource base and the environment to be maintained when people are being forced, through poverty, to destroy the base on which they depend."

There was momentary relief when the sudden collapse of the Soviet Union sent shock waves through Europe and the United States, sparking short-lived talk of "new peace dividends." But these were never cashed in. It was not long before the West, led by the United States, was once again heading into war. On August 2, 1990, Iraq invaded Kuwait, setting off the Gulf War, drying up the "peace dividend."

Meanwhile, the defeat of Soviet Communism meant that the West's economic policies, spreading across the globe, were virtually unchallenged. Globalization began to represent an intricate web of finance interactions, including mind-numbing speculation and trading, that had taken on a life of its own. As some in the West debated the impact of globalization, the East knew at least one thing for sure: It was having a devastating effect on traditional cultures. Asian nations were being inundated, as never before, with Western images, foods, and values. Kentucky Fried Chicken and McDonald's restaurants were proliferating. The young generation began to forsake traditions, snapping up Nike shoes and Banana Republic T-shirts, among other Western fads. None of this was exactly new, but the speed of change was.

As early as 1978 the Asian bishops had a good idea what secularization and the emerging global economy would bring to their traditional communities—and they were already worried. Consider the assessment they offered in the final statement of the FABC second plenary assembly, in Calcutta, in November 1978.

> The modern world, despite its undeniably great achievements, brings about the gradual disintegration of our traditional societies and the effects on people's lives that follow on it. The loss of a sense of belonging in community, depersonalized relationships, disorientation and loneliness,—these have become part of the lives of so many of our people. With its accompanying secularization, too, with its worship of technology, narrow materialism and secularism, its fever for consumerism, its ideological pluralism—realized in diverse ways in different societies—our age quite swiftly erodes religious values and often suffocates the aspirations of the human spirit, especially among the young. The generations growing up in our time tend to lose the sense of God, the sense of his presence in the world, of his providence over their lives.[5]

In the early 1970s, the Asian bishops, recognizing the dimensions of the challenges, decided to seek partners. They opened talks with other religious leaders. This decision helped contribute to transforming Catholic attitudes—as well as the way Catholics began to be perceived by the other religions of Asia. Catholics, approaching other religions more openly, unleashed good will. Nevertheless, the decades that followed witnessed interreligious tensions, particularly in areas where Muslims and Christians lived side by side.

During the Cold War, many in Asia perceived the world as largely divided between the U.S. and Soviet blocs. After the Cold War, the perception of an "East–West" bipolar world started to give way to another one, a "North–South," rich–poor, bipolar world, especially in Islamic Asia. The Gulf War also played into this perception. Extremist Muslims took advantage of this perception, connecting Christianity with rich persecutors and Islam with the poor persecuted. Attacks against Christians in Muslim countries such as Pakistan and Indonesia grew. Muslim–Christian tensions in the southern Philippines festered. In India, pockets of Hindu extremists began to target Christians. Upper-caste Hindus, threatened by Christians who worked to empower and convert low-caste *dalit*s and tribals, began targeting Christians.

In the early 1970s, the Asian bishops decided they needed to engage their churches more deeply in the lives of the peoples and places of Asia. They needed to "dialogue" with Asian cultures, meaning that they needed to inculturate the Catholic faith. This represented sound strategy both as a protective measure and in order to touch more actively the core sentiments and needs of the people. This placed the Asian leadership in a kind of a bind. On the one hand, the Vatican cautioned the Asians to go slow on inculturation. On the other hand, Asian nationalists were targeting Catholics, whom they viewed as maintaining close ties to the West. These contradictory pressures sparked intense questions among the Asian leadership concerning the nature of Catholic identity. These issues were to linger and fester. The last time the Asian bishops gathered in plenary session, in Thailand in January 2000, for example, one workshop focused on the causes of violence against Catholics in Asia. The workshop listed the following as three major reasons for it:

- The growth of small nondenominational Christian evangelical groups who have purposely isolated themselves from local cultures and traditions. These Christian fundamentalists openly condemn the majority religions, like Islam, Hinduism, and Buddhism in their attempts to convert people to Christianity. Catholics get lumped in with these groups.

- The visibility of Catholic outreach programs that have concentrated on their own communities, further isolating Catholics from the mainstream.

- The growth of conservative Catholics—helped by some in the Vatican—who oppose renewal efforts and are becoming vocal to the extent of dividing the community and thus paralyzing local churches from adapting to change in conformity with the needs of the times.[6]

CHRISTIAN–MUSLIM CONFLICT

In some Muslim nations Christian evangelization continues to be illegal. Laws spawn acts of persecution against Christians. World attention focused briefly on Pakistani blasphemy laws when on May 6, 1998, Pakistani Bishop John Joseph of Faisalabad, in a desperate attempt to draw attention to ongoing persecution, stood outside a courthouse and shot himself in the head with a pistol. A few days before Joseph shot himself, a Christian man, Ayub Masih, had been condemned to death at the courthouse for blasphemy against Islam. His alleged crime was that he had spoken favorably of British author Salman Rushdie, author of *The Satanic Verses*. Muslim officials called for Rushdie's death in 1989, forcing him into hiding. Joseph said the charges against Ayub Masih had been trumped up to force fifteen Christian families out in a local land dispute. For Joseph, the persecution of Ayub Masih symbolized the plight of all Christians in Pakistan. Masih—a name given to all Christians in Pakistan—was the fourth Christian sentenced to death for blasphemy in that country since the early 1990s.[7]

While religiously motivated violence between Muslims and Christians has been isolated, when it has flared up it has been bloody. Often Muslim–Christian violence results from complex social, political, economic, and cultural conditions. The disturbing fact is that these conflicts tend to become simplified to a confrontation between Christians and Muslims. One of the most publicized conflicts began on January 19, 1999, as Muslims around the world were celebrating the end of the fasting month. On that day a fight broke out on the island of Ambon in Indonesia between a Christian public transport driver and a Muslim youth. Such fights were commonplace, but this one escalated into a feud between Christians and Muslims that continued for months. Much of the central part of the city of Ambon, the capital of Maluku province, and many neighborhoods in other parts of Ambon and neighboring islands were eventually burned to the ground. Some thirty thousand people were displaced in the conflict, which took thousands of lives.

Some religious conflicts have deep historical roots. In the Philippines, Muslim–Christian conflict dates back to the colonial times of the sixteenth-century Spanish conquistadors. These conflicts continued during the period of American rule and through the postcolonial period. At the beginning of the 1970s, the Muslim minority on Mindanao, in the southern Philippines, relaunched its struggle for an independent Islamic state. Under Marcos, the Philippine army responded with force, sending the army to put down the rebels. After an agreement was signed in 1976, allowing partial autonomy, fighting resumed in 1978. After years of guerilla warfare, President Aquino's government, in 1989, offered administrative autonomy to the thirteen provinces, but only four accepted. Rebel forces numbering some fifteen thousand have been launching terrorist attacks and kidnappings since.

Reacting to complex social, economic, and political shifts, the Asian theologians continued to reflect on the life of Jesus and what he means to diverse Asians. Through these efforts the essentials of the triple dialogue have held up well. At the center is the idea of liberation from social injustice, a theme generally bypassed and neglected by much Western Christology—with the exception of the liberation theologians. The uniquely Asian contribution to Catholic Christology, growing out of the context of Asia in the late twentieth century, has been the linkage of the Christian social justice mission with Asian spirituality, a linkage of a dialogue with the poor and a dialogue with other religions. The Asian theologian most noted for making this link has been Aloysius Pieris of Sri Lanka, who once wrote that "our desperate search for the Asian face of Christ can find fulfillment only if we participate in Asia's own search for it in the unfathomable abyss where religion and poverty seem to have the same common source: God, who has declared mammon his enemy" (Matt. 6:24). Thus, the "church must be given time to step into the baptismal waters of Asian religion and to pass through passion and death on the cross of Asian poverty. Until this ecclesiological revolution is complete, there will be no Asian Christology."[8]

BANDUNG

As central as the "triple dialogue" had become to Asian Catholic thinking, it seemed under sharp attack as the bishops gathered in Bandung, Indonesia, in July 1990 for their fifth plenary session. Larger historical forces sweeping through Asia, growing pressures in Rome, and internal episcopal doubts had clouded the future. The bishops had come to a crossroads. Prayerful discernment was required. Looking back, church observers still recognize the importance of the moment. Felix Wilfred, the noted Indian theologian, called Bandung "one of the most important moments in FABC history."[9] Had the bishops been naïve? Overly ambitious? Faced with increased poverty, secularization, fragmentation of cultures, a rise in religious extremism, and scrutiny in Rome, might the bishops now reconsider their commitments in Bandung? The moment called for decisive leadership. It seemed appropriate to have chosen a forward-looking theme for their gathering: "Journeying Together toward the Third Millennium." As noted in the preceding chapter, the meeting began with an address by Joseph Tomko, Prefect of the Congregation for the Evangelization of Peoples. It was his first plenary gathering. His critical remarks raised serious questions about the directions of Asian theologians and Asian pastoral approaches. The Asian bishops, always polite, always hospitable, listened carefully. Then for the next ten days they labored in workshops, and discussed the future as they shared meals and prayers. They knew they would have to affirm the course they were on or set a new one. Whatever they did, their words would send out echoes throughout the church.

The deliberations led to the writing of a final statement that began with a sober assessment of the times. Asia, they wrote, not only faces a crisis; it faces "a crisis of survival." They acknowledged the influx of new wealth into the region but added, "It has benefited mainly a tiny elite." The context they found themselves in, the bishops explained, had its roots in the colonial period and was still causing division and oppression in the present. They wrote:

> A striking change in many of our societies is the breakdown of the nation-state. Typically the nation-state in Asia was usually the creation of the colonial powers; boundaries were set up with little regard for traditional ethnic and cultural groupings. Hence, it is not surprising that we now witness a variety of "secessionist" movements, and, tragically, widespread ethnic and communal conflict and violence. One reaction to this situation is the growth of "statism"—the imposition of artificial harmony through oppressive state power.

On the rise of fundamentalism, they wrote:

> Elsewhere, the struggle for power spawns militant fundamentalism, by which a majority group or a powerful minority imposes its values on the rest of society. Religious fundamentalism has its attraction to some believers for primarily religious reasons. But such attraction is too often exploited by persons and groups whose motive is political power and social control, or economic greed.

On modernization, they wrote:

> Modernization offers bright promise for our future. Even so, the whole process of modernization is fraught with ambiguity. Modernization often leads to social and cultural dislocation. Traditional values and attitudes are called into question. Traditional symbols lose their power. The beneficiaries of modernization are too often infected with secularism, materialism and consumerism. In some countries there has arisen a new middle class which is highly consumerist and competitive, and in general insensitive and indifferent to the overwhelming majority of poor and marginalized people.

On poverty and migration, they wrote:

> Poverty likewise drives both men and women to become migrant workers, often destroying family life in the process. Political con-

flict and economic desperation have driven millions to become refugees, to living for years in camps that are sometimes in effect crowded prisons. Within many Asian societies, graft and corruption remain a source of serious injustice.

On exploitation of the young, they wrote:

Asia is home to vast numbers of young people. But too many of them face a future of unemployment and consequent frustration. The most basic and fundamental human right to life is denied to the unborn child by the practice of abortion. Child labor (even bonded labor) is still prevalent. Our youth, who are 60 percent of the Asian population, tend to be influenced by an education, the media and social pressures which perpetuate this reality of injustice, and youth themselves are often victims.

On human rights and oppression, they wrote:

Connected too with these injustices are other violations of human rights. We see forms of cultural imperialism, with the imposition of majority values, or of values of an assertive minority on the rest of society. Access to education and employment is denied or limited on the basis of religion, caste, political stance, economic status, or ethnic origin. Those in these societies and elsewhere who speak and act in the name of justice are subject to imprisonment and other forms of punishment. All of these injustices are interconnected. Taken together, they amount to a crisis of survival.

On injustice and exploitation, they wrote:

We are deeply conscious, therefore, that within our context of change there is the unchanging reality of injustice. There remains in Asia massive poverty. Hundreds of millions of people are debarred from access to natural resources. Exploitation of the environment destroys precious resources and thus destroys the material and spiritual habitat of many of our peoples. Militarization involves the wasting of scarce resources on armies and armaments rather than the using of these resources to meet genuine and pressing human needs. Traditional patterns of discrimination against women continue in force. In situations of poverty and injustice it is usually women who suffer the most. We see this in the flourishing of exploitative tourism, where women and children are driven into prostitution—this is both a matter of sexual morality and also a matter of structural injustice.[10]

The Asian bishops' assessment of the times cut no corners. Having set the context, they then went on clearly and without qualification to reiterate their commitment to the poor, to inculturation, and to dialogue. There was no wavering. They would not change course. The course they had been on for nearly two decades was, in their opinion, the correct one, and they had to go forward whatever criticisms might come their way. Whatever the cost.

Years later, Bandung would stand out in the minds of many of the Asian Catholic leaders as a pivotal moment. In 1974 the Asian bishops, at their first FABC plenary assembly, invited the churches of Asia to join into dialogue. Now at Bandung the bishops strongly affirmed that approach. They reiterated their commitments. The Asian response to the gospel demands was to push forward. Christianity was about liberation—total liberation from poverty, hunger, and economic exploitation as well as from the new materialistic values sweeping through Asia.

Addressing their mission at Bandung, the Asian bishops offered an alternative path and an alternative ecclesiology, one they felt fit Asian needs. They wrote:

> Mission includes: being with the people, responding to their needs, with sensitiveness to the presence of God in cultures and other religious traditions, and witnessing to the values of God's Kingdom through presence, solidarity, sharing and word. Mission will mean a dialogue with Asia's poor, with its local cultures, and with other religious traditions.[11]

Entering into a dialogue with culture only enhanced the bishops' desire to preserve Asia's traditional values—respect for spirit, for community, for transcendence—and moved them to become a louder countercultural voice against the growing secular materialism and the neo-liberal economics spreading from the West. Over the years different theologians have commented on this Asian Catholic perspective and the challenges it posed. Some years later, Jesuit Michael Amaladoss, professor of theology at Vidyajyoti College in New Delhi, India, spoke about the call to be countercultural. He put the challenge this way:

> We are reflecting during these days on the impact of the dominant liberal capitalist economic and commercial systems on our societies and on the challenges they pose to us as witnesses to Jesus' Good News of the Reign of God. The poor are not only increasing in number but are becoming poorer. The resources of the earth, common to all, are being abused by a few and depleted and destroyed. Social

inequalities follow the growing economic inequalities and give rise to tensions and violent conflicts. We have seen how the economic and commercial systems are supported by the political systems, whatever be their democratic façades. The political regimes are further sustained by military systems that impose internal and external control to facilitate economic and commercial activity. The military systems are in turn promoted and sustained by the industrial complex through the production and sale of arms. We are also realizing how this network of exploitation and control today has global dimensions. We understand how the monetisation of the economy has given rise to financial markets in which, through speculation, money makes more money. We realize that the only effective way of witnessing to and promoting the Reign of God in this situation is to adopt a two-pronged strategy. On the one hand we have to show in practice that people can meet their needs through alternative technologies and alternative economic and commercial practices. On the other hand the people must progressively gain participative control of the systems that govern their lives and, in this manner, humanize and socialize them. This strategy has to be pioneered by small groups of people who link themselves into networks, nationally and internationally, to put pressure on the powers that be so as to bring about progressive change. I would like to suggest that such a strategy will not be effective unless it is accompanied by a cultural transformation, namely a change in people's world-views and systems of values. The roots of such a cultural transformation will be a spirituality that motivates, inspires, and enables people to search for a fuller life for all. Any spirituality today, in a world of religious pluralism, can only be human and global, cutting across religious frontiers. The mission of the Good News in such a context requires counter-cultural communities who do not believe in the power of money or numbers or even of truth, perceived in the abstract, but in the power of the Spirit and in their own call to serve.[12]

Peter C. Phan, professor of religion and culture in the department of religion and religious education at the Catholic University of America, called the Asian bishops' views on mission nothing short of a "Copernican revolution." Putting their vision into an ecclesial context, he says, it "de-centers the church in the sense that it makes the center of the Christian life not the church but the Reign of God." The Asian bishops continued to say, Phan explains, that their mission is not to expand the church and its structures in order to enlarge its sphere of influence, but rather "to be a transparent sign and effective instrument of the saving presence of the Reign of God, the reign of justice, peace, and love, of which the church is a seed."

The Asian bishops at Bandung spoke of their determination to hold to the mission of building the reign of God. Their call was to work for justice and peace and to do this in communion with the poor. This is how Catholicism would put an Asian face on Jesus. This is how they would bring life to the gospel. This is how they would critique the material order. Five years later, they recommitted themselves to continuing their journey at their sixth plenary meeting in Manila:

> We Asians are searching not simply for the meaning of life but for life itself. We are striving and struggling for life, because it is a task and a challenge. But life is a gift too, a mystery, because our efforts to achieve it are far too short of the ultimate values of life. We speak of life as a becoming—a growing into, a journeying to life and the source of life.[13]

However, the Asian bishops were not the only Catholics with their eyes on the road ahead. Pope John Paul II had been giving a lot of thought to the subject as he pondered Asia and the new millennium. In November 1994 he caught the church by surprise when he announced in an apostolic letter entitled *Tertio Millennio Adveniente* his plans to hold several regional synods as part of the millennial preparation. One of these would be a synod on Asia. In his letter he cited an "urgent need for a synod" to "illustrate and explain more fully the truth that Christ is the one Mediator between God and man and the sole Redeemer of the world, to be clearly distinguished from the founders of other great religions." The Asian bishops were among those who were surprised by the call for a synod. They had not asked for a synod. They did not share the pope's sense of urgency. The Asian bishops did not publicly disagree with the pope's assessment, but it worried more than a few. At a minimum the bishop of Rome and the bishops of Asia had differing ideas about church priorities and which issues posed the greatest challenges to the future of Asian Catholics. With a synod coming, these differences were bound to become more public in the years ahead.

CHAPTER 11

Called to Rome

*These are the elements of crucial
importance in the task of preaching
the Gospel in Asia, today:*

· Inculturation, *which renders the
local church truly present within the
life of our people.*

· Dialogue *with the great Asian religions,
which brings them into contact with the
Gospel, so that the seed of the Word in
them may come to full flower.*

· Service of the poor, *uniting with them
in their struggle for a more human world.*
      —Asian bishops, Manila, 1970

The idea of a synod on Asia took the church, Asian Catholics included, by surprise. Word first surfaced in Pope John Paul's Apostolic Letter *Tertio Millennio Adveniente* (The Coming of the Third Millennium), which he promulgated on November 10, 1994, five years to the day from the fall of the Berlin Wall. Pope John Paul has been an anniversary-conscious pope; the date was not accidental. It was his way of saying, "With Communism behind us, we can move freely with Christ into the future." His exhortation focused on preparations for the millennial celebration. Part of that preparation was to include a series of regional synods—on America, Asia, Oceania, and Europe—each within the theme of "evangelization." More specifically, the pope spoke of "the new evangelization." The Special Assembly of the Synod of Bishops for Asia took place from April 19 through May 14, 1998, in Rome. It included bishops from the Middle East, the Persian Gulf countries, South Asian countries, Central Asian countries, Southeast Asian countries, Asian Siberia, and the countries of the Far East.[1]

Synods go far back into Christian history. In modern times the idea resurfaced at Vatican II as council fathers grappled with the issue of how to maintain the spirit of collegiality after the bishops had returned to their dioceses at the end of the council. Their answer was to hold periodic synods at which the bishops of the world would gather with the pope to think and act collectively to chart the course of the church. Specific guidelines, however, were not drawn up as to how the process would take place. After early attempts following the council to draft synod statements, the bishops found that it is easier simply to make recommendations and leave the final word to the pope. Quickly the synods became consultative in nature.

At the time John Paul announced the plan for the regional synods there had been fourteen since the council. The initial intention was to have them serve as a counterbalance to traditional Vatican bureaucracy, a meaningful step toward true collegiality. However, Vatican machinery eventually took over synod planning and procedures. By 1994, synods had become watered down and somewhat predictable. As for the synods themselves, the appointed bishops would come to Rome, would take turns sharing eight-minute presentations in the synod hall and would gather in language groups to discuss the ideas selected by Vatican officials from the presentations. The whole process distilled controversy and led to bland recommendations set before the pope. It has been said that the whole synod process was like taking a feast of tasty dishes and blending them into a tasteless porridge.

Over the years I attended five synods as a journalist. A principal frustration has been that they are always conducted in secret. The press is not allowed into the synod hall to listen and report. The penchant for Vatican secrecy is legendary. The argument offered for secrecy is that some episcopal comments—for example, those made by bishops living in nations hostile to the church—should not be made public. The media has responded, saying it could accommodate, but the Vatican has not relented. Sadly, the life and vitality of the church, as seen in the varied views of the bishops, are not adequately shared as a result of the cloak of secrecy. Within the inner circles of church power, disagreement is viewed as a sign of weakness, not health. Even initial comments made during the first week of the month-long synod, which the Vatican distills before handing them out to the press, are not debated. Each bishop simply reads his statement and sits down. There is no discussion.

The normal synod process begins some two years before a synod, when the Vatican sends to the bishops its ideas about the topics to be discussed. The document is called a *Lineamenta*. In the case of the Synod on Asia, Rome sent out the *Lineamenta* to forty Asian conferences on September 3, 1996. Most Asian episcopal conferences used it as an occasion to evaluate their pastoral work and goals. Many engaged in consultative processes before writing their responses. Once the responses were sent back to Rome, they were to be gathered by the Secretary General of the Synods of Bishops, Cardinal Jan P. Schotte, who was responsible for running the synod. His staff was to take the papers and from them write a new document called the *Instrumentum laboris*, the synod's official working document. Officially called a Special Assembly for Asia of the Synod of Bishops, its theme was "Jesus Christ the Savior and His Mission of Love and Service in Asia: ' . . . That They May Have Life, and Have It Abundantly.'"

The Asian synod *Lineamenta* released by Rome took the form of a seventy-page booklet, published in English and French. It was divided into an introduction, six chapters, and a conclusion. A series of questions related to each of the chapters. In the preface, Schotte noted that the announcement of the synod first appeared in John Paul's Apostolic Letter *Tertio Millennio Adveniente* and went on to explain that the *Instrumentum laboris* would be developed using responses received in Rome before August 1, 1997. Chapter 1 of the *Lineamenta* offered a description of the real-life situations in Asia today, highlighting the fact that Asia has had a proud history of being the mother of many races, peoples, and religions and that "the cultural and religious values on the continent are deeply felt and enduring. . . ." Chapter 2 presented highlights from the history of evangelization in Asia, pointing to the accomplishments of the early Syrian Church in India, the work of the Franciscan missionaries in the thirteenth century and that of the Jesuits in the sixteenth century. Chapter 3 developed a presentation of a Christian anthropology in which the work of the Triune God is illustrated along with "Asia's natural longing for God and the fullness of life." Chapter 4 was a theological presentation of salvation in Jesus Christ, treating Christ as the one and only Savior. Chapter 5 painted the work of the church as continuing the mission of Jesus Christ in the Spirit. Chapter 6 called for a renewed understanding of mission in Asia today and concluded by highlighting "the role of Mary, Mother and Model of Evangelization." The conclusion of the *Lineamenta* spoke of the need to use the synod to spawn spiritual renewal in Asia and to usher in a "new beginning" in evangelization efforts in Asia.

The response of the bishops of Japan was the first to surface publicly in 1998, several months before the opening of the synod. It quickly became world news. The Japanese bishops offered a stinging rejection of the proposed synod agenda—and the first indication that this synod would be anything but ordinary. Putting Asian diplomacy aside, the Japanese bishops were forceful and direct in their rebuke of the outline of subjects proposed by Rome. They said flatly that the synod cannot succeed if non-Asian, Vatican directives were to determine the content and process of the gathering. Then instead of answering questions asked by the Vatican's *Lineamenta,* they came up with a list of their own issues and questions, proposing a synod more in tune with their views of Asian realities. The stark tone of the Japanese document revealed serious tensions between them and Rome. It underscored serious differences with regard to issues of culture, theology, and mission. It represented a radical repudiation of the Roman approach to running synods. "Since the questions of the *Lineamenta* were composed in the context of Western Christianity, they are not suitable," the Japanese bishops wrote. "From the way the questions are proposed, one feels that the holding of the synod is like an occasion for the central office to evaluate the performance of the branch offices." To succeed, the Japanese bishops stated, the issues addressed and the process by which they are addressed must stem from the minds of Asians, not Vatican officials. "The decision concerning the global direction of the synod should not be made by the Roman secretariat, but should be left to the bishops from Asia."

The Japanese bishops went on to say that language barriers further complicate the synod. Just translating the *Lineamenta* took three months, they noted. They then suggested that:

- all synod proceedings include Asian languages in addition to the Italian, English, French, German, and Spanish normally used in synods;

- extra time be given to translating the synod's working document, the *Instrumentum laboris*, into Asian languages;

- provisions be made for simultaneous translation of synod speakers from English and French into Asian languages;

- activities be included to "work toward . . . a new paradigm to include the varying realities and cultures of Asia" and its spiritual traditions;

- the synod's agenda not be determined until after it has been convened and Asian bishops decide on it;

- committee chairpersons be chosen by the Asian bishops and not by Vatican bureaucrats; and

- participating bishops be permitted to consult with experts chosen by the local bishops.

The Japanese bishops' document paid special attention to the then twenty-five-year-old Federation of Asian Bishops' Conferences, the FABC, saying that its deliberations were not adequately represented in the Vat-

ican *Lineamenta*. The Japanese bishops proposed that the practice of having a succession of bishops give reports be replaced with greater reliance
on the conclusions of representatives of the two blocs of bishops who
would make up the synod, the East Asian, or FABC bishops, and the Middle East Asian bishops. This, they said, would focus the scope of the
synod and assure a better chance of developing a concrete plan. The
Japanese bishops further suggested that language groups be dissolved
and replaced with clusters of bishops who meet around themes or religious cultures. They asked for the involvement of women, pointing out
that women are frequently objects of discrimination in Asia. They called
for inviting "experts in dialogue" from other religious traditions. Admitting that Catholicism in Asia faces formidable challenges, the Japanese
bishops said that the synod must not be aimed at "discovering how the
Asian church can be propped up by the Western church," but rather
must be a meeting in which the bishops of Asia "have an honest
exchange and learn how they can support and encourage one another."
The Japanese bishops said they found a "defensiveness" in the *Lineamenta*, especially in its Christology. "If we stress too much that 'Jesus
Christ is the one and only Savior,' we can have no dialogue, common
living or solidarity with other religions," they wrote. "The church, learning from the '*kenosis*' of Jesus Christ, should be humble and open its
heart to other religions to deepen its understanding of the mystery of
Christ." They deplored the image of the church in the *Lineamenta*, saying that it "is not as rich or deep as that of Vatican II, especially the
images of 'the church as people of God' and 'the church as servant'"
which, they said, are not stressed. "These two images have special meaning for the church in Asia, which in order to serve God's kingdom lives
in a minority position with and for others." The Japanese bishops said
that the "proclamation of Christ," stressed over and over in the *Lineamenta*, must give way to dialogue with other religions. In place of a
spirit of triumphalism, they emphasized the need for "compassion with
the suffering" if evangelization is to be successful. The Japanese bishops
reminded Rome that the association with the poor "has been the central
evangelization theme" to emerge from repeated FABC meetings. The
Western mind thinks in terms of distinctions, and these are found in the
Lineamenta, the Japanese bishops pointed out. "In the *Lineamenta* a
great deal is made, as in traditional scholastic theology, of 'distinctions'
and 'differences.' However, in the tradition of the Far East, it is characteristic to search for creative harmony rather than distinctions," the
bishops wrote. They went on to criticize the *Lineamenta*'s evaluation for
success in missionary efforts, rejecting number counting and stressing
instead fidelity to mission.

The Japanese bishops then proposed topics they would like to see discussed at the synod:

- development of Asian theology "based not on a Christ whom we only grasp in our minds, but who speaks to us in our hearts through his living presence and activity"

- a study of evangelization that includes a look at "the limits felt to the 'Western-type' of missionary activity used up to now"

- development of Asian celebrations and liturgies

- new commitments to living in solidarity with the poor

- efforts to form public sentiment toward respect for human life, human rights, social justice, peace, freedom and solidarity

- inculturation of the gospel in dialogue with other religions.

The Japanese bishops concluded their document with a plea to Rome to reconsider its relationships with local churches, a relationship "not based on 'centralization' but on 'collegiality.'" In terms of substantive theology, the Japanese response said little that had not been said by Asian bishops in their FABC papers and in their many gatherings in its twenty-five-year history. What was distinctly different, however, was the exasperated tone of the response. It read like a last-ditch effort to ward off a failed synod, a final plea to Rome to end its seemingly imperial attitude toward the Asian churches. As word of the Japanese response began to circulate, largely by means of the Internet, it began to send quiet shock waves through the church.[2]

An examination of more than a dozen responses from East and Southeast Asian bishops' conferences to the synod preparatory document, published in the *National Catholic Reporter*, revealed serious differences between the Asian bishops and Vatican officials on matters of church theologies and governance—starting, as one saw in the Japanese bishops' response, with the very purpose and process of the synod itself.[3] The degree of East Asian disillusionment was underscored by a request contained in the Indonesian bishops' response calling upon the synod to establish a mechanism "responsible for exploring the possibility of an East Asian patriarchate, at least endowed with autonomy comparable to that of the patriarchates in Oriental churches of the near East." This would, the suggestion reasoned, "relativize the primacy of the 'Western' church and enhance authentic inculturation of Christian faith." A patriarch has jurisdiction over all bishops, clergy, and people in a territory or in a specified rite (such as the Roman, Melchite, or Syrian rite). The division of the church into patriarchates goes back to the early years of Christianity. The Council of Nicaea, in 325, recognized the patriarchal status of Alexandria and Jerusalem in its canons and by inference that of Rome. By the time of Justinian, the title was reserved to these three sees plus Constantinople and Antioch. Patriarchates are an example of subsidiarity in church government. Each patriarch is responsible—according to the *New Catholic Encyclopedia*—"for the election of the bishops of his patriarchate in the best possible way."

While the length and tone of the Asian responses varied, most shared common visions, including strong commitments to inculturation, to the poor, to social justice, and to dialogue with other Asian religions. This seems altogether understandable, as these had been the themes developed by the bishops through the FABC in the twenty-five years that preceded the call to the synod. The responses also showed episcopal frustrations with growing centralization of authority in Rome. The Asian bishops' responses sent a united message to Rome: Evangelization efforts not grounded in Asian realities and Asian sensitivities are certain to fail.

On another front, the Asian bishops shared with Rome their deep concerns with the growth of Western consumer values brought on by the new economic forces they were feeling. Nearly every response made reference to a growing gap between rich and poor, further dividing the peoples of Asia. Besides the Japanese bishops, other Asian bishops also made it clear to Rome that they are not satisfied with some key suppositions in the synod preparatory document. The bishops' conference of Indonesia also took issue with the growth in centralized church authority. Citing Vatican II collegiality initiatives, the Indonesian bishops stated that "the specific responses of Asian churches should come out clearly as their contribution to the universal church as a 'communion of communities.'" They, too, said that evangelization as outlined in the *Lineamenta* "does not adequately reflect" the longtime approach of the FABC, which had encouraged the "triple-dialogue" with the poor, other religions, and cultures.

The chapter headings of the *Lineamenta* had an ecclesial focus in the eyes of some bishops' conferences—"Asian Realities," "Evangelization," "God's Salvific Design in History," "Jesus Christ as Savior to All," "Church as Communion," and "The Church's Mission of Love and Service in Asia"—moving them to criticize the format for being too institutionally oriented and not stressing enough the pastoral nature of the church. The *Lineamenta* had attempted to focus the synod on the theme "Jesus Christ as unique Savior of Asia." It stated that the primary task of the bishops of Asia is to "proclaim" Jesus Christ to all. Proclamation becomes the essential task, and dialogue with other religions is rooted in the clarity of this proclamation, the document stated. "The church in Asia has and wants to proclaim Jesus Christ to her brothers and sisters on the continent so that they may be enriched by the inexhaustible riches of

Jesus Christ," it said. "In turn, the church shall be enriched by the profound seeds of truth and goodness present among them through dialogue." The Asian bishops' conferences often responded that dialogue with other religions comes first and that in Asia it is the means of effective proclamation. For its part, the *Lineamenta* took a cautious, even at times suspicious, approach to interfaith dialogue. For example, it warned the Asian bishops against "false inculturation," which, it said, can occur when the focus of dialogue is not placed on Jesus Christ. "The church cannot abandon her faith in Jesus Christ for the sake of a false inculturation or irenicism, despite the fact that Asia has such a wide variety of cultures and religions," the *Lineamenta* stated. "If she did, the church would not be true to herself. It must be admitted that a Trinitarian faith may indeed be a stumbling block to cultures that are so diverse. Yet, if this faith is lived in love, service and humility, it will receive increasing acceptance, as it has at all times in the history of evangelization." The *Lineamenta* went on: "This lays a heavy responsibility on church leaders that they become truly Christlike in their lives. A life of witness wins hearts, not theoretical doctrines. . . . The Christian apostle is not just a social worker; nor is the Christian faith merely an ideology or a humanistic program."

Proclamation versus witnessing the faith: this issue of contention was to arise again and again in later exchanges between the Vatican and Asian bishops. The *Lineamenta* insisted that evangelization's primary task is to "proclaim" Jesus Christ as Savior. It lamented:

> for several theoretical and historical reasons, an opinion has been expressed from some quarters in Asia during the last three decades that the age of mission is over. Now is the time for dialogue and inculturation. Radical pluralism of religion and salvation seems to become a dogma itself. At times, one's culture is so absolutized that conversion is looked upon as violence done to the other. Others claim that the church's mission is only the proclamation of the values of the Kingdom, human promotion and liberation.

The *Lineamenta* insisted this is the wrong path. It stressed:

> the primacy of the proclamation of Jesus Christ in all evangelizing activities has been repeatedly stressed by the [Second Vatican] council and the magisterium of the church because it is of the essence of the faith and the very continuation of the saving event of Jesus Christ. . . . In the current theological, missiological and missionary situation of Asia, the proclamation of Jesus Christ is the central issue of the faith and life of the church. It is incumbent on the pas-

tors of the church to give priority to proclamation in all their pastoral planning. They must be seen primarily as evangelizers and only secondarily as administrators.

The Vatican document allowed a place for dialogue, but it was clearly a secondary place. "Even though dialogue is essential and forms part of every evangelizing activity of the church, it does not exhaust the whole reality of evangelization, nor is it a substitute for mission *ad gentes* [to the nations], and much less is it to be seen as something in opposition to the proclamation of Jesus Christ."

Addressing the subject of Mariology, the *Lineamenta* reminded the Asian bishops that the church must "look to Mary for her intercession, example, guidance, and strength. . . . On the eve of the third millennium, the church in Asia, therefore, turns to Mary for fresh inspiration, guidance and intercession for her challenging mission of proclaiming her Son to the peoples of Asia." Most Asian bishops' conference responses allowed Mary considerable respect, but did not echo the Vatican's bold admonitions. To the contrary, some conferences, including the Philippine conference, warned that Marian devotions sometimes are overemphasized and take the focus off a Christ-centered church. They also noted that these devotions often become tainted with superstitious beliefs.

Responding to chapter 1, "Asian Realities," the Asian bishops generally depicted increasingly harsh economic conditions across the continent. Conference after conference condemned the pernicious influence of growing consumerism and spreading economic hardships and stressed a church committed to social justice. The Indonesian bishops stated that besides its positive aspects, industrialization in Indonesia had produced such negative effects as the growth of materialism, consumerism, secularism, unemployment, poor working conditions, unjust remuneration, exploitation of women and children, restriction of labor organizations, inadequate land distribution, and the rapid increase of the tourism and sex industries. Industrialism, they wrote, was increasingly showing its effect on traditional ways of life, causing many, especially the younger generation, to disregard ancient cultural values. "Many still profess a religion but have no genuine faith," the bishops stated. The Indonesian conference was one of several that stated the need for the church to emphasize Jesus Christ as liberator. The Korean bishops warned of the decline of the family structure and a growing individualism caused by "rampant materialism, the breakdown of the traditional hierarchy of values." The Malaysian bishops said the church had not been able to stop "the negative influences arising out of economic development, affluence, consumerism, individualism." Taiwanese bishops warned that "money is becoming a god. There is no equal progress in morality and education. . . . Though the economic boom extends right through Asia, the plight of workers (local and foreign), which has become a global problem, hardly gets the attention of either civil or church leaders." The Taiwanese bishops added that the "whole of society is dominated by the quest for profits and consumerism. The traditional spirit of hard work and the simple life has been lost; the hierarchy of values is confused and disoriented; most people feel a spiritual emptiness. Unemployment is high, therefore people are more anxious to make money than to search for truth." The Philippine bishops spoke of the "massive poverty of the people, often caused by injustice; the scandalous gap between rich and poor; the concentration of power in the hands of the elite." The Indian bishops added another concern—rapid population growth. "No matter which way our national population is looked at, we admit that our country is approaching the limits of national resources as they are now being systematically abused. India," the bishops said, "had more than doubled her population within the first fifty years of her independence. . . . The country's population problem is not just a challenge for the Indian subcontinent; it is a problem for Asia and the world as well."

Also addressed in responses to the "realities" chapter were more local church concerns. For example:

- The Taiwanese bishops: "The church is still very hierarchical in structure. Though accepting some degree of democratization, she is not facing enough the equality of men and women."

- The Sri Lankan bishops: The faithful need to understand the important difference between "performing mere acts of charity and carrying out the church's evangelizing mission of love and service inspired by the social doctrine of the church. Very few in the Sri Lankan church, including the clergy, realize this difference."

Responding to chapter 2, "Evangelization," many Asian bishops' conferences expressed serious concerns that the *Lineamenta* failed to understand or reflect Asian religious conditions. The Indonesian bishops began their response to the issue by listing current challenges to evangelization efforts. These include new pressures from science and technology, a growing mass media culture, growing materialism, and the atmosphere of secularization. All these, the bishops stated, obscure "precious traditional cultural values." They attacked the *Lineamenta*, saying its approach to evangelization simply disregards the many years of experience contained in the writings of the Asian bishops since Vatican II. "The *Lineamenta* does not adequately reflect the [FABC's] view since its First Plenary Assembly in Taipei [in Taiwan] 1974," the Indonesian bishops lamented. "There—as also in the Fifth Plenary Assembly of the FABC in Bandung [in

Indonesia] 1990—Evangelization is linked with the triple dialogue: dialogue with the poor, dialogue with the religions and dialogue with the cultures." The Indonesian bishops cited structural problems in the *Lineamenta* saying its assessment of Asian realities appeared divorced from what follows. Chapter 1 of the *Lineamenta* on Asian realities, the Indonesian bishops wrote, "does not flow into the following chapters (it seems juxtaposed), whereas it is the FABC's main concern that evangelization should immerse itself in concrete life situations in order to save humans within the very conditions of their lives." The bishops of Thailand criticized the Vatican evangelization line from another angle, saying it did not support interfaith understanding enough. "Evangelization must establish good relationships with other religions through respect and acceptance of each other's values," they wrote. "Evangelization must recognize the traditions of other religions as friends or even relatives living together." The Vietnamese bishops questioned the *Lineamenta*'s suppositions as they pertained to evangelization in Asia and recalled approaches encouraged at the Second Vatican Council. "The first reason is that this continent is not virgin or fallow soil on which one can sow any kind of seed," they wrote.

> It is a land of very ancient religions and civilizations when compared to Europe. . . . The inhabitants are not without knowledge of God, quite the opposite: they have a certain experience of His presence, and invoke Him under different names such as "Sky," "Heaven," "Brahman," etc. Consequently, to "evangelize" in this particular case does not mean to present a God, a Christ, as totally unknown, but, in a certain way—perhaps borrowing from Buddhist language—it is "to make shine more brightly the Light" present but hidden; it is to help in "seeing the truth illuminated," which Vatican II recognized was partially present in other religions.

Responding to chapter 3, "God's Salvific Design," a number of the conferences raised questions dealing with church imagery contained in the *Lineamenta*. The Japanese bishops wrote that the imagery "is not as rich or deep as that [in the documents] of Vatican II. Especially, the images of 'the church as people of God' and 'the church as servant' are not stressed. These two images have special meaning for the church in Asia, which in order to serve God's kingdom lives in a minority position with and for others. Their absence would be unfortunate for the synod." Japan's bishops continued: "The central issues of service and dialogue developed by the [FABC] are two very important points for the Catholic church in Asia that are not sufficiently stressed in the *Lineamenta*. . . . The *Lineamenta* still reflects an ecclesiological pattern 'from above' and somewhat abstract. For the synod of Asian bishops, clearly the most appropriate model will be the church as 'communion of communities.'" The Philippine bishops also called for use of Vatican II imagery, saying the "main image of church that should be used in this section and throughout the document should be that of a co-pilgrim, companion and servant accompanying the peoples of Asia in the journey to full life." The Indian bishops said their "completely indigenous hierarchy" helps their church image. More than 90 percent of the nation's clergy and religious are Indian. "This has been a plus," the Indian bishops wrote. "However," they added, being "an overly clerical institution, the church's ways of thinking, speaking and acting not infrequently hinder her communication and hurt her credibility." The Indian bishops cited a contradiction within the church, saying the church "rightly proclaims freedom of conscience and religion, but in matters of grievances within the church her public image at times appears harsh and therefore one of counterwitness." Also on the negative side, the Indian bishops lamented that "the spiritual and mystical elements of Asian religions have been practically ignored" in the *Lineamenta*. "In place of understanding, appreciation and promotion of this different yet complementary world-view, we regret to observe that today within the church there is an atmosphere of fear and distrust. These are destructive of communion and collaboration for mission." The Indian bishops also dealt with the role of women in the church, saying "the structures of patriarchal traditions in Indian society and even in the church continue to offend and oppress women." Finally, they noted that "more and more faithful are vocalizing their dissatisfaction with some church institutions that appear to be more at the service of the rich, powerful and better-off sectors of our country."

Responses to the *Lineamenta*'s chapter 4, "Jesus Christ as Savior," were frequently unfavorable as well. The Japanese bishops said the document's Christology was too defensive. "This does not help the faith of Asian Christians," they wrote. "What is necessary is an open and spiritual Christology rooted in real life and alert to the problems of modern people. The Japanese bishops stated:

We should try to discover what kind of Jesus will be a "light" to the peoples of Asia. In other words, as the fathers of the early church did with Greco-Roman culture, we must make a more profound study of the fundamentals of the religiosity of our peoples, and from this point of view try to discover how Jesus Christ is answering their needs. . . . Jesus Christ is the way, the truth and the life, but in Asia, before stressing that Jesus Christ is the truth, we must search much more deeply into how he is the way and the life. If we stress too much that "Jesus Christ is the one and only Savior," we can have no dialogue, common living or solidarity with other religions.

The Japanese bishops seemed to delight in reminding Rome that "the world's great religions were born in Asia." The Philippine bishops also called for toning down the emphasis placed on Jesus Christ as Savior in the *Lineamenta*, saying it does not help interfaith dialogue—even though most of the Philippine population is at least nominally Catholic. In its response, the Philippine bishops' conference emphasized: "[interfaith] dialogue is not contrary to but is a mode of proclamation." The Indian bishops asked, "To what extent can [our] church learn from and collaborate with other religions to bring about God's Kingdom and peoples' integral liberation? . . . To be religious itself means to be interreligious . . . authentic dialogue does not seem to be well understood by many Christians." The Indian bishops then brought the issue of dialogue back within the Catholic Church. They stated that the "spirit and practice of dialogue is not restricted to interfaith matters among the Christian–Muslim, Christian–Hindu, Christian–Buddhist and Christian–traditional religions. It very much includes dialogue between the local church and the universal church as a communion of communions." This dialogical model, the Indian bishops wrote, is not only a tool; it is essential to being church. It is nothing less, they wrote, than "the new Asian way of being church, promoting mutual understanding, harmony and collaboration. This way of relating to and serving other religions is indicated by a careful reading of the signs of our times: It appears to us as God's will for Christian communities in Asia today. It is a timely answer to Asia's vast and varied problems, which threaten her very life." Some Asian bishops said they found in the *Lineamenta* an unwelcome return to church triumphalism. The Philippine bishops asked the Vatican to further explore "in an open and humble way" the "revelatory nature" of the religions of Asia and their impact on the church's proclamation of Jesus. Their response specifically warned against "triumphalism and a superior attitude" when discussing Jesus with religions that thrived long before thirteenth-century European explorers arrived in Asia.

The Philippine bishops suggested that the synod would prove more successful if it highlights Asia's rich contributions of contemplation and its "spirituality of harmony." The Korean bishops called for more study of the role of the great traditional religions in Korea. "They, too, play a part in the salvific economy of God," the Korean bishops wrote. "This understanding is essential for the inculturation of the gospel. Ignorance of these religions and their culture and a sense of superiority and exclusivism in religion should be eradicated." The Indonesian bishops called aspects of the *Lineamenta* "alarming." Its "dominant concern between the lines appears to be: 'too much (local) emphasis on dialogue, so that proclamation is not highlighted enough.'" The Indonesian bishops reasoned that proclamation of Jesus Christ "has to take full account of whatever good and true is found in other religions, and to proceed according to Christian principles of authentic inculturation." The Indonesian bishops went on to explain that "sincere Christian dialogue appreciates values of the Kingdom wherever they are found and provides room for indigenous Christians to make use of their religious traditions in order to express those values in ways familiar to them." They added: "In pluri-religious societies it is often difficult to directly and explicitly proclaim the central role of Jesus Christ in the economy of salvation. This proclamation must be adapted to concrete life conditions and to the disposition of the hearers." The Indonesian bishops concluded that "native religious values are not to be abolished but ought be purified through reflection in dialogue between Christian leaders and leaders of traditional religions. This may result in Christianity being enriched by traditional values and in a truly inculturated practice of Christian faith."

In responses to chapter 5, "Church as Communion," Asian bishops again asserted the need for interfaith dialogue and solidarity with the poor as the paths to effective evangelization. The Japanese bishops recalled that in the context of evangelization in Asia, "compassion with the suffering" had been identified time after time at the general assemblies of the Federation of Asian Bishops' Conferences "as a most important element." The Japanese bishops stated: "In missionary work among those of other religions, what is more important than convincing words is the attitude of standing by the side of the weak and powerless and showing them compassion."

The Indian bishops again defended dialogue "as the means to evangelization." "We can only do this by listening respectfully to our neighbors and dialoguing with them. Dialogue is not merely one ecclesial activity among many. It is a constituent dimension of every authentic local church," the Indian bishops insisted. "After Vatican II, to be church means being a faith community-in-dialogue." The Sri Lankan bishops suggested the same approach, even cautioning Rome to remember that they live in a "multireligious setting" in which Jesus Christ is viewed in many different forms. "Muslims accept Jesus as a great prophet, as he is mentioned in the Koran. Hindus treat him as an avatar, an incarnation of God. Buddhists see him as a social reformer and a great teacher, and for many others he is a great liberator. Generally speaking, there seems to be an awesome respect for this person Jesus Christ." The Sri Lankan bishops went on to explain that the uniqueness of Jesus and the church "has been a perennial problem and poses its own distinctive difficulties for authentic dialogue." A number of conferences also referred to the difficulties of building local churches in a postcolonial era. Many of the churches of Asia are traced to colonialism and its pernicious history. The Sri Lankan bishops reminded Rome that "Christ in Sri Lanka came in foreign garb. Hence, inculturation is becoming part of the missionary mandate for us. All impressions to the contrary must be carefully avoided. We must insist on Christ Jesus as a religious founder who came from Asia, which is such a rich continent in the history of religion." This leads to, the Sri Lankan bishops wrote, "the necessity of a missionary spirituality of dialogue." They added: "Our dialogue will be a two-way street. In this endeavor, we need to cultivate attitudes toward other religions that must be sincere. Hence, for us in Asia, religions are a part of the universal context in which the true identity of Jesus must find new expressions. While we affirm the uniqueness of Christ, we need to move toward a non-threatening articulation, an articulation that would be more conducive to dialogue in Asia." The Vietnamese bishops were also among those who made reference to the trappings of their colonial past, stating that the synod must pay special attention to the modest settings of local churches as well as to their "historical circumstances."

"Only a poor church," the Vietnamese bishops wrote, "will be able to adapt itself to a huge mass of poor people. A church that is humble and small will blend more easily with the poor masses of Asia. A church without power will more easily approach so many men and women who only ask for the right to live as men and women, to have enough to eat and to wear, to study and to find work." The Vietnamese bishops then asked: "Has not the time come to create new types of church, such as small communities that are more easily set up in society, especially that of the poor; poorer communities, without show, without obstructions that inspire discomfort and fear to those who wish to approach them; communities that are open rather than closed; communities that are more attentive to the whole of human living—and not just the purely religious—to help improve the physical and material life of the poor, to raise up their cultural level?" In an apparent reference to the Vatican's emphasis on proclaiming Jesus as Savior, the Vietnamese bishops replied: "Jesus did not proclaim the Good News only in words, but this Good News for him also meant that 'the blind see, the lame walk, the lepers are cleansed, the deaf hear and the dead come to life.'" The Vietnamese bishops also said that they found the *Lineamenta* to be "paternalistic" toward the people of Asia.

In their responses to chapter 6, "The Church's Mission of Love and Service," the Asian bishops described their options on issues of inculturation and missionary activity. The Indonesian bishops lamented that within the *Lineamenta* inculturation is mentioned only with passing reference, as "an interpretation of faith in context." They said this does "not do justice" to the subject. Inculturation, they insisted, should be a "way of life." "The Christian way of life should be authentic not only in the sense that it is in agreement with the '*Regula Fidei*' [rules of faith] but also in the sense that it expresses faith fully within and through the local culture," they wrote. "Inculturation is based on the mystery of incarnation and implies accepting God's word and expressing one's faith by using local cultural elements, in order that the church be fully accepted and the faithful, even society, consider the church as truly theirs. . . . " The Indonesian bishops continued, saying, "Inculturation also is a 'paschal' process: The local culture has to go through 'death.' . . . But traditional cultural faith expressions as imported from the 'West' also have to be critically examined and purified from whatever obscures the authenticity of faith."

As for local liturgy, the Indonesian bishops stated that "many ceremonies have been imported from the traditional church in the West, so that little room is left for a style of community life and of faith communication according to the rhythm of indigenous people. Clinging too much to the 'substantial unity of the Roman liturgy' may end up in rigidity that obstructs proper incarnation of Christian faith." The Indonesian bishops called for "urgent" development of Asian theologies, "Indonesian theology in particular," to help in the inculturation process. They then called for change within the church. "In order to promote the inculturation process, the universal church has to be more open and ready to change its own pattern of thinking and to allow local churches the freedom to think and act in response to concrete life situations, guided by the Spirit and led by the local hierarchy." In order for this to be achieved, the Indonesian bishops argued, local episcopal conferences "need greater freedom of decision-making with regard to inculturation." They noted that "continuous and serious study and experimentation by experts not only in liturgy but also in indigenous cultures are required, and wherever possible cooperation with interested groups from other Christian denominations ought to be promoted. Such efforts need to be wholeheartedly supported [and not restricted] by Rome." Finally, the Indonesian bishops asked: "Why should every change and adaptation in liturgy have the approval of the central ecclesial authority? Is the bishops' conference not competent to grant official approval? Does not pluriformity in unity (that is, 'Catholic') express the immense richness of God's glory?" The Japanese bishops similarly called for more inculturation in liturgy and religious life. "Though elements of cultural forms are found in liturgy, there have been no sustained efforts at inculturation in liturgy. . . . As a church, we have not sufficiently grasped the urgency and the importance or the necessity of inculturation." The Japanese bishops also spoke out against the underlying premise in the *Lineamenta*'s missionary viewpoint. They wrote: "A 'success orientation' of 'trying for better results' can only discourage the missionary. We need a vision of evangelization that gives joy and a sense of purpose to a Christian living as one of a minority in the midst of many traditional religions. An evaluation based not on the number of baptisms but rather from the point of view of 'How faithful have we been to our mission of evangelization?' is necessary."

The *Lineamenta* evoked a number of responses to Vatican admonitions to integrate Mariology into modern church life. Several conferences offered cautionary advice. The Japanese bishops, for example, while stating that novenas to the Blessed Virgin Mary are a popular form of devotion, noted "there are, of course, very real dangers in some of the devotional practices, which tend to be shallow, self-centered, individualistic and success-profit-oriented with little emphasis on accepting the will of God, recognition of the role of suffering and solicitude for the concerns of one's neighbor." Some conferences in responding to Rome suggested wholly different approaches to the synod. The Japanese and Indonesians were the most outspoken, with the latter calling for more encouragement and understanding from the West. Why must the synod examine church mission? the Indonesian bishops asked. Would it not be better "if the churches in Asia receive wholehearted encouragement rather than be reminded of their duties? Is it not perhaps better to take as a main theme 'Asian Spiritual Life,' 'Asian Religious Experience' or even 'Mysticism in Asia,' in order to foster values already alive in this continent?"

Some responses focused on canonical issues, including the granting of dispensations from priesthood. The Indonesian bishops asked why dispensations should be reserved "strictly to the central authority of the church? Why should one have to live for many years in 'sin' before he could be freed?" Throughout the responses to the *Lineamenta*, questions of who makes the decisions and how they are made are mixed with equally important questions of church mission and direction for the years ahead.[4]

The Vatican had much to consider after receiving the responses it had asked for, but probably did not quite expect to receive—at least in the form they were returned. The next step was to take those responses and use them as the basis of an *Instrumentum laboris*, the synod's official working document. The Vatican's *Instrumentum laboris* made only faint references to critical concerns raised by Asians. The 24,000-word working paper did not lay out an agenda for the synod. Instead, it went from narration to exhortation to assertion. Various episcopal responses to the *Lineamenta* had criticized its defensive tone. That tone still existed in the working paper—but less so. Meanwhile, urgent episcopal conference critiques lost their thunder in the homogenized language of the new document. Calls for an urgent upgrading of the role of the laity in evangelization, for example, were softened to: "Many responses mention that the laity seek to become more actively involved." Insistent criticisms of a lay/clerical gap became a call for "greater cooperation among the various states in the church." What ultimately emerged from a careful comparison of the working document and the responses to the *Lineamenta* of the Asian bishops were two radically different ecclesiologies. The Asian bishops worked out of the theologies of Vatican II, especially of its vision of the role of the church contained in *Gaudium et Spes,* the Pastoral Constitution on the Church in the Modern World, and the FABC pastoral reflections. Those theologies, as articulated by many of the Asian bishops' conferences, see the church committed to human liberation from both individual and social sins. The working document reflects a different view, concentrating on preaching Jesus as Savior of the World. The working document ignored Asian bishops' concerns that the Vatican had withdrawn from the Vatican II vision of the church's mission and that decision making had become too concentrated. Nowhere did the new document refer to the demand of the Japanese bishops' conference that the synod format be changed to allow the Asian bishops to take control of the synod's agenda and proceedings. Nor was there any reference to a request by the Indonesian bishops' conference to explore possibilities for establishing an East Asian patriarchate, to "relativize the primacy of the 'Western' church and enhance authentic inculturation of Christian faith."

The synod's general secretariat considered the bishops' responses during meetings held from September 30 to October 2, 1997. Its response was then translated into the official synod languages, French and English, making no accommodation to any Asian language. The new document roughly followed the outline of the original *Lineamenta*, consisting of an introduction, seven chapters, and a conclusion. It again developed the synod theme, chosen by John Paul, of "Jesus Christ the Savior and his mission of love and service in Asia, that they may have life and have it abundantly." The working document stressed the important preaching function of the church, particularly the call to Jesus Christ, Savior, as well as the unique role played by the church in God's salvation process. Chapter 4, "Jesus Christ: The Good News of Salvation," is described in the document as dealing with "the central aspect of the church's message of evangelization and her mission, i.e., the person of Jesus Christ, Son of God, Savior and Son of Man."

The document repeatedly exhorted the bishops to the "New Evangelization," a theme the pope had stressed throughout the 1990s. It stated that the success of the New Evangelization in Asia will depend "on how people come to recognize Jesus so as to respond to the perennial invitation to experience fullness of life in him through participation in the communion of the church, his body." It went on to say that it had found widespread support among the Asian bishops' responses to the *Lineamenta* for stressing the unique salvation path centered on Jesus Christ, as Savior, which probably came as a surprise to not a few bishops. The *Instrumentum laboris* at one point put it as follows: "Responses to the *Lineamenta* indicate that the overriding title for Christ among his disciples, associated with his mission to all humanity, is that of Savior and redeemer, who in freeing a 'people' from sin and all its effects—particularly death—has established a church, or worshiping community, called to give praise to God in Christ and through the Holy Spirit." It continued: "Acknowledging Jesus as Savior involves not simply confession of sin but a change of heart, that is, accepting Jesus Christ as lord of one's life in an ongoing process of conversion." A fair reading of the responses to the *Lineamenta* would probably not support the Vatican claim that it had found in them overwhelming support for stressing at the synod the New Evangelization with its preaching focus on Jesus Christ as Savior for all. The Asian bishops' conferences have written about evangelization far more subtly, stressing that it requires dialogue with other religions and the avoidance of undue focus on proclamation. The Indonesian bishops' conference, for example, in its response to the Vatican's *Lineamenta*, had said that "with regard to Christological concern expressed in the *Lineamenta*" the Federation of Asian Bishops' Conferences "makes attempts at an integral and holistic approach to the mystery of Jesus Christ by using 'inclusive language,' so that Christology truly becomes 'Catholic,' i.e., embracing all humans of whatever religious conviction." The Indonesian bishops' conference went on to say that Jesus Christ is best preached as the Savior "by a church that is in solidarity with people whose lives are marked by poverty, oppression, discrimination and all kinds of injustice." It cautioned that "in pluri-religious societies it is often difficult to directly and explicitly proclaim the central role of Jesus Christ in the economy of salvation." The Japanese bishops had similar concerns but were more blunt, writing, "If we stress too much that 'Jesus Christ is the one and only Savior,' we can have no dialogue, common living or solidarity with other religions. The church, learning from the *kenosis* [emptying, self-abasement] of Jesus Christ, should be humble and open its heart to other religions to deepen its understanding of the mystery of Christ." The Philippine bishops' conference wrote that it preferred a "witnessing" approach to the preaching of Jesus as Savior. "Witnessing is primary," they wrote. The Indian bishops' conference spoke of the "deficiency of our present Christology" in that "it sometimes uses exclusive

language, which deals with only one part of the great mystery of Christ."
"In union with the Father and the Spirit, Christ is indeed the source and
cause of salvation for all peoples," they wrote, adding "but this fact does
not exclude the possibility of God mysteriously employing other cooper-
ating channels." It then cautioned the Vatican that the *Lineamenta*
expression that Jesus Christ is the one and only Savior of the whole of
humankind should be understood in the Indian context "in a way that
takes seriously into account the multicultural and multireligious situations of our country." "In the light of the universal salvific will and
design of God, so emphatically affirmed in the New Testament witness,
the Indian Christological approach seeks to avoid negative and exclu-
sivistic expressions. . . . We cannot, then, deny, a priori, a salvific role for
these non-Christian religions," they wrote. The Indian bishops asked if it
is really necessary to choose one approach or another. "There is more
than one theology evident in the New Testament," they wrote. "This pluriformity of theology is catered to different churches of varied cultures
and life-situations. Christology is never a finished product but always in
process. . . ." "So today the churches around the world and here in Asia
need to create contextualized theologies of our one faith incarnated into
many cultures. . . . The agents of such contextualized faith expressions
are the local churches themselves under the guidance of 'a magisterium,
which is predominantly pastoral in character.'"

While focusing on salvation and the role of Jesus as Savior, the Vatican's working document glossed over other issues raised by a number of
Asian bishops' conferences. Several conferences, for example, identified
the church's association with its colonial past as a continuing handicap.
The Philippine bishops stated that they are conscious "of our baggage
from the past" and its "culturally imperialistic mission approach." They
called for a "self-emptying," "the unloading of our culturally imperialist
baggage," and an "openness to discern the footprints of the Lord among
Asian peoples—in their stories, traditions, cultures and religions." Only
faint echoes of such sentiments found their way into the working document. The working document mentioned colonialism only twice and
without any of the condemnatory tone evident in the bishops' responses.
Similarly, while Asian bishops' responses to the *Lineamenta* spoke of the
Catholic Church as being seen, in some instances, as foreign in Asia, the
working document preferred to replace foreign with "not totally Asian."
Several Asian bishops' conferences told Rome that it is not the Asian style
to challenge other religions but rather to enter into dialogue with them,
to search for points of agreement and downplay differences. The Japanese
bishops told the Vatican that its thinking had come out of "the traditional Western scholastic tradition with emphasis on distinctions and differences." The Japanese said they preferred seeking creative harmony. The

working document admitted that history and circumstance require dialogue, but insisted, in the final analysis, on the obligation to proclaim Jesus as Savior. "In this spirit," the working document states, "the church in Asia, engaged in the synod process, wishes to look to Jesus Christ, the Savior of all, in order to come to a proper understanding of the life she shares in him, to strengthen her union with him and to renew her dedication to her mission to all peoples of Asia." The issue of proclamation versus dialogue is at times subtle, but the distinction—and gulf between the two visions—became clear by the repetition of differing emphases.

The document also was reluctant to accord the title of "liberator" to Christ. It stated that "some [Asian bishops'] responses cautioned that the term 'liberator' in reference to Christ should be avoided." This struck some Asian bishops as unusual because no one remembers seeing such cautions in thirteen episcopal conference responses that became public. Several, on the other hand, specifically recommended use of the title. "The church is called to give concrete shape to the mission of Christ as 'liberator,'" the Indonesian bishops said. "Jesus Christ is presented as redeemer and liberator who fought injustice and oppression," the bishops of the Philippines wrote. The Sri Lankans made a similar statement.

Finally, the document ignored the recommendation made by several Asian bishops' conferences to adopt the see/judge/act method in analyzing Asian reality. This method had been associated with contextual theology. There was no use or mention of contextual theology in the working document. The word "liberation" appeared five times in the document, three of these in quotations from statements written by the Federation of Asian Bishops' Conferences. In their responses to the *Lineamenta*, many Asian bishops' conferences had objected to the way the Vatican had completely overlooked twenty-five years of FABC work, as if the tomes of Asian bishops' documents had never been written. The synodal working document gave the federation a slight but not large voice.

The different opinions over the future of the Catholicism in Asia contained in the exchanges were still largely private as the bishops prepared to gather for the synod. That would not remain the case. The stage was set. The curtain would go up April 19, 1998.

CHAPTER 12

Synod on Asia

The Way begot one,
And the one, two;
Then the two begot three
And three all else.
—*Lao Tzu*

The Synod on Asia opened on a clear spring afternoon, April 19, 1998, with a spectacular outdoor pontifical Mass in front of St. Peter's Basilica. It was celebrated with an eye for cultural sensitivity, using more than a dozen Asian languages. The *Gloria* was sung in Tagalog. The Gospel was proclaimed in Malayalam according to the Syro-Malabar rite. The general intercessions were read in Arabic, Chinese, Filipino, Korean, Tamil, and Vietnamese. The preparation of gifts was accompanied by an Indonesian dance troupe of men and women carrying flowers, incense, and candles while singing an Indonesian hymn. At the end of the Eucharistic Prayer, an Indian dance troupe performed a traditional love dance. No one in Rome ever recalled seeing anything like it before on Vatican grounds. Missing, however, was use of Japanese in the liturgy. It caused a stir among some synod participants who thought synod organizers had sent a message of displeasure. It was the Japanese bishops' conference that had been most critical of the proposed synod. Synod officials responded that the omission had been a simple oversight. Tensions were evident from the start.

Among the requests made by the Asian bishops before the synod had been a call for greater use of Asian languages. Responding to that request at a pre-synod news conference, Secretary General of the Synod, Belgian Cardinal Jan P. Schotte, said it was impossible to introduce Asian languages simply because there are too many of them, twenty-seven in all at the synod. He insisted that English and French would remain the two official synod languages and that they would be used throughout. He then made a point that had already been made by a number of Asian bishops in private conversations. The Asian bishops, unlike the African bishops, had not requested this synod. Indeed, they were not initially enthusiastic about it—and came reluctantly to Rome at its request.

In attendance at the synod were eleven Asian cardinals, six patriarchs with twenty-three bishops from Eastern rite churches, fifteen presidents of episcopal conferences with sixty-five other Latin rite bishops, ten superior generals of clerical orders, together with fifty-eight auditors and experts, five ecumenical delegates, and twenty-five heads of the departments of the Roman curia. Among the fifty-eight auditors and experts there were twelve laymen, eight laywomen, eight sisters, five priests, and two brothers. A single youth spoke for two-thirds of the Asian church membership, while sixteen women—among 236 men—stood for over half of those active in the church.

The papally appointed secretary for the synod, the *general relator*, Cardinal Paul Shan Kuo-hsi, set a tone for the gathering on the first day in an address intended to summarize discussions that had led up to the synod. He did not mince words. "The Catholic faith," he said, "will not be intelligible or attractive to the peoples of Asia if it continues to be a carbon copy of the Catholic Church in the West." Outlining the topics for synod discussion, Shan said the church's mission of love and service must begin with "a genuine regard and respect for all the peoples of Asia, their religions and cultures." Shan, the bishop of Kaohsiung, Taiwan, continued, saying there is "a serious need for inculturating the faith in the cultures of Asia and for shedding an appearance of being carbon copies of churches in Western societies." If the Catholic Church truly believes that the Spirit of God is at work in the world, he said, then it must "recognize the profound rays of truth and grace" present in other religions and be a living witness to "the fullness of revelation in Jesus Christ." Through dialogue, he insisted, the Catholic Church will discover the values it shares with other religions and philosophies, adding that an essential part of the church's mission is witnessing to the personal transformation that comes with conversion to Christ, "especially as seen in solidarity with the poor and defense of human rights." His speech was purposeful, covering the basic themes the FABC had been developing since the early 1970s. From that point observers became certain that it would be a most interesting synod.

Also at the outset, Cardinal Stephen Sou Hwan Kim of Seoul, South Korea, one of the synod presidents, spoke his mind, reminding Pope John Paul II, who was present in the hall, that the Asian bishops had worked together among themselves in a "collegial" atmosphere to build their vision for the last three decades. "While in full union with the church universal, we are to become Asian in our way of thinking, living and sharing our own Christ-experience . . . with those still seeking the face of God in his son, the savior of all," Kim said. "In the concrete, this means pro-claiming that Jesus is the Christ above all by living like him amidst our neighbors of other faiths and particularly with God's poor as did Jesus." Kim thus said yes to proclamation, as the Vatican had wanted, but placed his yes within the context of witness, as the Asian bishops had long insisted. Kim, speaking to an audience that included twenty-five top Roman curia officials, made specific reference to the faithful work of the Federation of Asian Bishops' Conferences.

So it started and so it went for the first week and a half of the synod, which I attended, as the Asian bishops spoke freely and from their hearts, taking turns in eight-minute speeches, or interventions. At the synod, unlike at any other in recent memory, each speech was followed by polite applause. The bishops were bringing Asia to Rome and through it to the West. Each day Pope John Paul II sat behind a long table in the synod hall, flanked by synod officials and facing the bishops and other synod par-ticipants who sat in tiered chairs. Sometimes the pope listened; just as often he read from a prayer book, glancing up occasionally. Language was a problem. For virtually all participants, neither English nor French is a commonly used language in their church. Further, the bishops did not even receive the full text of the interventions; they received sum-maries only.

From the start, however, the Asian bishops stuck to their convictions, repeatedly returning to themes they had developed in their pastoral work over the decades. On the first day several Japanese bishops offered unblemished critiques of Asian church life, saying Catholicism had grown slowly in the region because the church has been too Western, too paternalistic, and not adequately involved in Asian daily life. They insisted that successful evangelization in Asia will require more personal witness than words and will require that greater freedom be given to local churches and less uniformity imposed by the Vatican. Archbishop Leo J. Ikenaga of Osaka, Japan, the first bishop to address the synod, lamented before the 252 synod participants that evangelization in Asia had taken only "a few small steps" over the centuries.[1] Baptisms are few, he said, and, more important, Christian thinking has not entered into the mainstream of Asian society. One reason, he said, is that Western Chris-tianity, nurtured in Europe, has been preaching too masculine a God and emphasizing a division between God and the universe. The Asian church needs to stress the more "maternal traits" of God, so that Christianity can take on "a warmer, more approachable face," he said. Ikenaga went on to say that while the church traditionally preaches dogma and the cate-chism, Asians would be more receptive to the more "practical" approach that Jesus himself took—such as healing the sick. The next bishop to speak was Augustinus J. Nomura of Nagoya, Japan, who suggested that the church ought to present Christ to Asian people as a "spiritual master," as a guide who lights the way. The church needs a spirituality that is rooted in Asia and emphasizes witnessing over teaching, he said. "A gospel that is embodied in our own lives carries much more credibility and power of conviction than a gospel that has only been wrapped up in beautiful words, teachings and moral injunctions," he said.

Minutes later, Bishop Berard T. Oshikawa of Naha, Japan, told the synod that his primary concern is pastoral. He said the church does not need to look far to understand why Christianity has not grown in Japan. The reason, he said, is that "the norm for Christian life, for church discipline, for liturgical expression and theological orthodoxy continues to be that of the Western church." That may be good for the West, he said, but for places like Japan it "unfortunately becomes a very effective block" to pastoral development. He called for a new church model guided by the Asian bishops, making sure that "no imposition of any kind hinders the work of the Holy Spirit."

Oshikawa said this approach implies a redefined role for the Holy See, which should mediate church affairs with "prudence, flexibility, trust and courage." He added that this would mean "moving away from a single and uniform abstract norm that stifles genuine spiritualtiy, Asian liturgical expression, earnest Asian theoloical search, and real growth in maturity."

Archbishop Francis X. Kaname Shimamoto of Nagasaki, Japan, also speaking on the need for an authentic Asian Christianity, but seeming to want to make a point that he could use a Western language, was the only synod bishop during the first week to address the assembly in Latin. According to an observer, the other Asian bishops quickly placed earphones on their heads to listen to the translation. The pope did not use earphones. Nor, of course, did any of the members of the curia, sitting near the pope, apparently dare to pick up earphones to get the translation. Cardinal D. Simon Lourdusamy, of Bangalore, India, a member of the Congregation for the Evangelization of Peoples, also insisted that if Christianity is to take root in Asia, it must be inculturated and meaningful to local people. "The gospel cannot be proclaimed in a vacuum. Being the Word of Life, it addresses real life situations" such as poverty, disease, injustice, oppression of women and the abuse of the environment, he said. Bishop Kuriakose Kunnacherry of the Kottayam diocese in Kerala, India, lamented that the Second Vatican Council's call to accept and admire a variety of churches has yet to be understood and implemented. "The Asian communities are not to be disfigured so as to fit in the ecclesiastical structure in the Roman pattern," he said. Bishop Arturo M. Bastes of Romblon, Philippines, said the church needs to shift from a "Euro-centered to an authentically Asian church," from a "triumphalistic model of church to a church that identifies with the social conditions of the people." He was one of a number of bishops who spoke about growing Asian poverty under the forces of globalization and growing consumerism and materialism. Bishop Bunluen Mansap of Ubon Ratchathani, Thailand, spoke of his contact with Buddhist colleagues: "I feel inspired by their simplicity of life, their openness, their humane relationships, their unassuming ways; these are values I recognize as values of the Kingdom or of the Gospel." The bishop added: "Could it be said that this is the Good News that the Buddhist can offer us?"

Several Vietnamese bishops spoke about the need for inculturation of the faith. They used the example of ancestor worship, commonly practiced in Vietnam. The Catholic Church once condemned the practice, common throughout much of Asia, and for centuries it remained a serious obstacle to evangelization. Some say Rome's condemnation lost all hope of a Christian China. Then in 1965, the church finally accommodated and began to speak of ancestor worship within the framework of the communion of saints. Vietnamese and Chinese bishops both said the new Catholic allowance for allowing ancestor worship shows that respect for culture can go hand in hand with Christian teaching. "But the weight of history still holds many Vietnamese back," one Vietnamese bishop told the synod. The message was clear: Catholic teachings must accommodate to Asian realities.

The heart of the message the bishops attempted to deliver at the synod seemed to be summed up succinctly by another Vietnamese, the general secretary of the Vietnamese Bishops' Conference, Nguyên Son Lâm, bishop of Thanh Hoa, who said in an interview, "The churches of Asia must put on Asian clothes." To do this properly, the bishops said repeatedly, they need the authority to make decisions on matters of church life.

The synod theme, "Jesus Christ the Savior and His Mission of Love and Service in Asia," was chosen by Pope John Paul II. The bishops did not disagree. However, they made it clear they wanted to channel the theme through their Asian souls and Asian experiences. The church is most effective in its mission, the bishops countered, when it reaches out to the poor and preaches through example. Several bishops explained that the Asian "new way of being church" means living in solidarity with the poor and with greater lay/clergy collaboration. The themes that emerged in those first days focused on the need to establish a more balanced relationship between the central and local churches; the need for greater cultural sensitivity and diversity in Catholic religious expression; the need to affirm Christian life through service and solidarity with the poor; and the need to cooperate with the other religions of Asia in addressing the pressing social and economic crises of the times. Much was said about Asian poverty, including a worsening economic crisis in Asia at the time of the synod. Other common topics included calls for peace, human rights, migrant needs, the family support, the biblical apostolate, and education.

Bishop Orlando Quevedo of Nueva Segovia, Philippines, delivered a strong attack on the globalization of market forces and the manner in which they are further dividing rich from poor. "Clearly," he said, "the Spirit of the Lord is calling the church in Asia to be a church of the poor." He also made reference to the FABC's three basic insights during its history: The church must be a voice of the poor; dialogue is the path to effective evangelization; and the diverse cultures of Asia must be respected. "[Catholic] systems of belief are Western and foreign," he said. "Catholic uniformity must be replaced with Catholic diversity." He stressed the need to build local "basic ecclesial communities." Calling them "a new way of being church," he described them as similar to the basic communities of Latin America, except, he explained, that the local church initiates basic ecclesial communities. He said there are already some 47,000 such communities in the Philippines. A strong call for peace surfaced in the remarks of Japanese Bishop Stephen F. Hamao, then of Yokohama, Japan, site of a U.S. Naval base. He told the synod that working for peace and promoting respect for the environment should be the central concerns of the church in Asia. Peace is a Christian, interreligious and international project, he said. Respect for the environment is also a part of achieving harmony and promoting peace, in addition to being an obligation to future generations, he said. Bishop Carlos Filipe Ximenes Belo, then apostolic administrator of Dili, East Timor, and corecipient of the 1996 Nobel Peace Prize, said the church must continue to work on behalf of human rights. "The church's main contribution to the realization of human rights consists of a continuous and practical process of education . . . to make Christians more conscious of the dignity of the human person," he said.

Of particular note at the synod was the encounter between the bishops of the Near Eastern churches (from Palestine to Iran) and those of Central Asia (the southern states of the former Soviet Union) with those of the FABC (Pakistan to Japan, China to Indonesia). While the FABC churches had met regularly—and did not see the necessity of holding a synod—the ancient apostolic churches of the Near East, the Diaspora communities in Central Asia, and those of FABC had never met together in assembly before. Some observers remarked that this incipient pan-Asian awareness could prove to be the most notable accomplishment of the synod.[2]

The synod interventions revealed diverse Catholic experiences across the Asian continent. Bishops from South and Southeast Asia, for example, spoke of what they do or plan to do in contacts with willing Muslims, while most from the Near East said they can only hope Islamic believers in their areas will be open to dialogue someday. Eastern rite patriarchs, meanwhile, having seen Rome extend concessions to the Orthodox churches in efforts to win unity during the current pontificate, called for similar concessions, starting with greater autonomy within their own rites.

The Asians appeared confident. Joseph Kurian, a layman and judge from southern India, used his synod time to speak about the Asian traditions of "togetherness and communion." He then noted that future synods could be improved if they were more inclusive, allowing both laity and clergy into the decision-making process. (The Federation of Asian Bishops' Conferences documents, and especially the statements of the fourth plenary assembly in Tokyo, Japan, in September 1986, have repeatedly stressed the importance of the laity's active and full participation in the church's life and ministry.) Kurian concluded, expressing a not uncommon perception among Asian Catholics, that Asians "may have to take up the responsibility of re-evangelizing the church in the West of tomorrow."

One frequent theme heard in synod chambers had to do with who should have the final say on liturgies and translations. Currently the Asian churches must request approval from the Vatican for liturgical texts and other official documents translated by the local churches into Asian languages. This often presents problems, the most obvious being that Vatican personnel do not understand most of the Asian languages, and certainly not the nuanced language of prayer and spirituality. Stories abounded at the synod of Vatican rejections of Asian translations—translations that had been scrupulously thought through with the help of theologians, biblical scholars, and Asian linguists. Translations, it turns out, were often rejected by Roman bureaucrats who used the assistance of Asian seminarians studying in Rome. In other words, seminarians were second-guessing the work of their former professors and bishops who had sent them to Rome in the first place. "Can you image how humiliating that can be?" a priest from Indonesia asked. He told the story of Indonesian bishops who translated a liturgical text from Italian into Indonesian. Rome then asked that the translated document be submitted to Rome for approval. The Indonesians complied. Months later, Vatican officials asked the Indonesian bishops' conference if they could retranslate the document into Italian so it could be understood in Rome.

Addressing the synod, Philippine Bishop Francisco Claver, apostolic vicar of Bontoc-Lagawe, told the bishops it would be a "sterile exercise" to try to place blame on any single person for the lack of inculturation of the faith in Asia. The church must move on and trust the people to find ways of correctly expressing their faith in their own language and culture, he said. He added that it made no sense to send translations of liturgical texts to a foreign bishop, let alone a Vatican official, who does not speak that language or live in that culture. "The best judges of the correctness, even theological, of translations and texts are the faithful and clergy of the place where the language is spoken," he said.

A moment midway through the synod neatly encapsulated the clash of perspectives—Asian leaders pleading for the flexibility to meet local needs versus Vatican officials advancing a one-size-fits-all approach. It was Friday, April 24, and participating bishops had completed their second week of speeches. It was time to hear from heads of missionary orders. The superior general of the Missionaries of the Holy Family, Wilhelmus van der Weiden, delivered what quickly became one of the most talked about interventions. "During these days we heard a number of interventions with inculturation as the central theme," Weiden began, noting that a "really wide gap" had arisen between church principles and practice on the issue of inculturation. Citing Rome's refusal to grant experts in local churches the freedom to carry out liturgical inculturation, he isolated the central matter—trust—around which all synodal issues seemed to revolve. From the point of view of the Asian bishops, curial officials appear unwilling to permit local bishops to carry out the work of the church as they see fit. Weiden asked: "Are the Roman *dicasteries* [offices] so afraid for aberrations from that which is considered as the only true doctrine and the only true formulation of the liturgy? Must we not say that often the bishops' conferences with 20, 30 or more bishops and a number of theologians and specialists can better estimate what in liturgical matters is best for their flock than Roman authorities who often don't know the language and the culture of that country?" The superior general then cited scripture passages to show that lack of trust is nothing new to God's people. But the response required is the same, trusting the Holy Spirit. In this case, he argued, Rome needed to grant local churches more autonomy. He finished with a rousing plea to the Roman officials: "Be not afraid!"

Three interventions on women pointed to their serious marginalization in the life of the Asian churches. Filomena Hirota of the Mercedarian Missionaries of Berriz, in the name of the Japanese Religious Leadership Conference, spoke of the need for "a new way of being church in solidarity with the cry of women in a prophetic way," and then spelled out practical steps to ensure greater participation of women in church decision making.[3] Ecumenical delegate Agustina Lumentut of Indonesia stated: "There is a 'syn-odos', a 'walking together' with women from the same religion, but also from other religions. These shared experiences become a primary source for theological reflection, for re-reading the Scripture, a new perspective. As long as Asian women find the courage to tell each other their stories and share their experiences, they have hope." Then she challenged the bishops: "Women are walking together. But is the church walking with them?"

An especially dramatic moment occurred when Carmelite Bishop Francis Hadisumarta of Manokwari-Sorong, Indonesia, speaking on behalf of the Indonesian Bishops' Conference, said it makes no sense for bishops' conferences to translate liturgical texts into local languages, only to then submit them to the Vatican for approval from "people who do not understand our language. . . . What we need is trust: trust in God and trust in each other." He went on to say: "The Catholic church is not a monolithic pyramid. Bishops are not branch secretaries waiting for instructions from Headquarters! We are a communion of local churches. . . ." He continued, telling the synod that the Indonesian Bishops' Conference had been asking the Vatican for thirty years for permission to ordain married men known for their virtue, holiness, and stature within the local community. Because of a shortage of celibate priests, he said, the majority of Indonesian Catholics "live by the Word, rather than by Word and sacrament. We are becoming 'Protestant' by default," he said. "Cannot such pastoral concerns be worked out and decided upon by the local episcopal conference?" He said the Roman curia should become "a clearinghouse for information, support and encouragement rather than a universal decision-maker." He then concluded his intervention with some explosive questions: "This vision, where Episcopal Conferences would have the trust and authority to evangelize—in dialogue with the poor, with cultures and with other faith traditions—is both ancient and new. Do we have the imagination to envisage the birth of new Patriarchates, say the Patriarchate of South Asia, of Southeast Asia and of East Asia? . . . Thus, we envisage a radical decentralization of the Latin Rite—devolving into a host of local Rites in Asia. . . ."

Philippine Archbishop Leonardo Legaspi of Caceres also called for a change in the use of authority, telling his fellow bishops that the local Asian churches must place a new and different emphasis on the primacy of the pope in the church. The universal authority of the pope is "an essential part of our Catholic faith," he said. It "is not primarily concerned with juridical power over local churches and peoples, but is above all a doctrinal and pastoral ministry of service which enhances those very values of harmony, peace and love which make possible dialogue and coexistence with Asian governments and religions." Melkite Bishop Cyrille Salim Bustros of Baalbek, Lebanon, called for a reaffirmation and strengthening of the autonomy of the Eastern rite Catholic churches. He said the election of bishops by Eastern rite synods should not have to be approved by Rome. Bishops' appointments traditionally have been the privilege of the patriarchs; the pope is the "patriarch of the West," which gives him the power to appoint bishops in the Latin rite church, but not in the Eastern rites, he said. The Eastern rite synods should be allowed to establish dioceses outside their traditional territories and appoint pastors for their faithful wherever they live, without needing Vatican approval, he said. And, Bustros added, the Eastern rite churches that have married clergy in their traditional homeland should be allowed to have married clergy in all their dioceses.[4]

Despite such straight talk, the mood of the synod was cordial. The Asian bishops, many of whom came to Rome with few expectations, nevertheless seemed upbeat in the early days. One bishop, explaining why he felt so positive, shared the story of Mahatma Gandhi who returned from negotiations with India's British colonial occupiers unsuccessful in his efforts to win his nation's freedom. "You have failed," he was told by a despondent nationalist. "We have won," Gandhi replied. "We have engaged them in a discussion of our freedom." Another bishop was all smiles after he finished addressing the synod, having spoken on the need to inculturate the faith in his local church. Minutes later at the coffee bar, he beamed to a fellow bishop: "We've got the ideas; we've got the theologies; the rest will follow." At the same time, the bishops and theologians I spoke with were realistic, saying they believed little significant change is possible during the John Paul II pontificate. Their feeling, however, was that time is on their side. These bishops are characteristically patient men. Some said they hoped that the synod would provide new momentum for change in Asia and would place the Asian church on view before the universal church.

There were 191 interventions in all during the first phase of the synod. Asian bishops repeatedly returned to the themes of the "triple dialogue," the dialogue with religions, cultures, and the poor. Given that they shared the synod with Middle Eastern bishops and that church concerns are as varied as life itself, it is significant that interventions were as focused as they were. Days before the synod opened, FABC staff set up a temporary headquarters in a few rooms inside the Philippine embassy to the Vatican across the street from the synod hall. Key Asian bishops and other FABC leaders soon were meeting there to discuss strategies and help the bishops translate their thoughts from local languages into English and sometimes French. Staff members also helped bishops draft interventions or find biblical texts supporting episcopal thoughts. One of the federation's rooms was equipped with a copying machine and computers with e-mail and Internet connections. Asian theological journals were available. Throughout each day, Asian bishops found the temporary headquarters a comfortable place to think, meet, or relax. One federation staff member, Jesuit Soosai Arokiasamy, editor of the Delhi-based theological monthly *Vidyajyoti*, was straightforward in speaking of the federation's synod efforts. "Our goals," he said, "are basic: to help the bishops and enrich the process." In the end, the synod became an FABC platform to unveil to the world its vision, its mission—its "new way of being church."

A study of the interventions affirmed this consistency: twenty-three dealt with interfaith dialogue; eighteen with the need for a more participative and collegial church; sixteen with inculturation; eleven with the need of the church to accompany the poor and marginalized; and ten with the challenge of economic globalization. Another ten dealt with questions of Asian spirituality and God-experience; seven with youth; and another seven with the church in China. Six interventions focused on the ancient Apostolic Churches of the Middle East; five took up the question of women; five more the laity; four were on schools; four on ecumenism; four on indigenous peoples; four more on family life. Most of these interventions—76.3 percent—can be clustered around four main topics: dialogue with other Asian churches and faith traditions (22.5 percent), dialogue with cultures (21.4 percent), dialogue with the poor (17.2 percent), and an acknowledgment that the Asian church is a church of the laity (15.2 percent). These have been core to the FABC vision for decades.[5]

The synod work is most visible in its first phase. This is when participants have their say. Some religious and lay women attended the synod, but were not voting participants. During the second phase participants break down into language groups after synod organizers issue their *Relatio post disceptationem*, a mid-synod report that is supposed to summarize the speeches. It is at this stage that those in charge begin to steer the course of the proceedings. They have the authority to decide which interventions become themes for further discussions. During the Asian synod, the mid-synod report, it was revealed, was written several days before the interventions had been completed, upsetting many bishops. Not surprisingly, the report largely represented the view expressed by Cardinal Joseph Tomko, Prefect of the Congregation for the Evangelization of Peoples, that evangelization must start with the person of Jesus and his unique role in the salvation of all peoples. At a news conference on the afternoon of April 29, several Asian bishops tried to put a positive face on the report, saying that further discussion on "emphasis" will continue. Bishop Joseph Vianney Fernando of Kandy, India, told reporters that "a number of Asian fathers had already noted that key phrases and ideas important to them had been left out of the report." The report contained fifteen questions that to many synod participants sounded defensive and out of step with their thinking on key church matters. As an example, some questioned why the bishops were being asked, "How can the church deal with some unorthodox trends among theologians?" when the issue was never raised as a concern by the bishops during the initial interventions. Nevertheless, most groups answered making strong statements of encouragement for their theologians. The fifteen questions, one synod member complained, reflected "a discontinuity" from the main trends of the interventions. One of the few women participants at the synod expressed her disappointment that none of the fifteen questions dealt with women. She said women had become "almost invisible" in the discussions although in many Asian churches women constitute 60 to 70 percent of the faithful.

During the third week of the synod, discussions continued as synod participants met in eleven language groups. Tensions persisted, according to several bishops. The participants were grouped as follows: eight English-speaking, two French-speaking, and one Italian-speaking. Most working groups initially stuck with the questions, as the planners requested. Soon, however, over the course of thirteen meetings, most groups drifted back to earlier themes, to what they referred to as the needed "triple-dialogue" with religions, cultures, and the marginalized. Several Asian bishops complained that curial members tried to dominate the discussion groups. Bishop Hamao of Yokohama, Japan, told a reporter, "We came thinking they [the curia] would listen to us and learn something about the local churches of Asia. We did not expect they [curia members] would try to teach us." Hamao used the example of Cardinal Alfonso Lopez Trujillo, president of the Pontifical Council for the Family, who spoke for forty-five minutes at the beginning of a discussion group session. An Indonesian synod participant said he tired of hearing Cardinal James Stafford, president of the Pontifical Council for the Laity, talk at length about the need to maintain unity with the pope.

Following several days of work, the group leaders reported the outlines of their group's discussions to the larger assembly. At this point it was clear that liturgical texts and the question of who should finally approve them became a central focus of attention. One English-speaking group recommended that Asian episcopal conferences be given "full authority" to create liturgical commissions to produce and approve translations, which the curia should ratify without question. Another noted the "general feeling" that greater freedom must be granted to bishops' conferences and to the regional councils of bishops in regard to liturgical matters, as "they know the situations best." Still another recorded a "strong consensus" that local churches should be given full responsibility for translations of liturgical texts. So did two other English-speaking groups. One English-speaking group added that the attitude of curia members with regard to matters of inculturation of liturgy had not been helpful. The group said that Latin rite liturgies are simply Western liturgies translated into local Asian languages, an approach the group said is inadequate. It also said that local Asian bishops needed to be taken more seriously by Rome in the development of liturgies since the local bishops know the people, languages, and cultures. Several English-speaking groups asked permission to use the sacred scriptures of other religions in Catholic liturgies. Other work groups, including one French-speaking group, disagreed with this approach. A number of the working groups pointed out that effective evangelization continues to be hampered by the perception that Catholicism in Asia is "Western" and "foreign." The umbilical cords of colonialism have not been fully severed, said one English-speaking group. "Our Christian faith must by all means shed its reputation as a foreign religion and become better inculturated, taking on an Asian face everywhere without in any way compromising or diminishing Christ's gospel teachings," Philippine Bishop Claver reported on behalf of one working group. "The inculturation of the liturgy requires greater use of vernacular languages and indigenous symbols." Speaking about the relationship between Rome and the local churches, an English-language group reported that "collaboration" had to be strengthened. It recalled that in 1931, Pius XI formulated the principle of subsidiarity, a principle reaffirmed by a 1985 synod of bishops. "This principle of governance has to be practiced," the group report noted. "In principle, when it is possible and effective, the decision-making has to be shared at all levels, and more trust has to be manifested." One working group said that to promote greater communion, local churches should not be considered as separate units but as part of the universal church. Unity in diversity must be rightly understood and practiced in a spirit of mutual charity, the group said. Unity, not uniformity, is the goal. Group leader Archbishop Leonardo Z. Legaspi of Caceres, Philippines, suggested that members of various Vatican departments "exhibit more fully pastoral attention and charity to whom they minister. A warm and welcoming attitude does much to promote ecclesial communion." One synod participant said that the Italian-speaking group "tended to sound more curial" because it had a greater proportion of members of the curia in it than did the French-speaking or English-speaking groups. The conclusions drawn up by the working groups were aimed at formulating propositions to be presented to the pope.[6]

It was the task of the Secretary General of the Synod, Belgian Cardinal Schotte, charged with running the synod, to oversee the process, at every turn assuring that Vatican control over the synod is not lost. Through it all, the Asian bishops seemed patient—and resigned. If the Asian bishops never flinched from their pastoral perspectives, they never really expected them to be fully represented in the final fruits of the synod. As one of the Asian cardinal moderators reportedly said: "We should not become over excited by curial machinations. Yes, they have filtered out our contributions. When we return to our countries, we shall also be filtering their documents." The story was told at the synod of a Filipino bishop who, dining one afternoon with the pope, asked him: "Your Holiness, do you see any difference between the American and the Asian synods?" The pope replied: "No, I don't. Each has the same secretary general." The Filipino bishop laughed and said: "Yes, Your Holiness, the same secretary general, the same methodology, the same pope."

Eventually, the language groups pooled their thinking and submitted their work to the secretariat's office for final editing. When the propositions came forward, Indonesian and Japanese bishops, among others, complained their ideas had not been included. The issue of "subsidiarity" and its use—or abuse—had been on the minds of many bishops, several bishops told me. Yet it was absent from the propositions. One synod participant, referring to the propositions, said, "Most of this could have been written 20 to 30 years ago."

After further discussion, editing, and voting, fifty-nine propositions emerged to be presented to the pope.[7] In the editing process many ideas expressed by the Asian bishops simply disappeared. The term "Asian churches" became "the Catholic Church in Asia"; "other Christian churches" was changed to "other Christian confessions." Words like "subsidiarity," "decentralization," "deregulation," and "democracy" simply fell off the table. The final proposition topics moved from local church (diocese) directly to universal church (Rome), no mention of bishops' conferences. Proposals on enhancing the authority of episcopal conferences disappeared. The one form of collaboration between local churches that survived was mutual help through prayer and finance. Without a word, FABC theology was subsumed into official curial ideology.[8]

At one level the synod ended more with a whimper than a bang. Looked at as a moment when the Asian bishops confidently paraded their pastoral teachings before the wider church, it was a historic—and revealing—month. Father Peter C. Phan, the Vietnamese professor of theology at Catholic University of America, said this of the synod:

What was new is not what the Asian bishops said but that they said it and how they said it at the synod. What they said had been said, at length and with power and depth, for almost 30 years, ever since the founding of the FABC in 1972, in its numerous plenary assemblies and in the documents of its several institutes. But at the synod, they said it again, to the whole church, and with surprising boldness and refreshing candor. . . . The synod was the first official recognition that the churches of Asia have come of age. . . .[9]

More practically the synod allowed bishops to have month-long encounters with fellow bishops from other parts of Asia. Friendship and fellowship were created or renewed.

The larger meaning of the synod could also be gleaned in the official closing remarks by Cardinal Julius Darmaatmadja of Indonesia on May 13, 1998. The cardinal described the synod as a "process of walking together" during which participants had the opportunity to experience the rich variety of the local churches of Asia and the many forms of ecclesial communion on the local and regional levels:

> For almost a month now, we have truly experienced a process of walking together. This synodal experience has allowed us to come to know many particular churches of Asia with which we had not previously come into contact. We feel spiritually renewed by having been with one another and having sought together ways to make the particular churches of Asia fully and deeply present as the one Church which desires to serve the many and varied concerns of the Asian people.

He went to say:

> Considering all the challenges in Asia, we feel that the synod theme is quite relevant. "Being Church in Asia" today means "participating in the mission of Christ, the Savior, in rendering his redemptive love and service in Asia," so that Asian men and women can more fully achieve their integral human development, and "that they may have life, and have it abundantly" (Jn 10:10). . . . In addition to offering hope and new life in Jesus Christ and serving directly people who are needy in so many ways, we must also take part in the task of striving to improve unjust structures, whether in the economic, political, cultural or governmental realms, as well as of building a new culture of life characterized by love, truth, honesty and justice.

There was nothing triumphal in Darmaatmadja's remarks, nothing confrontational. Full of resolve, he and the other Asian bishops left Rome with new commitment and a better understanding of the obstacles they faced in the months and years to come.

CHAPTER 13

Home Again

The Kingdom of God is within you.
—Luke 17:21

I do not want my house to be walled
in on all sides and my windows to be
stuffed. I want the cultures of all the
lands to be blown about my house as
freely as possible. (But) I refuse to be
blown off my feet by any.
—Mahatma Gandhi

Two subjects that were never publicly raised during the synod—but were on a lot of minds—had to do with Pope John Paul's age and health. It is said in Catholic circles that nothing is deader than a dead pope. In life our popes are hailed; in death, they are forgotten. Some have said it would be healthier if we exalted our popes less in life and offered more lavish praise after death. But that is not the way it is.

The synod took place in the twentieth year of John Paul's pontificate. It ended three days before the pope's seventy-eighth birthday. What was not being said—at least aloud—among the Asian bishops and others during the synod was that John Paul's pontificate had to be in its last years. The bishops of Asia desperately want change. They want greater local authority to make pastoral decisions. However, they are respectful men and know the way the church operates—and how it does not. So they knew they needed to let their so-called Asian patience carry the day. But something else was at play. The bishops and others viewed the work of the synod as helping to set an agenda for the next conclave, that gathering of the College of Cardinals that elects the new pope. And they could be helping to draw up an agenda for the next church council, one that would truly allow Catholicism to become the universal religion it is meant to become. Issues of how to achieve collegiality and how to use authority were at the top of virtually every bishop's "needs attention" list. Under

John Paul's pontificate it made little sense to push for change that could not occur.

It would be wrong to believe that the Asian bishops anticipated change going into the synod. It would be just as wrong to believe they expected it coming out of the synod. These men are realists. These are wise and worldly bishops. What they hoped for was modest affirmation. What they feared was that their visions, based on the triple dialogue, would come under further attack.

Truth is, the Asian bishops were eager to get back home. A month away from Asia and they were missing family and compatriots; they were also missing their Asian cuisine. Ravioli is fine; but for many Asians it is not a substitute for rice or the rich and spicy foods that make Asian cuisine special. There was something else afoot. After the synod, it would be only a year and a half before there would be another plenary assembly of the Federation of Asian Bishops' Conferences. It would begin on January 3, 2000, in Sam Phran, Thailand. Unlike the synod, the FABC meeting would take place on *Asian soil*—and Asians would run it. The running of the Synod on Asia was kept entirely in the hands of curial officials. The FABC gatherings, by contrast, would be the products of Asian minds.

In the months that followed the Asian synod in the spring of 1998, the Vatican kept the pressure on the Asian leadership. Two actions in particular seemed aimed at sending a message from Rome to the East:

- August 1998: Ratzinger's office censured certain ideas in the work of Indian Jesuit Anthony de Mello, who died more than ten years earlier. De Mello's work was accused of uncritically blending ideas from Eastern and Western traditions and of promoting "religious indifferentism."

- October 1998: Jesuit Jacques Dupuis took a leave of absence from the Gregorian University in Rome in order to answer charges against him concerning his book, *Toward a Christian Theology of Religious Pluralism*, in which he argued that Christ as God's Eternal Word can be active in non-Christian religions. Dupuis' response ran to some 118 pages, but failed to satisfy Vatican concerns. Dupuis spent thirty-six years in India before joining the theology faculty at Rome's Gregorian University. He served for many years as an adviser on interreligious issues to Vatican offices. It took him three years before Rome cleared his name.

These events had clouded Rome–Asia relations, putting the brakes on further serious publishing. Even completed manuscripts were being held up. "Why take grief?" the attitude seemed to be. It was in this context of uncertainty and tension that the bishops awaited Pope John Paul as he traveled to New Delhi, India, for a brief trip beginning November 6, 1999. The purpose of the trip was to unveil his response to the synod. He had wanted to offer his response on Chinese soil, in Hong Kong. However, Beijing had turned him down. India was the first alternative. Days before the pope's arrival Hindu fundamentalists were in the streets protesting. They didn't want the pope in India. When the then seventy-nine-year-old pontiff arrived, he responded to his critics, saying to the media: "Let no one fear the church." In the same breath, he asserted that everyone has the right to "freedom of belief and worship" and reiterated the command to preach the gospel to all nations.

PAPAL RESPONSE

John Paul's official response to the synod came in the form of a thirty-thousand-word document called *Ecclesia in Asia.* It covered a range of topics, responding to sanitized recommendations that had come out of the synod. Its principal message was the one Rome had broadcast before and during the synod: "Jesus Christ is humanity's one and only Savior." In this sense, *Ecclesia in Asia* held few surprises. Most of the document was laced with phrases such as, "preaching . . . the saving Death and Resurrection of Jesus Christ must be your absolute priority" (*Ecclesia in Asia* §2), "proclaim with vigor in word and deed that Jesus Christ is the Savior" (§9), "Jesus is the greatest gift which the Church can offer to Asia" (§10), "the disciples of Christ in Asia must . . . be unstinting in their efforts to fulfill the mission . . . the love of Jesus the Savior" (§50). This is how John Paul explained evangelization:

> There can be no true evangelization without the explicit proclamation of Jesus as Lord. The Second Vatican Council and the Magisterium since then, responding to a certain confusion about the true nature of the Church's mission, have repeatedly stressed the primacy of the proclamation of Jesus Christ in all evangelizing work. . . . The Church in Asia is all the more eager for the task of proclamation knowing that "through the working of the Spirit, there already exists in individuals and peoples an expectation, even if an unconscious one, of knowing the truth about God, about man, and about how we are to be set free from sin and death." This insistence on proclamation is prompted neither by sectarian impulse or the spirit of proselytism nor any sense of superiority. The Church evangelizes in obedience to Christ's command, in the knowledge that every person has the right to hear the Good News of the God who reveals and gives himself in Christ.

Reactions by the national press in India were dominated by the impression that the pope had called for a new missionary era for Asia in general and India in particular. This raised many fears among Asian religious leaders, so many that the archbishop of New Delhi, Alan de Lastic, felt the need to respond that the pope had not called for new conversions and that he had only spoken of "inner conversion," not the changing of religions. "The whole episode," wrote one Asian church observer, "shows that it makes a real difference when certain issues are addressed in Rome, in the context of old ecclesial traditions and ways, or when the same problems are presented outside this context in Asia or in India."[1]

Virginia Saldanha of Mumbai, India, a lay member of the Federation of Asian Bishops' Conferences, said that the document was received in India with "a lot of unease." "The problem is it has been written by men who are far removed from our reality in the streets of India." She noted that a Muslim had asked her how she would feel if a command had gone out to the Muslims of the world to go out and convert the whole world. "Would you not feel threatened?" she quoted him as asking.

Reactions overall were mixed. *Ecclesia in Asia,* wrote Father Peter C. Phan, was a "typical" John Paul II work, "with its rather forbidding length, its frequent insistence on complete orthodoxy, its abundant citations of the pope's own writings, and its emotional peroration with a prayer to Mary."[2] The professor of theology at Catholic University of America said the document begs two questions: "Has the exhortation said anything new and important for the churches of Asia that either had not been said before by these churches themselves or could not have been said except thanks to the work of the synod itself? To both parts of the question, the answer is frankly no."[3]

Maryknoll missioner James H. Kroeger, professor of systematic theology, missiology and Islamics at the Jesuit Loyola School in Manila, called it a "rich" document, characterized by a spirit of "gratitude, celebration and optimism."[4]

Filomena Hirota of the Mercedarian Missionaries of Berriz, an Asian synod participant, said she had the same difficulty reading *Ecclesia in Asia* that she had during the synod itself. "I saw in the new document the phrase which some of us at the synod tried hard to have taken away: 'The heart of Asia will be restless until the whole of Asia finds its rest in the peace of Christ, the Risen Lord.'" Hirota explained that she had difficulty understanding a sentence such as "There can be no full evangelization without the explicit proclamation of Jesus as Lord." She said she knew many women and men committed to the Good News of Jesus who are witnessing to the gospels in Asia with their very lives.

Cardinal Stephen Kim Sou-hwan of Seoul, South Korea, the synod *general relator*, put a positive face on *Ecclesia in Asia.* The pope, he said, "added his personal stress that Jesus Christ is the only Savior, though dialogue is needed." Bishop Vincent Ri Byong-ho of Chonju, another Korean synod delegate, liked the fact that the pope had stressed that Jesus was Asian and that appropriate means of preaching to Asians are necessary.

Jesuit Michael Amaladoss, an Indian and former Jesuit assistant general, called *Ecclesia in Asia* "a document *for* Asia but not *from* Asia." He said its tone and style "are very un-Asian." He added, however, that "one can pick up encouraging quotes to support any activity in which the church is engaged."[5]

Precious Blood priest Bob Schreiter, professor of theology at Catholic Theological Union in Chicago and past president of the American Society of Missiology and the Catholic Theological Society of America, said that while the document calls for "sensitivity to the special needs and contexts of the diverse populations of Asia," it reduces evangelization "almost entirely" to proclamation of the Word.

During the Asian synod many bishops spoke of the need to engage in dialogue with other religions and to learn from them. Implicit in this thinking is the idea that the Holy Spirit exists within other religions. In *Ecclesia in Asia*, however, the pope warns against making "a false separation between the Redeemer and the Holy Spirit," saying this "would jeopardize the truth of Jesus as the one Savior of all."

Society of the Divine Word priest John Prior, who worked as the press liaison for English-speaking media at the synod, did a study of *Ecclesia in Asia*.[6] He found that the pope quoted himself in sixty-eight out of 240 footnotes, or in 28.3 percent of all the references. By contrast, he quoted from Vatican II documents only fifteen times, or in 6.2 percent of all references. "Conciliar teaching has receded into the background," Prior stated. He also noted that proposals from the working groups on the need to reform the Roman curia, to democratize and decentralize the Latin rite and to allow much greater scope to the local churches to forge ahead with deep inculturation never found their way to the recommendations that went to the pope. *Ecclesia in Asia* "has not a single direct reference to any intervention by an individual bishop, nor to interventions by bishops in the name of their conferences. There are no direct references to regional episcopal bodies such as the Federation of Asian Bishops' Conferences (FABC) or the Council of Oriental Catholic Patriarchs (COCP)."

Shortly after the pope delivered *Ecclesia in Asia* to the one hundred bishops who had gathered in New Delhi to receive him, Indonesian Cardinal Julius Darmaatmadja, the president delegate of the synod, offered a response. His speech was viewed as especially important not only because he is considered to be one of Asia's more influential church figures but also because his words represented the first official Asian response to the exhortation. Malaysian La Salle Brother Edmund Chia, who has been active in the FABC for many years, did a comparison between *Ecclesia in Asia* and Darmaatmadja's response.[7] Chia notes that from John Paul's perspective the new evangelization is necessary because "after two millennia, a major part of the human family still does not acknowledge Christ." Darmaatmadja sees the new evangelization as the Asian churches "taking on the face of Asia," a process "that is meaningful for Asian society, particularly for the poor and underprivileged." *Ecclesia in Asia* sees other religions as "a great challenge to evangelization," while the cardinal says it is the church that must be open to learning from these other religions. Pope John Paul stated that "there can be no true evangelization without the explicit proclamation of Jesus as Lord." The cardinal responded, "Yes . . . but for Asia, there will be no complete evangelization unless there is dialogue with other religions and cultures."

While Darmaatmadja's remarks represented the first individual Asian response to *Ecclesia in Asia*, the January 2000 deliberations of the FABC were the first collective Asian response. The gathering took place at a pastoral center outside of Bangkok. The week-long meeting drew 160 bishops and other Asian church leaders. Once again, Cardinal Joseph Tomko, Prefect of the Sacred Congregation for the Evangelization of Peoples, was the featured representative from the Vatican. Speaking the first day, he told the Asian bishops that analysis of *Ecclesia in Asia* was the gathering's "main duty." His directive, however, went largely unobserved. No workshop or session was devoted to it. No one delivered a talk about it. No official assessment was offered. Meanwhile, after Tomko spoke he faced some rough grilling by several bishops who wanted to know what he had meant when, in his address, he warned them about allowing "weak Christology" into Asia. Asked to be more specific, he replied that a weak Christology was one that portrayed Jesus as simply a wise person or prophet— but not as the Son of God. Pressed further if he had encountered any such Christology in their midst, Tomko replied he had not. Another bishop then facetiously asked Tomko if Rome would recognize an Asian Christ "if it ever saw one." The question brought widespread laughter.

Archbishop Orlando Quevedo of the Philippines, considered a key strategist, delivered the opening address. Drawing from statements of previous FABC plenary assemblies, he spoke of a series of movements that are weaving together the Asian vision of a renewed church. He listed these: becoming a church of the poor and of the young, becoming Christian communities driven by an integrated spirituality, and becoming communities that empower the laity to generate and serve life.[8] The tone of Quevedo's remarks was thoughtful, affirming, and forward-looking. In the days that followed, the bishops drew up a list of challenges facing Asia: globalization, religious fundamentalism, politics, ecology, and militarization. Among those groups needing special attention the bishops listed women, youth, families, indigenous peoples, migrants, and refugees.

During the ten-day gathering, which I attended as a journalist for the *National Catholic Reporter*, the bishops repeatedly spoke about the importance of building local communities and invigorating them through service and Christian example. They did not contradict anything the pope had said in *Ecclesia in Asia* as much as they seemed to look beyond the document. Privately many bishops expressed frustration with Rome's inability to understand their circumstances. At the same time they expressed respect for the pope and for the office of the papacy. It is helpful to remember that Pope John Paul II was twenty to thirty years older than most of the bishops who attended the Thailand assembly. Asians are both respectful and deferential to the elderly. The Asian bishops are no exceptions.

During the gathering, the bishops consoled and affirmed one another. They shared stories of personal hardships. An Indonesian bishop explained the complexities of working as a priest in heavily Muslim areas. One priest had worked for years in one such area doing simple social work. Eventually he was approached quietly by a young Muslim man who asked to be baptized. If word got out of such a baptism, the bishop explained, it could lead to the man's execution and also to violent attacks on local Catholics. The priest told the man he could not baptize him and suggested he travel to another area of the country where a baptism might be possible. The story was told of another bishop, who, lacking priests, ordained two married men. Several bishops expressed disappointment that Rome did not trust them more with making decisions critical to the health of their local churches. Many bishops deplored the growing gap between rich and poor in their countries. A Filipino priest spoke about his role in heading the newest church mission in the world, the Mongolian church. He has eighty-seven Catholics in his flock, most of them converts and most of them youngsters who had left the sewers and streets to take up shelter in his home. He continues to do much of his ministry work in the sewers, he said.

The final statement released by the FABC at that plenary session highlighted concerns that the bishops viewed as critical. At the top of their list they placed the issue of globalization, which, they said, continues to be unregulated by juridical and ethical norms and is adding to the millions who live below the poverty line. Globalization, they wrote, is also accelerating the process of secularization in Asia and it is helping to spawn extremist fundamentalism, as bewildered people and cultures react to it.

The final FABC document celebrated Asian freedom from colonialism. It then went on to say that "corrupt governments, a growing concentration of wealth among the few and international economic 'restructuring'" are causing great hardships. It lamented the deterioration of the environment and growing concentrations of people in urban areas, linking these to global economic forces. Facing overwhelming and complex forces, the bishops said, Asia requires "integrated" responses by churches and religions working together in the wider societies.

"We need to feel and act integrally," meaning that spiritual, social, economic, and interreligious programs need to be linked if they are to have the force necessary to fulfill the church's true evangelization mission. In workshops and large discussions, the bishops made frequent references to the need to help their people develop deeper spiritual lives and to combine these with work on behalf of social justice. They affirmed their commitment to the "triple dialogue"—with culture, other religions, and the poor.

UNEXPECTED EVENT

The bishops concluded their work in Thailand feeling that they were on solid footing and, despite some differences with Rome, that they were managing to collaborate. Tensions between the Vatican vision for the future of Asia and the Asian bishops' own vision grew substantially before the year was out when the Congregation for the Doctrine of the Faith released *Dominus Iesus* on September 5 at a news conference hosted by Cardinal Joseph Ratzinger.[9] *Dominus Iesus* essentially argues that while followers of other religions can be saved (though only in a mysterious fashion and only through the grace of Christ), they nevertheless live in a "gravely deficient situation" compared with Christians, who alone "have the fullness of the means of salvation." Some observers saw in *Dominus Iesus* the beginning of a movement against the theology of religious pluralism similar to the one the Vatican had been waging against liberation theology in the 1980s. Like liberation theology, which sought to align Catholicism with movements for social justice in Latin America, the theology of religious pluralism, which sees the Holy Spirit operating in all religions, is rooted in the Third World, particularly in Asia. At his news conference, Ratzinger said the new document had been prompted in part by the "worrisome influence" of the "negative theology" of Asia on the West. He said *Dominus Iesus* aimed to combat the post–Vatican II "ideology of dialogue," a not very veiled reference to the Asian bishops' pastoral initiatives embedded in the triple dialogue. Ratzinger said that dialogue falsely rejects the "urgency of the appeal for conversion." Some of the major points of *Dominus Iesus* include:

- Revelation in Christ is complete and cannot be complemented by other religions.

- Sacred writings of other religions may have elements that "maintain a life-relationship with God," but only the Old and New Testaments are "inspired texts."

- Whatever the Holy Spirit brings about in other religions "serves as a preparation for the gospel and can only be understood in reference to Christ."

- Non-Catholic Christian churches have "defects," and Protestant communities are not "churches" at all in the proper sense.

- Prayers and rituals of other religions do not have a "divine origin."

- Catholics must be committed to "announcing the necessity of conversion to Jesus Christ."

The Vatican condemned religious pluralism in these words:

The church's constant missionary proclamation is endangered today by relativistic theories that seek to justify religious pluralism, not only *de facto* but also *de jure* (*in principle*). . . . Some of these can be mentioned: the conviction of the elusiveness and inexpressibility of divine truth, even by Christian revelation; relativistic attitudes toward truth itself, according to which what is true for some would not be true for others; the radical opposition posited between the logical mentality of the West and the symbolic mentality of the East; . . . the metaphysical emptying of the historical incarnation of the Eternal Logos, reduced to a mere appearing of God in history; the eclecticism of those who, in theological research, uncritically absorb ideas from a variety of theological and philosophical contexts without regard for consistency, systematic connection, or compatibility with Christian truth; finally, the tendency to read and to interpret sacred scripture outside the tradition and the magisterium of the church. As a remedy for this relativistic mentality, which is becoming ever more common, it is necessary above all to reassert the definitive and complete character of the revelation of Jesus Christ. . . .

Reactions to *Dominus Iesus* were generally negative. Critiques viewed the document as too dogmatic and too rigid and a return to pre–Vatican II triumphalism. The declaration that followers of other religions live in a "gravely deficient situation" struck most observers as both insensitive and arrogant. Even prominent Catholic prelates seemed embarrassed by it. Australian Cardinal Edward Cassidy, former secretary of the Pontifical Council for Promoting Christian Unity, told Rome's *Corriere della Sera* newspaper that "neither the time nor the language of the document were opportune."[10] Bishop Walter Kasper, secretary of the Pontifical Council for Promoting Christian Unity, said that while he agreed with the basic principles in the document, it lacked "the necessary sensitivity." Cardinal Carlo Maria Martini of Milan described the document as "theologically rather dense, peppered with quotations, and not easy to grasp." He, too, faulted its tone. Cardinal Roger Mahony of Los Angeles wrote in *The Tidings,* the archdiocesan newspaper, that it "may not fully reflect the deeper understanding that has been achieved through ecumenical and interreligious dialogues over these last 30 years or more."

The Institute of Missiology Missio in Aachen, Germany, which follows Catholic mission work closely, stated that *Dominus Iesus*

> is not doing justice to the serious theological reflection done, especially by theologians from Asia, but also from the other continents, in the fields of christology, pneumatology, ecclesiology and theology of religions. . . . The issue at stake . . . is whether the great plurality in the content and methodology in theological reflection, which has developed in recent years, can be considered to be a legitimate expression of the emergence of a world church since Vatican II. . . . The document seems to refute nearly all theological advances made during the last 30 years by theologians in Asia, Africa and Latin America as incompatible with Catholic orthodoxy.[11]

Father John Prior, a missionary in Indonesia for more than a quarter century, said it smacks of "cultural arrogance." "Apparently we are allowed to dialogue with members of other faith traditions, although we have nothing to learn doctrinally," he told *National Catholic Reporter* Vatican Affairs writer John Allen.

Said Mohammed Sammak, a Muslim who directs a dialogue with Christianity in Lebanon: "Islam is suffering from fundamentalism, and this gives the extremists an excuse to pounce and say, 'See, we told you, they do not respect us.'"[12] "They will ask us moderates, 'Why are you making peace with them? Why do you want to dialogue with them?' It makes my job much more difficult."

Some observers expressed concern that the document would erode church authority, as had, for example, the 1968 birth control encyclical *Humanae Vitae.* They argued that Catholics involved in interreligious dialogue might be forced to assent to *Dominus Iesus'* theological principles only to ignore them in practice when they encountered members of other religions.[13]

La Salle Brother Edmund Chia, in Bangkok, had practical reasons to criticize the document: "Religious pluralism is an existential reality for many of us, and not just a theory or theological concept. . . . Some of us have relatives, parents, spouses or children who are adherents of other religions. We see that these people are good and holy not in spite of but because of the God and religions they believe in. It would therefore be a violation of our conscience to even suggest that baptism is necessary for their salvation."

The Vatican attack on religious pluralism was especially dispiriting to Jesuit Jacques Dupuis, who endured what he called a period of "very great suffering" while Rome investigated his writings. For Dupuis it was almost unimaginable that the church he had given his life to in service would turn on him. The investigation cast a shadow over him. He saw it as a grave injustice in that he was not allowed to respond to his faceless critics inside the Vatican. Then, finally, on February 26, 2001, the Congregation for the Doctrine of the Faith called off the inquiry after Dupuis accepted a "censure" for eight so-called "ambiguities" in his best-known book, *Toward a Christian Theology of Religious Pluralism* (Orbis), published in 1997. The censure also ended months of imposed silence. Most observers believe the Vatican's main concern with Dupuis' complex book had been his belief that other religions play a positive role in God's plan for humanity. The Vatican censure, officially known as a "notification," came at the same time the congregation lauded Dupuis for raising new questions and for his "attempt to remain within the limit of orthodoxy." Nevertheless, it listed several points that Dupuis and all other theologians were called upon to uphold:

- Jesus Christ is the "sole and universal mediator of salvation for all humanity."

- The revelation offered in Jesus offers everything necessary for salvation and has no need of completion by other religions.

- Elements of truth in other religions derive from Jesus.

- The Word of God and the Holy Spirit are not agents of salvation apart from Jesus Christ.

- Different religions are not ways of salvation complementary to the Catholic Church.

- Followers of other religions are called to be part of the Catholic Church.

- In themselves, other religions are not means of salvation because they "contain omissions, insufficiencies and errors."

Dominus Iesus and the Dupuis investigation did little to squelch talk that Pope John Paul II was no longer running the show. The gap between some of the pope's earlier writings and, more importantly, gestures and

the uncompromising nature of *Dominus Iesus* only fueled further speculation. For example, in October 1986 Pope John Paul had invited leaders
of other world religions to prayer services in Assisi, Italy, and in March
2000, he prayed at the Wailing Wall in Jerusalem, leaving behind a hand-
written note apologizing to Jews for the failings of the church. During
those celebrated events, he asked no one to convert, but rather used the
common language of penance and prayer.

A far more accommodating Vatican surfaced in October 2001, during
ceremonies marking the four hundredth anniversary of the arrival of the
Jesuit missionary Father Matteo Ricci in Peking [now Beijing]. As part of
those ceremonies, simultaneously taking place in Beijing and Rome, Pope
John Paul issued a letter calling for better relations between the Holy See
and China. The letter apologized for "past and present" wrongs committed by members of the Catholic Church. "I feel deep sadness" for errors
and limits of the past, he said. "I regret that in many people these failings
may have given the impression of a lack of respect and esteem for the
Chinese people . . . making them feel that the church was motivated by
feelings of hostility toward China."

Beijing responded cautiously, saying it would study the papal appeal.
A Chinese official quickly added China's long-standing caveats that diplomatic relations between the Holy See and China cannot happen until the
Vatican severs its ties with Taiwan and pledges not to interfere in China's
internal affairs. The latter is a code word for "We will appoint our own
bishops, thank you." The apology was viewed as being unlikely to break
the diplomatic logjam.

More significant, however, was the praise the pope lavished on Ricci
and his inculturation efforts. Ricci, a scholar, had been deeply aware of
the important role culture takes in Asian life. As John Paul noted in his
address, Ricci studied Chinese language, culture, and history for twenty-
one years before traveling to Peking to approach the emperor and his
court. He dressed as a Confucian scholar and taught mathematics and science—not catechism. "I am pleased here to recall," John Paul stated, "that
Ricci introduced himself as a celibate religious who sought no privilege
at court, asking only to be able to place at the service of His Majesty his
own person and the expertise in the sciences which he had acquired. . . ."

The Ricci story was a tragic episode in Asian Catholic history. He and
his fellow Jesuits were winning friends and gaining influence in high
places. Of all the "wrongs" committed "by some Catholics" that Pope
John Paul II referred to the most serious was one done by one of John
Paul's predecessors, Pope Clement XI in 1709. It was Clement who condemned the Jesuits' efforts at inculturation. That condemnation was a
fatal mistake, ending further missionary efforts and leading to a century

of hostility against Christians. What struck many observers was the contrast between the tone of John Paul's remarks concerning Ricci and the tone of *Dominus Iesus*. As the pope noted, Ricci sought no privilege and asked only to serve. Curiously, that was the approach to evangelism advocated by virtually every Asian bishop who spoke at the April 1998 Synod on Asia—an approach dismissed by Vatican prelates who insisted on the primary need to proclaim Jesus as unique Savior to the World.

CHAPTER **14**

New Century Vision

*The Lord executes justice for the
oppressed; gives food to the hungry. . . .*
—*Psalm 146:7*

*Christianity must assume into the
full Christian life of our peoples what
is good, noble and living in our cultures
and traditions as well as bring to
fulfillment whatever seeds of the Gospel
have been planted in Asian cultures
previous to evangelization.*
—*Asian bishops, Calcutta, 1978*

The challenges facing the human family in the new century are daunting. Population, hunger, poverty, resource depletion, injustice, cultural dislocation, nationalism, weapons production, environmental degradation, climate change: all these are part of lists that are all too familiar. Meanwhile, human wisdom seems not to have kept abreast with human intelligence. As a result, the forces of destruction appear more powerful than the resolve to contain them. Curtailing human shortsightedness for long-term planetary benefits will require every bit of human ingenuity that can be mustered. It will also require unprecedented international cooperation, including that of the major religions and wisdom traditions of the world.

Transcending national boundaries, the Catholic Church will inevitably play a role in setting the climate for interreligious cooperation. Its agenda must be a worldly agenda. "The joys and the hopes, the griefs and the anxieties of the men of this age, especially those who are poor or in any way afflicted, these are the joys and hopes, the griefs and anxieties of the followers of Christ." With these bold words, embedded in the opening lines of *Gaudium et Spes,* the Pastoral Constitution on the Church in the

Modern World, promulgated by the Second Vatican Council on December 7, 1965, the Catholic Church opened to the modern world and its needs. A church founded on the belief of an incarnate God had to place itself at the service of the world. But how that was to be done, what theologies would compel the mission, what pastoral visions would embrace the mission, were left to the faithful to work out. The work continues. In the end, it will undoubtedly take many theologies and many pastoral approaches. That said, not all visions and approaches will carry the same energy or speak with the same authority. Those that have come out of the lives of the poor or responses to the poor, such as in Latin America, have already revolutionized the way countless Christians do theology, envision church, and engage the world. For many Catholics, Latin American theologians transformed their very understanding of church and church mission.

Less known to the world, Asian theologians, working with their bishops and grounded by similar commitments to solidarity with the poor, have shaped another dynamic pastoral vision, one that could help direct the church and its mission in the new century. The Asian vision has grown out of decades of responses to Asian needs, but it is one that deserves the attention of the wider Catholic assembly. Recognizing the rich diversity of societies, cultures, and religions, while understanding the fundamental injustices that define the world today, the Asian vision seems fitting indeed. Enthusiastically and unapologetically, Asians boldly call it "a new way of being church."

By their very nature, visions pave the road ahead. They offer direction. They generate hope and enkindle the faith of the community. Asian Catholics quickly admit that there remains a considerable distance between their vision and what, after three decades, they have been able to implement. The record is spotty. Recent episcopal appointments in Asia, as elsewhere, have often placed cautious men in key positions of authority. This has not speeded the process. At the same time, these appointments have not undermined the vision, which has come together through consensus and over several decades.

For centuries Asian Catholics have been viewed as living at the far edges of the Catholic Church. They have been seen as living in "mission" territory. Few in the West had any reason to pay attention to these brothers and sisters of faith. Why, after all, should anyone in the West? Wasn't Asia "backward?" What could its theologians know about the church? About theology? Wasn't Europe the center of civilization? Didn't Europe spawn the Renaissance? Isn't Rome the seat of the bishop among bishops? The pope himself? So relatively few in the West paid attention. The Asian bishops and their theologians were left to be. However, since the council, driven by their desire to inculturate the faith and make it relevant to the lives of Christians, the Asian Catholic leadership worked to build a vision of faith. Several elements allowed this to happen. The first was the coming together of bishops and theologians from throughout Asia in an umbrella organization that allowed the leadership, for the first time, to listen to each other and learn that they shared many common concerns. Looking out together, what these leaders saw was widespread poverty, hunger, and oppression as well as the crushing weight of the modern secular world on their traditional societies. Soon they began to think and discern together and in the process they began to assemble their thoughts in pastoral statements. They dealt with ordinary needs: life, jobs, spiritual identity, food, community, dialogue, building ties with families and neighbors (most often of different religions). Another element enabled the new vision: trust. Asian theologians and their bishops have trusted each other. They have worked together virtually seamlessly in writing their many pastoral statements. They have shared a sense of common purpose. Arguably no other theologians and bishops have worked together as closely since the Vatican Council. The result has been an unparalleled burst of vision and energy. This has come to life through scores of major statements supported by countless others produced in journals, books, seminars and other gatherings. These in turn have triggered countless programs and local initiatives throughout Asia. It needs to be remembered that education and scholarship are highly esteemed throughout Asia. Teachers are revered. Theologians, focused on the spiritual order, are especially honored. In many Asian languages, bishops address their theologians using the word "master." It is not difficult to imagine that Asian bishops respect and willingly cooperate with their theologians, who have been influential in the development of the Asian pastoral vision during the past several decades.

The foundational tripod of the Asian pastoral vision has involved the local church, contextual reflection, and consensus building. Meanwhile, the vision emerged largely out of sight and out of mind of Rome's cautious radar screens. The 1970s and 1980s were critical decades for the foundational development in Asian theology. It was also a period in which the Vatican was focusing on Latin America and its theologians.

This Asian pastoral vision is spawned by theologians who place great emphasis on the bonds of trust between God and humanity. They trust God's providence in Asian history. They trust a Spirit present in the world and active in its many Asian cultures, religions, and traditions. They trust that being a follower of Jesus, serving as he called others to serve, evangelizing with their lives is what Jesus requires of them today. In the final analysis, they trust the work of Catholic evangelization to God.

Some in the Vatican have found this approach wanting. These critics of the Asian leadership insist that evangelization requires the explicit proclamation of Jesus as unique Savior to the World. The Asian leadership responds with a "yes, but. . . ." Being an evangelizer in Asia, the Asians say, both *does* and *does not* mean "proclaiming" Jesus as Savior, at least in the verbal sense. Asians have little difficulty holding to these seemingly different positions. The Asians say, "Okay, we will proclaim, but we will do it by witnessing to the gospel, to the teachings of Jesus." In some instances, proclaiming Jesus as Savior, they note, would be an act of suicide. In others, it would be simply counterproductive. What is important is that Christians live hopefully with a commitment to building the reign of God.

The Asian pastoral vision is gospel-based. It focuses on the teachings of Jesus. It sets its sight on living out the gospel in the world. It is not in this sense "institutionally oriented." Its primary goal is not building church structures. These will follow the more essential mission, the outward mission of "integral liberation," liberation at every level of existence, from the personal to the communal to the national to the global. It calls for liberation from distractions such as lust and greed as well as from unjust social and economic structures that impede harmonious relationships. The Asian vision is essentially nonviolent. It places high value on harmony. Where harmony is missing, the Asian vision seeks to restore it through dialogue. The Asian vision of church is a humble vision. It makes no effort to impose. God, after all, is already everywhere. The Asian vision rather seeks to find, to understand, and to experience community and God. It is an open vision. It seeks harmony, or as other Asian traditions put it, enlightenment.

This sense of oneness applies as well to the way local churches throughout the world should relate to one another. The Asian vision of church does not deny the primacy of the bishop of Rome, but emphasizes the need for all local churches to learn from one another and share with one another their special gifts. The Asians envision a networked church of local churches, void of any single dominating culture or template. In this sense the Asian vision is a remarkably universal vision of church. One could say it is a post-Western church.

In an age that pays increasing attention to ethnic and cultural diversity, in an age that sings of new technologies that network the planet, the Asian decentralized vision of church seems fresh and fitting. It is Eastern yin to the Western yang. In the school of yin-yang the universe is run by a single principle, the Tao, or Great Ultimate. This principle is divided into two opposite principles, or two principles that oppose each other in their actions, yin and yang. Under yang are the principles of maleness, the sun, creation, heat, light, Heaven, dominance, and so on; and under yin are the principles of femaleness, the moon, completion, cold, darkness, material forms, submission, and so on. Each of these opposites produces the other: Heaven creates the ideas of things under yang; the earth produces their material forms under yin. Creation occurs under the principle of yang; the completion of the created thing occurs under yin. This production of yin from yang and yang from yin occurs cyclically and constantly, so that no one principle continually dominates the other or determines the other. Could it, however, be that human history, shaped by new global transportation and communication, has only recently gotten to a new point of the meeting of yin and yang? Could it be that our church, molded over centuries in the West, is now encountering its complementary half? Could it be that these two halves now must find ways to integrate together? Could it be that they need each other to prosper, even to survive? Is this the meaning of being Catholic, belonging to a universal church in the third millennium after Christ? The answers to these questions will take years to sort out. But we already have clues. Eastern religious practices are already finding homes in the West. Western Christians who have lived in the East—the "bridge builders"—have come home to say that much can be learned from the East. Tens of thousands of Asians, meanwhile, many of them refugees, many of them still marginalized in their new homes, are saying the same thing.

What follows are a few summary points of the social, economic, and cultural forces that have helped shape the context out of which the Asian vision of church has emerged and is still emerging. Also listed are a few of the vision's basic spiritual, pastoral, and theological components.

· Demographics, poverty, and injustice

In 1960 the world's population stood at 3 billion; by the end of the century, it had doubled to 6 billion and is expected to reach 9 billion by 2050. Most of these new people—most of these new Catholics—live in poverty. At the dawn of the new century, some 3.5 billion of the planet's 6 billion people lived in East, Southeast, and South Central Asia—most living on less than two dollars a day. The United Nations projects that this region will have to feed nearly 1 billion more mouths by the year 2025.

The poor will increasingly outnumber the rich—and by wide margins. In Europe, North America, and Japan populations are leveling out. Combined, they will be slightly lower by 2050 than they are today, a bit over 1 billion. The poorer nations, however, are expected to double in population in the next fifty years, growing to about 8 billion. Already, the gap between the world's richest and poorest human beings is mind-numbing.

As the world entered the twenty-first century, one United Nations report found the world's richest fifth consuming more than sixty-six times the materials and resources of the poorest fifth. The world's 225 richest people, including sixty from the United States, had a combined wealth of $1 trillion, equal to the income of the poorest 2.5 billion of the world's poor.[1]

To be an Asian Catholic almost invariably means to experience poverty or at least to confront it every day. Responding to this reality, the Asian bishops at the first plenary meeting of the Federation of Asian Bishops' Conferences in 1974 stated that they must enter into a dialogue with the poor. This involved, they wrote, "a genuine experience and understanding of the poverty, deprivation and oppression of many of the Asian peoples." The theme of poverty and the need to work for justice have remained constant priorities throughout the Asian church documents. At the same time some theologians have faulted the bishops for not having developed a systematic analysis of the causes of poverty and for not getting the contents of these documents to the many of the tens of thousands who make up the churches in Asia.[2] The Sri Lankan Jesuit theologian Aloysius Pieris speaks of involvement with and commitment to the poor of Asia as the one condition of the possibility of a truly inculturated Asian liturgy. Asian theologians have made that point repeatedly.[3]

At the end of an important week-long Asian Catholic gathering entitled "Colloquium on Church in Asia in the 21st Century" in Pattaya, Thailand, in August 1997, Archbishop Orlando Quevedo of Cotabato, Philippines, the president of his nation's Catholic Bishops' Conference, in a closing homily, asked:

> If I am then asked today: What is it to be holy? What is it to be a good and faithful servant? . . . My answer would have to be this: In faith and love, I have to be at the heart of the struggle of the little people, as Jesus was. I have to be at their side to proclaim a prophetic word, disturbing the mighty, strengthening the little ones, to help build with them a new form of global communion that begins in the heart of the poor and, in pain but with unshakable trust in the power and wisdom of God, reaches out to other peoples everywhere. There is no doubt that a fountain of new life shall spring from this village we lovingly call Asia, if we all move in the Spirit of Jesus towards communion and solidarity.[4]

Asian Catholics provide an enormous opportunity to the universal church. They open a window onto human poverty and suffering from which the Word of God can be heard.

• Globalization

For many in the West, the issue of globalization remains largely academic. Debates concerning its merits continue on campuses and in think tanks. The same is not true in Asia, where the impact of globalization—whether one embraces it or not—is creating havoc. The painful economic "adjustments" that globalization advocates say are required as the underdeveloped nations of the world join the global economy fall almost entirely on the poorest of the poor. The weight is crushing people, societies, and entire cultures. Whether one wants to advance the process of globalization or resist it, the impact on the poor of Asia is undeniable and immediate. Globalization offers most Asians little hope they will benefit significantly in their lifetimes. That relatively few reap great financial rewards from globalization while most find their lives disrupted and pushed further into poverty is a moral issue that cannot be ignored. The Asian bishops, while not providing economic answers, have made their thoughts on globalization clear. At the seventh plenary of the FABC in Bangkok in 2000, the bishops placed globalization at the top of their list of challenges to be faced in the years ahead. "We view the Asian economic scenario with great pastoral concern," they wrote. "While the process of economic globalization has brought certain positive effects . . . it has enabled only a small portion of the population to improve their standards of living, leaving many to remain in poverty. Another consequence is excessive urbanization, causing the emergence of huge urban conglomerations and the resultant migration, crime and exploitation of the weaker sections." They then linked economic globalization with cultural globalization. The spreading mass media, influenced by Western values is "quickly drawing Asian societies into a global consumer culture that is both secularist and materialistic," causing "incalculable damage."

Asian Catholics offer to the universal church a unique vantage point on the effects of globalization, the perspective of its suffering victims.

• Fundamentalism

Many Asian Catholics have personally experienced the effects of rising fundamentalism. It has grown in Asia as a reaction to the disrupting pressures of globalization, secularization, and the breakdown of traditional societies. Searching for stability, many Muslims and Hindus have turned to fundamentalist religion. Some have abused religious symbols and ideas, taking up violence to right wrongs, real and imagined. Some extremists have attacked Christians, viewed as Western agents in Asia. Christians, too, have acted violently. As tensions have grown, violence has broken out in countries such as Pakistan, Indonesia, India, and the Philippines. Most acts of violence have received little attention in the Western press. This changed in the wake of the terrorist attacks on the United States on September 11, 2001. When Islamic militants turned their guns the following month on a Catholic church in the central Pakistani city of Bahawalpur, the reports appeared in papers around the world. The massacre killed fifteen Protestants who were using the church at the time. The killings came in the wake of U.S. bombings of Afghanistan carried out as part of Washington's war against terrorism.

Suddenly the dimensions—and threats—of religious-motivated violence grew in human consciousness. Never did interreligious dialogue seem more needed and more important. Little is as likely to shape the twenty-first century—for better or worse—as much as the interactions of the world's religions. If they learn to cooperate and work together on behalf of peace, this young century could be a turning point in the human journey. If they fail to do so, violence and death will likely be the twin hallmarks of the new century. In this light, the work of the Asian Catholic leadership on behalf of interreligious dialogue becomes all the more important.

Asian Christian–Islamic channels of communication are especially important. The Christian and Islamic worlds live side by side in dozens of nations. At their plenary gathering in Bangkok in 2000, the Asian bishops seemed to understand the critical nature of the situation. We are "painfully aware of the rise of religious fundamentalism," the Asian bishops stated, adding that their vision of a "renewed church," based on dialogue with the other Asian religions, would encourage "social and cultural activities" that would bridge communities and religions, building harmony. They noted that Asian Christians, living in multireligious communities, are especially well situated to encourage healthy religious renewal, working with other religious leaders to "draw nourishment from their own roots in this time of globalization." "We must endeavor to promote the human rights of all people, regardless of caste, color, creed or religion, by raising our voices against all such violations," they stated.

Asian Catholics offer the universal church models of dialogue and channels of communication that can, if properly used, help assuage violence in the new century.

• Politics and corruption

Most of Asia has been free from external colonization for at least a half century; however, the quest for democracy has not come easily. The ruling elite still has its way. The results of elections in Asia are often questionable. Frequently, after elections, the governed have very little say in governance. Many elected officials simply pursue their own interests. Meanwhile, there is often a tendency toward centralization of power and decision making. Pervasive corruption is too often a reality. Governments, meanwhile, are forced to adopt policies and practices, such as the structural adjustment policies, dictated by the International Monetary Fund, the World Bank, and the World Trade Organization. These policies are often devoid of a human face and social concern. Economic models for modest revenue and resource management seem few and far between. Out of this context of suspicion and corruption, the Asian Catholic leadership, especially in nations such as India and the Philippines, has developed alternative democratic community models called basic Christian communities. Today in many parts of Asia these gospel-inspired communities are growing. Given the spirit of sharing and dialogue that characterizes these communities, they present themselves as an important means to promote critical consciousness and the beginnings of self-determination. As the gospel is preached to the poor and as these communities lay claim to the liberating message of the gospel, it makes sense that they take up issues that affect their lives at the local, national, and global levels. Such conscience building, focused on empowering the poor and women, is occurring in many parts of Asia.

Another major Asian contribution to the wider economic/social and ecclesial discussion has been the encouragementof "basic inter-faith communities" and "basic human communities." These terms are found in many Asian writings and also in many FABC documents.

While basic Christian and inter-faith communities are not unique to Asia they have been an essential element in the emerging integral Asian pastoral vision, one that disavows the notion of a personal spirituality set apart from the goals of community building, justice, and peace.

· Local church and contextual theology

The starting point of virtually all the Asian pastoral reflections has been the local church. It is a context that includes widespread poverty and marginalization of peoples. The Asian bishops made their own "preferential option for the poor" nearly three decades ago, calling upon their churches to become churches of the poor. This radical involvement with the poor and the oppressed is what initially directed Asian theology. It has been a theology that has emerged from the vantage point of the poor. In the Philippine context, the term "grass-roots poor" is used and refers to "peasants, workers, fisherfolk, poor urban dwellers, cultural minorities." In the Korean context, the term *minjung* is used, referring to those who have been politically oppressed, economically exploited, and socioculturally marginalized by the ruling elite. While different contexts in different Asia nations led to different analyses, there is general agreement that a liberating theology in Asia must be the work of the poor and the marginalized. It is they who must reflect on and share their faith experiences as theologies are developed. Much Asian theology has been emerging out of the struggle of oppressed people for personal and societal liberation.

At the same time Asian theologies are also being derived from the contexts of histories of rich cultures and religions. These Asian theologies have no problem seeing the hand of God in Asian rituals and the sacred writings of other world religions. They see the eternal Christ in these religions. The Asian mind, meanwhile, accepts the mutuality among various religious traditions and appreciates the inexhaustibility of God's providence. It has little difficulty embracing religious pluralism because it does not operate from an Aristotelian logic of exclusion (either/or) but rather from the yin-yang logic of complementarity (both/and). Thus, ambiguity and paradoxes are aspects common to the Asian psyche.[5]

Sri Lankan theologian Aloysius Pieris points to the fact that the uniqueness of Christ or Christianity is never the starting point for Asians when relating with other religions. Such a paradigm, he maintains, follows from a hierarchical structural model that quantifies everything into higher or lower, better or worse. In Asia, such comparisons are alien because people are generally able to hold more than one thing, event, or person with equal worth. Asians, therefore, have no problem acknowledging more than one lord or savior and more than one path of salvation.[6]

Asian theologies have special relevance in a world of enormous poverty and diverse cultures that require greater interreligious dialogue.

• Dialogue as proclamation

The Asian bishops embraced the "triple dialogue" as their pastoral path in Taipei in 1974: dialogue with religions, cultures, and the poor. Since then they have repeatedly written about the need for such dialogue, so much that it has been the Asian Catholic pastoral mantra. This mantra, in turn, acknowledges the richness of Asian cultures and religions as well as the need for Catholics to learn from them. Dialogue, then, is not simply a technique. It is a way of life; it is the means of inculturation, the means to the reign of God, the means to harmony, and the means to understanding the will of God.

Dialogue with the poor gives the church its fundamental grounding, its soul, its pathway to redemption and enlightenment. For it is in this dialogue that the voice of Jesus is discovered anew. Dialogue, then, is quintessentially Christian and Asian. Meanwhile, it does not set out to conquer or convert as much as it attempts to understand and to witness. It proclaims the Gospels by following their teachings, by living the Beatitudes. It proclaims the Word by working to build the reign of God. It seeks understanding and cooperation with other religions to build communities, nations, and a more peaceful world. It engages cultures better to inculturate the faith. The Asian bishops deny that dialogue somehow contradicts the need to proclaim Jesus as Savior. To the contrary, they insist that dialogue and proclamation work together as one.

Over the years the key role of dialogue as a means of church building has grown. Asians today speak freely of at least five types of dialogue: First, the dialogue of life. People in their diverse life situations mingle freely with each other and share their joys and sorrows. Second, dialogue of action. It promotes human rights, democratic liberties, and freedom from oppressive structures. Third, dialogue with the poor. Fourth, dialogue with religious experience and cultures. Fifth, dialogue of theological exchange.

Asian Catholics, in their call for dialogue, model what they call the "new way of being church." In an age of religious strife and in a period that begs for greater cultural and religious understanding, it is a model that deserves attention in Asia and beyond.

· Solidarity with the marginalized

The poor speak with special clarity. Their messages carry little baggage. Churches that speak on behalf of the poor or in concert with them do so authentically. Members of these churches share common bonds and experiences wherever they may be. They understand each other. One senses that the Asian bishops, a small but important segment within the wider Catholic hierarchy, are, unlike other elements in that hierarchy, on the correct side of history, that they, more than others in their ranks, have successfully sorted through the myriad issues that face men and women of vision and have chosen the marginalized of the world. This choice makes these bishops, these modern apostles, beacons of hope in an otherwise dark time. The Asian bishops are subversives because they live and operate outside the cash-flow rivers of modern corporate life. These bishops lead pre-corporate churches with post-corporate worldviews. Whether their vision eventually dies from a lack of courage to implement it or whether it will somehow dissolve and eventually disappear, amalgamated into larger, less distinctive ecclesial forces, remains to be seen. For the moment, vulnerable, uncertain of the future, they are staying their quiet course. The wider church owes them gratitude and respect.

The Asian bishops have earned their authority. It is an authority easily recognized by the marginalized, both outside and inside the church. As voices of the marginalized, these Asian bishops speak a language that is readily understood by the marginalized everywhere. Over the years I have had many conversations with African American, Hispanic, and Asian American Catholics who feel they live at the edges of the wider U.S. culture and church. Most have experienced both the burdens of poverty and the cross-cultural pressures that come with living in more than one culture. While these minorities may have felt isolation in the past, this is changing now. Slowly, the "old" European-crafted twentieth-century church is giving way to a "new" global church of the twenty-first century. This global church should do a better job of weaving together the voices of the hitherto marginalized within the church. The so-called Catholic minorities in the West (who are actually "majorities" in the global church context), when exposed to Asian Catholics, understand them—and are understood by them.

The church is challenged as never before, given the transformation that is taking place within it. What bothers Asians as well as minority Catholics in the U.S. church is the lack of trust by traditional authorities. The most symbolic manifestation of this lack of trust can be found in Rome's refusal to allow the Asian bishops to authorize their own liturgical translations from Latin into their own Asian languages. Asian bishop after Asian bishop repeated this request during the Synod on Asia—only to be denied permission. From the Asian viewpoint, these denials send out a bewildering message of distrust. U.S. minorities, struggling with their own local episcopal authorities, have experienced similar misunderstandings and similar pain in getting their views heard at the centers of church power.

The marginalized of the church have special bonds that transcend location, which come out of backgrounds of shared adversity.

• Spirituality of harmony

In communion with their theologians, the Asian bishops have repeatedly focused on the importance of harmony, an age-old Asian calling.

Eventually, the Asian bishops adopted the notion of harmony into their pastoral vision. In fact, it became the principal underlying spiritual theme of that pastoral vision. In reflecting on the theme of harmony at an important gathering of Asian church leaders, the participants noted that despite many forces of fragmentation in Asia, a hunger for harmony is widespread. It exists in religious and philosophical traditions, in a thirst for peace, for greater human dignity, in a longing for equality.[7] Traditional Asian cultures provide many resources from which signs of harmony can be cultivated, the bishops wrote. "Sensitivity in human relationships, close ties of love and cooperation in families are highly valued in our cultures. Furthermore, traditionally, the various groups in Asian societies were held together harmoniously through forces of syncretism, spirit of tolerance, mysticism and through messianic movements."[8] Asian mysticism, found in union with the Absolute, with the divine, is at the heart of Asian prayer and is another component of the call to spiritual harmony.

Through Asian eyes, Christianity can be interpreted as a religion that fosters harmony between humanity and God, among the peoples of the earth, and with the cosmos itself. The doctrines of creation, covenant, and the people of God, but particularly those of the reign of God and the Trinity, are all ways of expressing the mystery at the heart of Christian faith: God is involved in human history and calls creation to harmony in community.[9] Starting at a personal level, the Christian notion of harmony opens in various stages from within oneself through neighbor and nature to God. Looked at another way, the test of true harmony lies in the acceptance of diversity *as richness*, the Asian bishops have stated.[10] They did not simply write, "the test of true harmony lies in the acceptance of diversity." They added the words "as richness." Harmony also means establishing dialogue in order better to see the church and its mission through the eyes of other religions as a way to better measure if it is living up to its ideals. Pluralism of culture and religion, thus, is seen as a component of God's providential plan for humanity. As Asians see it, how could it be otherwise? Could God have arrived in Asia with the missionaries only five centuries ago? For Asian Catholics, this would be preposterous. No, God has been present in the religions of Asia over the millennia.

Catholics are called to discover the many manifestations of God in these religions and cultures through dialogue. Could it be that the Spirit has ordained the churches of Asia to show the universal church what it really means to live in harmony with the other great wisdom and religious traditions of humankind? Implicit in this required life of dialogue is the continuous search for the true meaning and relevance of Christ. Through Asian Catholic eyes, the Christian story is a story of restoration.

It is a story of Christ who enters history to restore harmony. The pathways to harmony—prayer, contemplation, dialogue, building of the reign of God on earth—come from being open to the entire creation process and responding to it, as Jesus responded to it.

Pentecost was the culmination of Christ's redemptive work of restoring harmony to humankind. It was then that the apostles became filled with the Spirit. With bonds of unity and harmony, they began to speak in other languages. Pentecost was a historic sign that the disharmony of humanity, manifested in the confusion of language at Babel, had been remedied and that the way to harmony of all humanity had been decisively opened. Envisioning their "new way of being church," the Asian bishops offer a new and harmonious pastoral vision. It is a vision that initially started in the East, with Jesus, went West into Europe and then to the New World, then back to Asia, to be transformed in the East at the dawn of a new millennium. It is at once an old and a new story, an old and a new vision, renewed for the new needs of new peoples. After several stages of evolution and permeation, it is no longer a Western vision; nor is it uniquely Eastern. It is a new vision for a new global age. Spawned in timeless Asian values, it awaits discovery.

We don't choose our apostles. They emerge. They speak out. They inspire. They connect to us and help point the way. They speak in Asia. It is a new moment. It is a Pentecost in Asia.

Nations and Religions in Brief

Bangladesh

1 archdiocese; 5 dioceses; 253 priests; 98 seminarians; 55 brothers; 1,015 sisters; 252,000 Catholics in population of 125 million.

Formerly the eastern portion of Pakistan. Officially constituted as a separate nation Dec. 16, 1971; capital, Dhaka; official language, Bengali. Religious affiliation: Muslim, 86.8%; Hindu, 11.9%; other, 1.3%, including Protestant, .02% and Catholic, .02%.

One of the poorest countries in the world; predominantly rural and agricultural; annual per capita income, $210; literacy rate, 32%; staggering population density, 829 persons per square kilometer; population projection, 210 million in 2045.

Christianity first arrived in Bangladesh in 1576 through Portuguese missionaries who came along with traders. The majority of Christians, perhaps a little more than half, are indigenous tribal peoples, many of whom live on either side of the long Indian border. The constitution guarantees religious freedom, but it also states that Islam is the state religion. While churches enjoy freedom of worship, the government tends to be wary of Christian activity. Sunday is a regular working day. In Muslim society, Friday is observed as a Holy Day. Christian churches continue to be heavily dependent on foreign sources. Dhaka is one of the fastest growing cities in the world, causing major population adjustments and conflicts in culture.

Brunei

Apostolic Prefecture; 3 parishes; 2 priests; 2 seminarians; 2,100 Catholics in a total population of 314,000.

Located on the northern coast of Borneo; became fully independent state Jan. 1, 1984; formal name, Negara Brunei Darussalam; capital, Bandar Seri Begawan; official language, Malay. Religious affiliation: Muslim, 67.2%; Buddhist, 12.8%; other, 20%, including Protestants, 0.6% and Catholics, 0.6%. Most Christians are Chinese who have migrated from Hong Kong and other areas of China. These are skilled workers and not permanent residents. Ecclesiastical jurisdiction of Miri Diocese, Malaysia.

Annual per capita income, $12,135; population density, 52 persons per square kilometer; population projection, 700,000 in 2045.

Brunei is a small state. The government is centered in the sultan. The present sultan can trace his lineage back twenty-nine generations. The celebration of Christmas is banned; Christian materials, especially the Bible, are not allowed to be brought into Brunei. Evangelism is not permitted among the Muslims.

Cambodia

Apostolic Vicariate; 2 Apostolic Prefectures; 2 bishops; 35 priests; 11 seminarians; 6 brothers; 57 sisters; 19,000 Catholics in a total population of 11.5 million.

Situated between Vietnam and Thailand. A republic in Southeast Asia; capital, Phnom Penh; official language, Khmer. Religious affiliation: Buddhist, 95%; Muslim, 2%; other, 3%, including 0.13% Catholic.

Annual per capita income, $106; population density, 60 persons per square kilometer; population projection, 37 million in 2045.

The Khmer people practice Theravada Buddhism, which came through Thailand from India. Christianity first came to Cambodia in the sixteenth century by way of Portuguese merchants and navigators. In 1970, the Christian community comprised around 65,000 believers, of whom 60,000 were Vietnamese. During the civil war of 1970–1975, Cambodian Christians made remarkable efforts to inculturate their faith and liturgies. Beginning in 1975, under the Khmer Rouge, most priests and women religious and other Catholics were killed as part of a national purge that saw the deaths of between 2 and 3 million persons.

China, People's Republic of

138 dioceses; 70 officially recognized bishops, 39 publicly unofficial, 20 not publicly known; 2,200 priests (three-quarters ordained in past twelve years); 1,000 seminarians, trained in nineteen approved major seminaries and five preparatory seminaries; 700 others have been trained in unofficial seminaries; 2,000 officially recognized women religious, plus 2,000 unofficial; 5,000 churches and chapels. There were 3.5 million to 4 million Catholics in 1949; today there are about 10 to 12 million Catholics out of a total population of 1.2 billion.

People's republic in eastern part of Asia; capital, Beijing; official language, Mandarin Chinese. Religious affiliation: nonreligious, 59.2%; Confucian, 20.1%; atheist, 12%; Buddhist, 6%; Muslim, 2.4%; Christian, 0.2%; other, 0.1%.

Annual per capita income, $564; population density, 127 persons per square kilometer; population projection, 1.4 billion in 2045.

Christianity was first introduced to the Middle Kingdom by a Nestorian missionary, Alopen, in the seventh century. Nestorianism remained in China for 210 years. Various Christian missionaries returned to China in the thirteenth and fourteenth centuries. Some 30,000 Christians were believed to be living in China by 1338. Jesuits entered China in the sixteenth century, including Matteo Ricci, noted for his inculturation efforts. Following his death in 1610, other missionary orders entered China, leading to debates about the practice of ancestor worship among the Chinese, and to the "Rites Controversy," culminating in the decree of Pope Clement XI in 1704 forbidding Chinese Christians to take part in sacrifices to Confucius or to practice ancestor worship. Because of the Rites Controversy, the golden age of Catholic missions in China came to an end. More missionaries came to China in the 1820s and 1830s, a period that culminated in the Opium War of 1839 and Treaty of Nanjing in 1842. For the rest of the nineteenth century, Western powers waged war against China, and missionaries were seen by Chinese as working side by side with the imperialist powers. In Chinese eyes, Christians who sided with the West were most often no longer seen as Chinese. The birth of the People's Republic in 1949 signified an end to the history of foreign missions in China. Waves of repression against Christians continued until 1979. By then, institutional Christianity had been virtually eliminated. Since then, China's "open door" policy has seen a rebirth of Christianity under official government controls.

East Timor

2 dioceses; 118 priests; 138 seminarians; 16 brothers; 331 sisters; 736,000 Catholics or 86% of total population of 852,000.

Island nation in eastern Indonesia; former Portuguese colony invaded by Indonesia in 1975 and annexed the following year; under United Nations auspices voted for independence in 1999; capital, Dili.

Catholicism was introduced by the Portuguese and was the religion of about 30% of the population until the time of the Indonesian invasion in 1975. East Timorese flocked to the church in the years that followed. The church was the only East Timorese institution able to function officially during the occupation, and it provided solace and sanctuary to the people. Jose Ramos Horta and Bishop Carlos Filipe Ximenes Belo, both of East Timor, were awarded the Nobel Peace Prize in 1996.

Hong Kong

1 diocese; 1 cardinal; 1 bishop; 59 parishes; 337 priests; 19 seminarians; 73 brothers; 559 sisters; 347,000 Catholics or 3.7% of total population of 6,690,000.

Was placed under British administration in 1841. For several years after 1949, there was an influx of Chinese church leaders and missionaries from China to Hong Kong. Today, there are 260,000 Protestants from fifty denominations constituting 950 congregations in Hong Kong. One of the best-known Catholic institutions is the Hong Kong Catholic Center, established in 1945 to meet the spiritual needs of business people and the armed forces.

India

1 patriarchate (titular of East Indies); 1 major archbishopric (Syro-Malabar); 23 archdioceses; 118 dioceses; 18,320 priests; 9,885 seminarians; 2,453 brothers; 78,044 sisters; 17.5 million Catholics in a total population of 970 million.

Republic on the subcontinent of south central Asia; capital, New Delhi; official languages, Hindi, English. Religious affiliation: Hindu, 80%; Muslim, 11%; Christian, 2.4%, including Catholics, 1.8%; Sikh, 2%; Buddhist, 0.7%; other 3.9%.

Annual per capital income, $276 per person; population density, 300 persons per square kilometer; population projection, 1.55 billion in 2045.

The origin of Christianity in India is a matter of controversy. Legend holds that St. Thomas the Apostle arrived in southern India in 52 C.E. The South Indian tradition of St. Thomas's arrival is preserved in oral tradition. This tradition is usually called the Malabar tradition, which is a very ancient tradition. Members of the Syro-Malabar church, an Eastern rite of the Roman Catholic Church, trace their history to Thomas.

The second wave of Christianity came with early Catholic missionaries. The Portuguese, led by Jesuit Francis Xavier (1506-1552), expanded from their bases on India's west coast making many converts, especially among lower castes and outcastes. Xavier's body remains on public view in a glass coffin at the Basilica of Bom Jesus in Goa.

The third wave was largely Protestant and came with the onset of British colonialist rule in the nineteenth century. The fourth wave grew in the twentieth century, as Christian missionaries began to evangelize among tribal groups and *dalits*, otherwise known as outcastes.

Indonesia

8 archdioceses; 26 dioceses; 2,754 priests; 2,670 seminarians; 933 brothers; 6,791 sisters; 5.8 million Catholics in a total population of 204 million.

Republic in the Malay Archipelago, consisting of some 3,000 islands; capital, Jakarta; official language, Bahasa Indonesia. Religious affiliation: Muslim, 87%; Christian, 9.6%, including Catholics, 2.8%; Hindu, 2%; Buddhist 0.6%; other 0.8%.

Annual per capita income, $663; population density, 108 persons per square mile; population projection, 320 million in 2045.

In the sixteenth century the Portuguese brought Catholicism to parts of Indonesia. Some missions grew to over 100,000 faithful. In 1605 the Dutch United East-India Company forced Catholics to become Reformed Christians. In 1799, the Dutch state took over the assets of the bankrupt Dutch company, proclaiming freedom of religion in 1806. Catholic missionary work in the nineteenth century concentrated on Flores, Central Java, North Sumatra, West Kalimantan, North Sulawesi, and Timor. Christian churches today tend to conform to government policy. In 1984-85, all Christian churches had to officially recognize the government's founding principles of tolerance based on *Pancasila*.

Japan

3 archdioceses; 13 dioceses; 1,788 priests; 226 seminarians; 257 brothers; 6,594 sisters; 500,000 Catholics in a total population of 126,410,000.

Archipelago in the northwest Pacific; capital, Tokyo; official language, Japanese. Religious affiliation: Shintoist and similar, 39%; Buddhist, 38%; Christian, 3.9%, including 0.39% Catholic; other, 19.1%.

Annual per capita income, $37,000 per person; population density, 332 persons per square kilometer; population projection, 100 million in 2045.

Most scholars agree that the introduction of Christianity into Japan began with the arrival of Francis Xavier and his Jesuit colleagues in 1549. By 1614 there were some 300,000 converts in a population of 20 million. Government decrees prohibiting Christianity followed, and European missionaries were expelled. Japan's second encounter with Christianity came in the nineteenth century. Christians have played major leadership roles in social welfare, education, and health. Even though most Japanese show little interest in church membership, many have a high regard for Christian institutions and the role that Christians have played in the modernization of Japan. Although less than 1% of Japanese are Christian, as many as 30% of Japanese couples choose to have their marriages in Christian churches or chapels. This suggests that the social stigma against Christianity in the postwar period has ended.

Laos

4 Apostolic Vicariates; 15 priests; 17 seminarians; 1 brother; 82 sisters; 37,000 Catholics in a total population of 5,160,000.

People's republic in Southeast Asia; capital Vientiane; official language, Lao. Religious affiliation: Buddhist, 58%; tribal, 33%; Christian, 1.8%, including 0.6% Catholic; Muslim, 1%; other, 6.2%.

Annual per capita income, $259; population density, 21 persons per square kilometer; population projection, 13.5 million in 2045.

The first Christian mission to Laos was attempted in 1642 by the Jesuit Jean de Leria. He stayed five years and was forced out under pressure from Buddhist monks. The next efforts to bring Christianity to Laos came in the late nineteenth century, but were accompanied by intermittent periods of persecution.

Macau

1 diocese; 85 priests; 7 brothers; 179 sisters; 28,000 Catholics or 0.06% of the total population of 430,000.

Former Portuguese-administered territory in Southeast Asia across the Pearl River estuary from Hong Kong; reverted to Chinese control Dec. 20, 1999.

When the Portuguese established their first settlement off the coast of South China in Macau in 1553 there were priests among them. The Catholic presence has existed since. Today the church in Macau is becoming fully Chinese, although it still takes care of some 9,000 Portuguese-speaking Catholics.

Malaysia

2 archdioceses; 6 dioceses; 222 priests; 67 seminarians; 67 brothers; 483 sisters; 712,000 Catholics in a total population of 21 million.

Parliamentary democracy in southwest Asia; capital, Kuala Lumpur; official language, Malay. Religious affiliation: Muslim, 52.9%; Buddhist, 17.3%; Chinese folk-religionist, 11.6%; Hindu, 7%; Christian, 6.4%, including 3% Catholic; other, 4.8%.

Annual per capita income, $3,000; population density, 60 persons per square kilometer; population projection, 39 million in 2045.

Soon after the Portuguese capture of Malacca in 1511, a Catholic Franciscan arrived to become the first parish priest there. The early days of Christianity were largely focused on chaplaincy work among the Portuguese and later the British. Significant numbers of Christians are found among the Chinese, Indians, and aborigines. Christians are largely found in urban centers. A 1991 census found the Christian population had grown by 12.5% in ten years. Many denominations, including the Catholic Church, are witnessing renewal of church life in recent years.

Mongolia

1 mission; 5 priests; 2 seminarians; 2 brothers; 10 sisters; 3,000 Catholics in a total population of 2.4 million.

Republic in north central Asia; formerly under Communist control; capital, Ulan Bator; official language, Khalkha Mongolian. Religious affiliation: Buddhist.

Annual per capita income, $378; population density, 1.6 persons per square kilometer; population projection, 4 million in 2045.

The underlying worldview of the Mongols is shamanism, but Tibetan Buddhism remains the dominant religion.

Myanmar

3 archdioceses; 9 dioceses; 471 priests; 296 seminarians; 78 brothers; 1,247 sisters; 570,000 Catholics in a total population of 44.5 million.

Socialist republic in Southeast Asia; formerly Burma; name changed to Myanmar in 1989; capital, Yangon (Rangoon); official language, Burmese. Religious affiliation: Buddhist, 89.1%; Christian, 4.9%; Muslim, 3.8%; other, 2.2%.

Annual per capita income, $955; population density, 68 persons per square kilometer; population projection, 91 million in 2045.

The first Christian missionary arrived in 1554. The wars between Myanmar and the British in the nineteenth century resulted in the final British annexation in 1885. Under colonial rule, missionaries made many converts, especially among tribal groups. Consequently, a division along ethnic, cultural, and religious lines developed between the Christian ethnic minorities and the Buddhist Burmese majority. When military governments took over, beginning in 1962, foreigners, including missionaries, were expelled. Today Christianity remains the religion of ethnic minorities.

Nepal

1 Apostolic Prefecture; 43 priests; 31 seminarians; 2 brothers; 91 sisters; 6,000 Catholics in a total population of 22 million.

Constitutional monarchy, the only Hindu kingdom in the world, in central Asia; capital, Katmandu; official language, Nepali. Religious affiliation: Hindu, 86%; Buddhist, 8%; Muslim, 3.3%; other, 2.7%.

Annual per capita income, $144; population density, 150 persons per square kilometer; population projection, 58 million in 2045.

Sandwiched between China and India, Nepal is a mountainous country. Nepal's first contact with Christianity came through the periodic travels of Jesuits and then Capuchins in the 1600s. Occasional mission activity has continued. The first resident missionary of the modern era was Jesuit Marshall Moral, who moved to Katmandu in 1951 and started St. Xavier's School. The largest numbers of Christians are among tribal groups.

Pakistan

2 archdioceses; 4 dioceses; 277 priests; 129 seminarians; 49 brothers; 732 sisters; 1 million Catholics in a total population of 131 million.

Islamic republic in southwest Asia; capital, Islamabad. (Formerly included East Pakistan, which became the independent nation of Bangladesh in 1971.) Religious affiliation: Muslim, 97%; Christian, 1.6%, including 0.8% Catholic; Hindu, 1.4%.

Annual per capita income, $412; population density, 150 persons per square kilometer; population projection, 255 million in 2045.

Early missionary activity took place in the sixteenth to mid-eighteenth centuries. In the past two decades, Catholic social development work has taken on a larger dimension. The National Commission for Justice and Peace has given new identity to what it means to be Christian. The doors to government jobs are closed to Christians. Apostasy from Islam carries the death penalty. The law of evidence requires two Christian men for every one Muslim, the witness of a woman being half that of a man, and the witness of a Christian woman being half that again. The law of blasphemy, taking the name of the prophet of Islam, has been divisive and has led to numerous accusations.

Philippines

16 archdioceses; 50 dioceses; 7,112 priests; 6,781 seminarians; 1,167 brothers; 10,369 sisters; 62 million Catholics in a population of 75 million.

Republic, an archipelago of 7,000 islands off the southeast coast of Asia; capital, Manila; official languages, Filipino, English. Religious affiliation: Catholic, 82%; Aglipayanan, 6%; Muslim, 4%; Protestant, 4%; other, 4%.

Annual per capita income, $733; population density, 248 persons per square kilometer; population projection, 150 million in 2045.

Christianity arrived with the early Spanish expedition in 1521. Islam antedated Christianity in the Philippines by 150 years. By 1565, Islam had advanced as far north as Manila, but Christianity pushed it back south, with a line drawn in southern Mindanao and southern Palawan. Catholicism was found to be congenial with traditional Filipino animistic religion. The healing powers of baptism and the belief that Christian ceremonials and symbols were effective against the dreaded evil spirits drew masses of Filipinos to the new faith.

Singapore

1 archdiocese; 137 priests; 24 seminarians; 55 brothers; 233 sisters; 144,000 Catholics or 3.7 percent of the total population of 3.8 million.

Independent island republic off the southern tip of the Malay Peninsula; capital, Singapore; official languages, Chinese, Malay, Tamil, English. Religious affiliation: Buddhist/Taoist, 54%; Muslim, 15%; Christian, 12.6%, including 3.7% Catholic; Hindu, 3.6%; other, 14.8%.

Annual per capita income, $16,300; population density, 5,300 persons per square kilometer; population projection, 4.5 million in 2045.

With the establishment of a British settlement in Singapore by Stamford Raffles in 1819, Protestant and Catholic missionaries began work among the European residents and then the Asians. While Catholics outnumbered Protestants in 1970, the situation was reversed in 1980. During these years many older denominations experienced charismatic renewal. Meanwhile, Christians have been involved in many areas of social welfare.

South Korea

3 archdioceses; 11 dioceses; 2,490 priests; 1,844 seminarians; 524 brothers; 7,869 sisters; 3.8 million Catholics in a total population of 46.4 million.

Southern part of peninsula in eastern Asia; formal name, Republic of Korea (1948); capital, Seoul; official language, Korean. Religious affiliation: Christian, 25%, including 8.1% Catholic; Buddhist, 70%; Confucian, 3%; other, 2%.

Annual per capita income, $7,433; population density, 458 persons per square kilometer; population projection, 53 million in 2045.

It is significant to note that the founding of the Catholic Church in Korea came about by the spontaneous efforts of the Koreans themselves. Missionaries from the West came after an indigenous church had been founded. Persecutions began almost immediately, as Christians were charged with abolishing the practice of ancestor worship. Mass executions of Catholics took place in 1791, 1801, 1839, and 1846. The number of martyrs during the first one hundred years of Catholic history has been estimated as high as 10,000. In Korea, Christianity grew faster than in Japan or China. One of the reasons cited was that the exploitive colonial power in Korea was not the Christian West but Japan, thereby making it patriotic to be Christian.

Sri Lanka

1 archdiocese; 10 dioceses; 889 priests; 443 seminarians; 230 brothers; 2,263 sisters; 1.25 million Catholics in a total population of 18.7 million.

Independent socialist republic, island southeast of India (formerly Ceylon); capital, Colombo; official language, Arabic. Religious affiliation: Buddhist, 69%; Hindu, 15%; Muslim, 8%; Christian, 7.5%, including Catholic, 6.6%; other, 0.5%.

Annual per capita income, $574; population density, 283 persons per square kilometer; population projection, 24 million in 2045.

Christianity came to Sri Lanka with the arrival of the first Franciscan missionaries in 1542. It took new shape with the arrival of new European missionaries beginning in 1842. In 1886 the Catholic hierarchy was organized under an archbishop resident in Colombo, but it was not until the 1930s that church leadership gradually felt into the hands of national leaders. Independence gave the Buddhist majority greater voice. The constitutions of 1972 and 1978 made Buddhism the religion of the government while tolerating other religions. Christians are equally divided between the two major ethnic groups, the Sinhalese and Tamil.

Taiwan

1 archdiocese; 7 dioceses; 675 priests; 160 seminarians; 100 brothers; 1,070 sisters; 310,000 Catholics in a total population of 23 million.

Democratic island state (also known as Formosa) 100 miles off the southern coast of mainland China; capital, Taipei; official language, Mandarin Chinese. Religious affiliation: Confucianist/Tao, 48%; Buddhist, 43%; Christian, 7.4%, including 1.3% Catholic; Muslim, 0.5%; other 1.1%.

Annual per capita income, $12,475; population density, 593 persons per square kilometer; population projection, 25 million in 2045.

Christianity in Taiwan can be traced back to the Dutch and Spanish missions in the 1620s. The second wave of missionaries appeared in the 1860s. From 1915 onward, Taiwan fell under Japanese rule. In the 1940s all foreign missionaries were expelled as the Japanese forced the Taiwanese people to accept Shintoism. As a result, all Christian institutions were shut until the end of the war. During the postwar period the various Christian churches experienced new growth.

Thailand

2 archdioceses; 8 dioceses; 614 priests; 255 seminarians; 115 brothers; 1,388 sisters; 265,000 Catholics in a total population of 61 million.

Constitutional monarchy in southeast Asia (formerly Siam); capital, Bangkok; official language, Thai. Religious affiliation: Buddhist, 95%; Muslim, 4%; Christian, 0.5%, including 0.4% Catholic; other, 0.5%.

Annual per capita income, $2,042; population density, 115 persons per square kilometer; population projection, 70 million in 2045.

Although there were a few Christian missionaries in the area as early as the fourteenth or fifteenth centuries, the first Western missions were established by the Portuguese in the sixteenth century. Christians experienced persecution in the early eighteenth century. Christianity in the nineteenth and twentieth centuries experienced slow but steady growth in this heavily Buddhist nation.

Vietnam

3 archdioceses; 22 dioceses; 2,306 priests; 1,514 seminarians; 1,207 brothers; 9,312 sisters; 5 million Catholics in a total population of 78 million.

Country in southeast Asia, reunited officially July 2, 1976, as the Socialist Republic of Vietnam; capital, Hanoi; official language, Vietnamese. Religious affiliation: Buddhist, 67%; Cao Dai, 10.3%; Catholic, 6.4%; Hoa Hao, 2%; Muslim, 0.6%; Protestant, 0.9%; other, 12.8%.

Annual per capita income, $370; population density, 224 persons per square kilometer; population projection, 118 million in 2045.

Christianity appears to have entered Vietnam in the first decades of the sixteenth century. In the early seventeenth century the bulk of missionary work was carried out by the Jesuits, including the notable French priest Alexandre de Rhodes, who is credited with romanizing Vietnamese script, a move that significantly increased Vietnamese literacy and allowed the population to read the Bible. Christians faced significant persecutions during the seventeenth and eighteenth centuries. More than 130,000 died for their faith. After the partition of the country into North and South in 1954, some 700,000 Catholics came south, swelling church ranks. The northern Catholics were largely cut off from the outside world —and the renewal of Vatican II—by the Communists. In 1975, Catholic institutions were closed in the south as well. In the late 1980s, restrictions on the publication of religious works were eased considerably.

Primary sources: *2001: Catholic Almanac* (Huntington, Ind.: Our Sunday Visitor Publishing Division); *The 21st Century World Atlas, 2000 English Edition* (Naples, Fla.: Trident Press International); *A Dictionary of Asian Christianity* (Grand Rapids: William B. Eerdmans Publishing Company, 2001).

Preface: Apostles among Us

1. Thomas Bamat, "Popular Catholicism: Global Paradox and Promise," *America* 180, no. 19 (May 29, 1999): 6.

2. Gaudencio B. Rosales, D.D., and C. G. Arévalo, S.J., eds., *For All the Peoples of Asia: Federation of Asian Bishops' Conferences Documents from 1970 to 1991*, Vol. 1 (Maryknoll, N.Y.: Orbis Books; Quezon City, Philippines: Claretian Publications, 1997), xxi ("The Time of the Heirs").

Introduction: Asian Odyssey

1. The term "Pentecost in Asia" is found in Catholic Asian literature. For example, Maryknoll missioner James H. Kroeger, of Loyola School of Theology in Manila, has used the phrase in papers he has written, an early reference appearing as in "Continuing Pentecost in Asia: Introducing Ecclesia in Asia," *Journal of the Loyola School of Theology* [Manila] 13, no. 2 (1999): 3-13. Also, "Asian Synod—Asian Pentecost: Introducing Ecclesia in Asia," *SEDOS Bulletin* 32, no. 1 (January 2000): 8-11.

Chapter 1
New Way of Being Church

1. After each synod session, the Vatican Press Office distributes summaries of the daily episcopal interventions. This is from the Vatican summary of Archbishop Fumio Hamao's remarks.

2. J. A. G. Gerwin van Leeuwen, O.F.M., *Fully Indian, Authentically Christian* (Bangalore, India: National Biblical and Liturgical Center, 1990), 5.

3. Gaudencio B. Rosales, D.D., and C. G. Arévalo, S.J., eds., *For All the Peoples of Asia: Federation of Asian Bishops' Conferences Documents from 1970 to 1991*, Vol. 1 (Maryknoll, N.Y.: Orbis Books; Quezon City, Philippines: Claretian Publications, 1997), xxi ("The Time of the Heirs").

4. *New York Times*, November 25, 1970, section 1.

5. *For All the Peoples of Asia,* 1:xvii.

6. Peter Hebblethwaite, *Pope Paul VI: The First Modern Pope* (New York: Paulist Press, 1993), 564.

7. *For All the Peoples of Asia,* 1:xxiii.

8. Miguel Marcelo Quatra, O.M.I., *At the Side of the Multitudes: The Kingdom of God and the Mission of the Church in the FABC Documents (1970-1995)* (Quezon City, Philippines: Claretian Publications, 2000), 7.

9. *For All the Peoples of Asia,* 1:xxiii.

10. Ibid., 1:8-10.

11. Quatra, *At the Side of the Multitudes,* 8.

12. *For All the Peoples of Asia,* 1:5.

13. Ibid., 1:6.

14. Stephen Kim, "Founding Father Reflects on FABC's Origin and Development," *Asia Focus*, January 6, 1995.

15. *For All the Peoples of Asia*, 1:xviii.

16. Quatra, *At the Side of the Multitudes*, 9.

17. *For All the Peoples of Asia*, 1:xvii.

Chapter 2
Triple Dialogue

1. "Asian Pacific Presence: Harmony in Faith," pastoral letter by the U.S. bishops, 2001.

2. Gaudencio B. Rosales, D.D., and C. G. Arévalo, S.J., eds., *For All the Peoples of Asia: Federation of Asian Bishops' Conferences Documents from 1970 to 1991, Vol. 1* (Maryknoll, N.Y.: Orbis Books; Quezon City, Philippines: Claretian Publications, 1997), xv ff.; also personal interview, January 16, 2001.

3. Miguel Marcelo Quatra, O.M.I., *At the Side of the Multitudes: The Kingdom of God and the Mission of the Church in the FABC Documents (1970-1995)* (Quezon City, Philippines: Claretian Publications, 2000), 10.

4. Bernard Fall, *The Two Vietnams: A Political and Military Analysis* (New York: Praeger, 1963), 153-54.

5. J. Benedict Dilag, C.M.F., "A Deep and Passionate Love for Christ and the Church," *Tinig Loyola* (Christmas 1997): 5-7.

6. Ibid.

7. *For All the Peoples of Asia*, 1:15ff.

8. Peter C. Phan, "Human Development and Evangelization: The First to the Sixth Plenary Assembly of the Federation of Asian Bishops' Conferences," *Studia Missionalia* 47 (1998): 205-27.

9. *For All the Peoples of Asia*, 1:20.

10. *His Gospel to Our People*, vol. 2 (Manila: Cardinal Bea Institute, 1976), 332.

Chapter 3
Spirituality of Harmony

1. S. J. Emmanuel, "Asian Churches for a New Evangelization: Changes and Challenges," SEDOS documents (www.sedos.org/English/Emmanuel.htm).

2. "Theses on the Local Church: The Theological Advisory Commission of the Federation of Asian Bishops' Conferences," 1991, FABC papers, no. 60, www.ucannews.com.

3. To Thi Anh, "Eastern and Western Cultural Values: Conflict or Harmony," *East Asian Pastoral Institute* (Manila, Philippines, 1974).

4. *The Way of Life of Lao Tzu* (New York: Mentor Books, 1955), 95.

5. Gaudencio B. Rosales, D.D., and C. G. Arévalo, S.J., eds., *For All the Peoples of Asia: Federation of Asian Bishops' Conferences Documents from 1970 to 1991, Vol. 1* (Maryknoll, N.Y.: Orbis Books; Quezon City, Philippines: Claretian Publications, 1997), 40ff.

6. Ibid., 1:31.

7. Ibid.

8. Ibid., 1:35.

9. Ibid.

10. Ibid., 1:35.

11. Samuel Rayan, S.J., "A Spirituality of Mission in an Asian Context," SEDOS document, available at www.sedos.org.

12. *Lumen Gentium* §16; *Nostra Aetate* §2.

13. *For All the Peoples of Asia,* 1:35.

14. Franz-Josef Eilers, S.V.D., *For All the Peoples of Asia: Federation of Asian Bishops' Conferences Documents from 1992 to 1996,* Vol. 2 (Quezon City, Philippines: Claretian Publications, 1997), 229ff.

15. Rayan, "A Spirituality of Mission in an Asian Context."

16. Ibid.

17. *For All the Peoples of Asia,* 1:xix.

18. Ibid., 1:xxv.

19. Georg Evers, "Christianity and Harmony, from the Past to the Present," *East Asian Pastoral Review* 29 (1992): 348ff.

20. Ibid.

Chapter 4
Tasting Poverty

1. José M. de Mesa, SEDOS documents, "Making Salvation Concrete and Jesus Real: Trends in Asian Christology" (www.sedos.org).

2. Information supplied by the Office of Human Development of the Federation of Asian Bishops' Conferences.

3. Gaudencio B. Rosales, D.D., and C. G. Arévalo, S.J., eds., *For All the Peoples of Asia: Federation of Asian Bishops' Conferences Documents from 1970 to 1991,* Vol. 1 (Maryknoll, N.Y.: Orbis Books; Quezon City, Philippines: Claretian Publications, 1997), 199ff. (BISA I, Final Reflections).

4. Ibid., 1:200.

5. Ibid., 1:xxv.

6. Ibid., 1:15; and Peter C. Phan, "Human Development and Evangelization: The First to the Sixth Plenary Assembly of the Federation of Asian Bishops' Conferences," *Studia Missionalia* 47 (1998): 205-27.

7. *For All the Peoples of Asia,* 1:204 ("BISA II").

8. Felix Wilfred, "Images of Jesus Christ in the Asian Pastoral Context: An Interpretation of Documents from the Federation of Asian Bishops' Conferences," *Concilium* (1993/2): 51.

9. *For All the Peoples of Asia,* 1:230.

10. Ibid.

11. Jonathan Yun-Ka Tan, "Theologizing at the Service of Life: The Contextual Theological Methodology of the Federation of Asian Bishops' Conferences (FABC)," *Gregorianum* 81, no. 3 (2000): 558.

12. Archbishop Angel Fernandes, "Dialogue in the Context of Asian Realities," *Vidyajyoti* 55 (1991): 548.

13. "FABC Must Continue Efforts That Make the Church Human," *Asian Focus,* January 6, 1995.

14. "OHD Helps Asian Church Become Church of the Poor," *UCA News,* May 3, 1991.

15. Ibid.

16. "What the Spirit Says to the Churches (Rev 2:7)," *Vidyajyoti* 62, no. 2 (February 1998): 124-33.

17. *For All the Peoples of Asia*, 1:231 ("BISA VII").

18. Franz-Josef Eilers, S.V.D., *For All the Peoples of Asia: Federation of Asian Bishops' Conferences Documents from 1992 to 1996*, Vol. 2 (Quezon City, Philippines: Claretian Publications, 1997), 5.

19. "Theologians Try to Add Asian Perspective to Catholic Social Teachings," *UCA News*, March 17, 1992.

20. *For All the Peoples of Asia*, 1:110.

21. Ibid., 1:114.

22. "Understanding Grows as Bishops Consider the Spirit at Work in Asia," *UCA News*, November 12, 1986.

23. "Let Christians and Muslims Have Dialogue in Pakistan," *Asia Focus*, August 19, 1994.

Chapter 5
Reign of God

1. A concise outline of the changes that took place in the Catholic Church's approach to mission can be found in an essay by Father Peter C. Phan, "Proclamation of the Reign of God as Mission of the Church: What for, To Whom, With Whom and How?" SEDOS document available at www.sedos.org.

2. Ibid.

3. Ibid.

4. Ibid.

5. James H. Kroeger, M.M., "The Church in Asia in Mission, *Ad Gentes*," FABC paper no. 92o. Seventh Plenary Assembly: Workshop Discussion Guide, *UCA News*, available at www.ucanews.com.

6. Ibid.

7. Gaudencio B. Rosales, D.D., and C. G. Arévalo, S.J., eds., *For All the Peoples of Asia: Federation of Asian Bishops' Conferences Documents from 1970 to 1991*, Vol. 1 (Maryknoll, N.Y.: Orbis Books; Quezon City, Philippines: Claretian Publications, 1997), 252.

8. Ibid., 1:57.

9. Ibid., 1:281.

10. Franz-Josef Eilers, S.V.D., *For All the Peoples of Asia: Federation of Asian Bishops' Conferences Documents from 1992 to 1996*, Vol. 2 (Quezon City, Philippines: Claretian Publications, 1997), 6.

11. Peter C. Phan, "Kingdom of God: A Theological Symbol for Asians," *Gregorianum* 79, no. 2 (1998): 295-322.

12. Ibid., 298.

Chapter 6
New Openings

1. *Minneapolis Star Tribune*, June 19, 2001.

2. Bishop John Tong spoke during the Asian synod at a lecture sponsored by SEDOS, the international missionary organization.

3. Richard Madsen, *China's Catholics* (Berkeley: University of California Press, 1998), 30.

4. Father Peter Julian Kelly, "Christianity and China: Background History Notes to Facilitate a Better Understanding of the Present Situation of the Catholic Church in China," St. Columban's Mission Society, website papers on China, www.columban.org.au/China/cac 98july.htm.

Chapter 7
East–West Bridges

1. Ken Wilber, *No Boundary: Eastern and Western Approaches to Personal Growth* (Boston: Shambhala, 2001), 21.

2. See Michael Amaladoss, "Response to Sung-Hae Kim," in *Mission in the Third Millennium*, ed. Robert J. Schreiter (Maryknoll, N.Y.: Orbis, 2001), 21.

3. Ibid.

4. Karl Joachim Weintraub, *The Value of the Individual: Self and Circumstance in Autobiography* (Chicago: University of Chicago Press, 1978).

5. Jeannette Batz, column in *National Catholic Reporter*, October 23, 1998.

6. Mary Evelyn Tucker, "Thomas Berry's Intellectual Journey," The Third Annual Thomas Berry Award and Lecture, State of the World Forum, United Nations Millennium Peace Summit, Waldorf Astoria Hotel, New York, New York, August 30, 2000.

7. Mary Evelyn Tucker, *An Introduction to the Work of Thomas Berry* (Lewisburg, Pa.: Bucknell University, Department of Religion), published on the Internet, www.ecoethics.net/ops/berrybio.htm.

8. Thomas Merton, *Asian Journal* (New York: New Directions, 1975), 4.

9. Lawrence Cunningham, with John Russell on Radio National, the Australian Broadcasting Corporation's national radio network of ideas, January 7, 2001.

10. James Forest, lecture at Boston College, November 13, 1995.

11. Ibid.

12. Paul Veliyathil, "East-West Dialogue: Thomas Merton, a Modern Arjuna," *Spirituality Today* 39 (winter 1987): 293–304.

13. Ibid.

14. Merton, *Asian Journal*, 101.

15. Ibid., 124.

16. Thomas Merton, *The Other Side of the Mountain: The Journals of Thomas Merton, Vol. 7, 1967–1968,* ed. Patrick Hart, O.C.S.O. (San Francisco: HarperSanFrancisco, 1998), 281.

17. Robert Hale, O.S.B. Cam., "Bede Griffiths and Thomas Merton," *The Golden String Newsletter* 7, no. 1 (summer 2000).

18. Bede Griffiths, *The Marriage of East and West: A Sequel to the Golden String* (Springfield, Ill.: Templegate, 1982), 13–15.

19. *National Catholic Reporter,* August 28, 1998.

20. *National Catholic Reporter,* September 4, 1998.

21. Ibid.

22. "Eruption of Truth," an interview with Raimon Panikkar by Henri Tincq, trans. Joseph Cunneen, in *Christian Century,* August 16-23, 2000.

23. "Panikkar at Santa Barbara," *Cross Currents* 29, no. 2 (summer 1979).

24. "The New Innocence," interview with Raimon Panikkar by Carmen Font, *Share International,* October 1996.

25. Ibid.

26. "Eruption of Truth."

27. "The New Innocence."

Chapter 8
Migrations and Settlements

1. Veltisezar Bautista, *The Filipino Americans from 1763 to the Present: Their History, Culture, and Traditions* (Midlothian, Va.: Bookhaus Publishers, 1998), in the U.S. bishops' pastoral of November 2001, "Asian Pacific Presence: Harmony in Faith."

2. Sucheng Chan, *Asian Americans: An Interpretive History* (Boston: Twayne Publishers, 1991).

3. U.S. bishops' pastoral of November 2001, "Asian Pacific Presence: Harmony in Faith."

4. Ibid.

5. Sucheng Chan, *Asian Americans.*

6. Franz-Josef Eilers, S.V.D., *For All the Peoples of Asia: Federation of Asian Bishops' Conferences Documents from 1992 to 1996,* Vol. 2 (Quezon City, Philippines: Claretian Publications, 1997), 278.

7. Census Bureau, "We Are the American Asians" (September 1993).

8. Pope John Paul II's homily during the opening Mass of the Synod of Asian Bishops (April 19, 1998).

9. *Ecclesia in Asia* §27.

10. "A Refugee's Odyssey Leads to Theological Peaks," *National Catholic Reporter,* February 11, 2000.

11. "New Pastoral on Asian- and Pacific-Americans Sheds Light on Overlooked Catholics," *National Catholic Reporter,* November 11, 2001.

12. U.S. bishops' pastoral of November 2001, "Asian Pacific Presence: Harmony in Faith."

Chapter 9
Taking Notice

1. *Catholic World News,* February 9, 1996; *National Catholic Reporter*, February 26, 1996, p. 2.

2. *National Catholic Reporter,* February 26, 1996, p. 2.

3. John Allen wrote an especially insightful article in the June 2, 2000, issue of the *National Catholic Reporter.* It outlines how six key Latin American cardinals got to the Roman curia after supporting right-wing governments in Latin America and opposing liberation theology.

4. S. J. Emmanuel, "Asian Churches for a New Evangelization: Changes and Challenges," *East Asian Pastoral Review* 36, no. 3 (1999).

5. Ibid.

6. Jacob Parappally, "Church's Dialogue with Culture and Religion," *Third Millennium (Indian Journal of Evangelization),* no. 4 (October-December 2000), available at www.sedos.org.

7. Ibid.

8. Ibid.

9. *UCA News* document, July 23, 1990, www.ucanews.com..

10. Cardinal Joseph Tomko, "Proclaiming Christ the World's Only Savior," *L'Osservatore Romano* [Eng.], April 15, 1991, p. 4. Partly the description was a misrepresentation. For instance what the cardinal quoted as an Indian theologian's views on conversion was in fact only that which the concerned theologian described as the Hindu view of conversion.

11. Quoted by John Allen, "Perils of Pluralism," *National Catholic Reporter,* September 15, 2000, p. 1. See also "Relativism: The Central Problem for Faith Today," *Origins* 26, no. 20 (October 31, 1996).

12. Ibid.; see also Wayne Teasdale, "Bridging the Infinite: Christians and Buddhists in Conversation," *Conscious Choice* (November 1998).

Chapter 10
Asian Crossroads

1. "The Asia Development Bank on Asia's Megacities," *The Asia Development Bank Population and Development Review* 23, no. 2 (June 1997).

2. United Nations Population Division, 1992.

3. John Vidal, "Losing Confidence in the Aid Trick," *London Guardian*, September 21, 1990.

4. UNICEF Annual Report, 1997; World Health Organization, 1998; Human Development Report, "Globalization with a Human Face," 1999.

5. Gaudencio B. Rosales, D.D., and C. G. Arévalo, S.J., eds., *For All the Peoples of Asia: Federation of Asian Bishops' Conferences Documents from 1970 to 1991, Vol. 1* (Maryknoll, N.Y.: Orbis Books; Quezon City, Philippines: Claretian Publications, 1997), 30-31.

6. "Challenges of Religious Fundamentalism," workshop report at FABC Plenary VII, Sam Phran, Thailand, January, 2000.

7. *National Catholic Reporter*, May 7, 1999.

8. José M. de Mesa, "Making Salvation Concrete and Jesus Real: Trends in Asian Christology," *Journal of Missiological and Ecumenical Research*, 30, no. 1 (2001).

9. Wilfred made the remark in an interview in February 2001.

10. *For All the Peoples of Asia*, 1:273-89.

11. Ibid., 1:280.

12. Michael Amaladoss, S.J., "Mission in a Post-Modern World: A Call to Be Counter-cultural," SEDOS document, available at www.sedos.org.

13. FABC Sixth Plenary Assembly, Manila, January 10-19, 1995. Statement §9.

Chapter 11
Called to Rome

1. The *Lineamenta* and other documents from the Asian synod are found in *The Asian Synod: Texts and Commentaries,* edited and compiled by Peter C. Phan (Maryknoll, N.Y.: Orbis Books, 2002).

2. *National Catholic Reporter,* March 27, 1998.

3. *National Catholic Reporter,* April 10, 1998.

4. Ibid.

Chapter 12
Synod on Asia

1. *National Catholic Reporter,* May 1, 1998.

2. John Mansford Prior, S.V.D., "A Tale of Two Synods: Observations on the Special Assembly for Asia," *Vidyajyoti* 62 (1998): 654-65.

3. Ibid.

4. *National Catholic Reporter,* May 8, 1998.

5. John Mansford Prior, S.V.D., "The Asian Synod in Action: Unfinished Encounter: A note on the voice and tone of Ecclesia in Asia," *East Asian Pastoral Review* 37 no. 3 (2000). Prior is a Divine Word Missionary (S.V.D.) who has been working in Indonesia since 1973. He is presently secretary of Candraditya Research Centre for the study of Religion and Culture. John was liaison with the English-speaking press during the Synod for Asia.

6. *National Catholic Reporter,* May 15, 1998.

7. *National Catholic Reporter,* May 29, 1998.

8. Prior, "A Tale of Two Synods."

9. Peter C. Phan, *"Ecclesia in Asia:* Challenges for Asian Christianity," *East Asian Pastoral Review* 37, no. 3 (2000): 215-32.

Chapter 13
Home Again

1. Georg Evers (Institute of Missiology Missio, Aachen, Germany), "The Continental Bishops Synods: Lost Chance or New Beginning?" *Jeevadhara* 30, no. 177 (2000): 313-29.

2. Peter C. Phan, *"Ecclesia in Asia,* Challenges for Asian Christianity," *East Asian Pastoral Review* 37 no. 3 (2000): 215-32.

3. Ibid.

4. Maryknoll Father James H. Kroeger, "Introducing Ecclesia in Asia," *Vidyajyoti* 64, no. 1 (January 2000): 11.

5. *National Catholic Reporter,* December 3, 1999.

6. John Manford Prior, S.V.D., "A Tale of Two Synods: Observations on the Special Assembly for Asia," *Vidyajyoti* 62 (1998): 654-65.

7. Edmund Chia, F.S.C., "Of Fork and Spoon or Fingers and Chopsticks: Interreligious Dialogue in *Ecclesia in Asia,"* SEDOS documents, available at www.sedos.org. Chia is a Malaysian La Salle Brother with graduate degrees in psychology and religious studies.

8. Ibid.

9. *National Catholic Reporter,* Sep. 15, 2000. For the complete text of *Dominus Iesus* and a balanced set of positive and negative reviews of the document, see Stephen J. Pope and Charles Hefling (eds.), Sic et Non: *Encountering* Dominus Iesus (Maryknoll, N.Y.: Orbis Books, 2002).

10. Father Richard McBrien, *"Dominus Jesus:* An Ecclesiological Critique," Lecture given at the Centro Pro Unione in Rome, January 11, 2001.

11. On the initiative of the Pontifical Mission Aid Society, the Institute of Missiology Missio e.V. (MWI) was founded in 1971 as an incorporated society. The Institute's statutes define its purpose as the promotion of philosophical and theological research and teaching in the field of Catholic mission work. At the time of this writing the statement may be found at www.mwi-aachen.de/Agora/uk agora domi.html.

12. *National Catholic Reporter*, October 6, 2000.

13. *National Catholic Reporter*, September 22, 2000.

Chapter 14
New Century Vision

1. *Christian Science Monitor*, November 6, 1998, section 1.

2. Tissa Balasuriya, "Theologian Asks More from BABD as New Century Dawns," *Asia Focus*, January 6, 1995, 8.

3. Aloysius Pieris, "Inculturation: Some Critical Reflections," *Vidyajyoti* 57 (1993): 645.

4. "Colloquium on Church in Asia in the 21st Century" (Office of Human Development, Manila, Philippines), 502.

5. Edmund Chia, F.S.C., "Dialogues with Religions of Asia, Challenges from Within," paper presented at SEDOS Annual Research Seminar, Rome, May 19-23, 1998. (1) (Part II).

6. Ibid.

7. Gaudencio B. Rosales, D.D., and C. G. Arévalo, S.J., eds., *For All the Peoples of Asia: Federation of Asian Bishops' Conferences Documents from 1970 to 1991*, Vol. 1 (Maryknoll, N.Y.: Orbis Books; Quezon City, Philippines: Claretian Publications, 1997), Final Statement of the Eleventh Bishops' Institute for Interreligious Affairs, 1:318, par. 4.

8. Ibid., 1:399, par. 6.

9. Ibid., Final Statement of the Tenth Bishops' Institute for Interreligious Affairs, 1:314, par. 6-9; Report on the Assembly of the First Bishops' Institute for Interreligious Affairs, 1:247ff.

10. Ibid., 1:249ff.